COOKING PEOPLE

COOKING PEOPLE

PEOPLE

THE WRITERS WHO TAUGHT
THE ENGLISH HOW TO EAT

Sophia Waugh

QUARTET

First published in 2013 by Quartet Books Limited
A member of the Namara Group
27 Goodge Street, London W1T 2LD
Copyright © Sophia Waugh 2013
The right of Sophia Waugh to be identified
as the author of this work has been asserted
by her in accordance with the
Copyright, Designs and Patents Act, 1988
All rights reserved.

A catalogue record for this book
is available from the British Library
ISBN 978 0 7043 7320 4
Typeset by Josh Bryson
Printed and bound in Great Britain by
T J International Ltd, Padstow, Cornwall

Elizabeth David recipes from *Mediterranean Food*
© Elizabeth David 1950

For my mother, Teresa Waugh, and in memory of my grandmother, Pamela Onslow, and my uncle, Michael Onslow, for the love of cooking

member a huge crock of sauerkraut which, when it was opened, released a storm of flies, heady with vinegar and freedom. There was a tart made of rose jam, which haunts all four of us to this day...enough said. The less successful experiments did have their own reward, though. We learned that cooking is about more than following a safe recipe and that there is room for a mistake.

The first question our parents asked any of us when we came home from friends was 'what was the food like?' or, after an extended stay, 'what was the best and worst thing you ate?' Family pride was great when, after two weeks with French friends and one meal during that time when I visited my parents, the best meal I'd eaten was that one cooked by my mother (fresh ox tongue with mustard and mushroom sauce, if you're interested). We at least knew that the French were not automatically better cooks than the English.

Visits abroad or to London involved restaurants, and restaurants were always treats; order anything you want and (unlike at home) you don't have to finish everything on your plate. My father's generosity in restaurants was legendary within the family. And always, always, the mantra was 'taste'. Taste what was on each other's plates, try everything at least once, learn to recognise the joy of textures and flavours and contrast.

Some elements of my childhood were definitely bizarre; I was educated at a state school but sent to Harley Street for my braces. Therefore, for me, a visit to the dentist was a huge treat. I'd go from Harley Street to Soho where my father would take me out to a Chinese lunch. He would take control of the ordering and a tower of wicker baskets would appear, one after another giving up their secrets in a splurge of colour, smell and taste.

A major part of our childhood was the summers spent in the Languedoc. My parents had lived there for a year when I was a baby,

3

and when I was nine bought a house near Castelnaudary. We spent our summers in France eating every bit of goose and pig you could imagine, and a few more. The farm down the lane was more old-fashioned than anything you would have found in England at the time. Racks of hutches lined a barn wall and my mother would choose a couple of rabbits for supper (*à la moutarde*, tender and delicious if bony). The farmers (two brothers and one wife – we never knew which of the identical brothers was the husband, and wondered if the wife was any wiser) kept their own geese and a pig, grew their own tomatoes and beans and made their own filthy (according to my parents) wine. They would lay the haricot beans out on sacking to dry in the sun, made their own *saucissons*, *boudin* (black pudding) and sausages, their own confit and cassoulet.

Ah, cassoulet. Mention Castelnaudary to any Frenchman and he will sigh, 'Ah, le cassoulet de Castelnaudary!' A rich stew made of haricot beans, sausage, confit of either duck or goose, pork and pork fat, it is one of the great peasant dishes not just of France but of the world. (Please allow for a little partisanship here.) It was – and still is – eaten at great feasts such as weddings, or the annual village fêtes. Our builder, Fat Francois, even ate it for breakfast before coming to work – once he said he was feeling so ill he'd had to force the cassoulet down his throat with two fingers. But he ate it anyway.

No part of an animal was wasted. Fussiness was not an option; we were each given one thing we were allowed to refuse. Mine was macaroons, my sister's was raisins, one of my brothers wouldn't eat mussels but only because he was worried they'd bite his throat on the way down and I don't remember my other brother ever turning up his nose at anything.

My mother owned few cookery books, and looks with bewilderment at the shelves and shelves of them that I have bought over the years. She had Mrs Beeton and Constance Spry (although I have no memory of her ever using the latter) and, of course, Elizabeth David. She uses cookery books a little more often now, but she is not churning out endless meals for four children. And even now, the books she uses are more likely to be Claudia Roden or Madhur Jaffrey, cooks of other cultures' dishes that she cannot be expected to know by instinct. In my childhood I think she mostly used cookbooks for bread and pastry, things that require exact proportions. The rest she mostly, or so it seemed to us, *knew*.

From early childhood I was encouraged to learn to cook. Not pizzas decorated with faces, nor endless cup cakes, but proper food. These are the first things I learned: salad dressing (no sugar, 'filthy German habit'), macaroni cheese (can never be too cheesy), corned beef hash, treacle tart, chocolate mousse. My first cookbook was Bee Nilson's *The Penguin Cookery Book*, a basic and trustworthy standard, given me by Father Christmas (although I didn't quite believe in him by then). My second was a hardback grey A4 index book into which I wrote down recipes and, later, cut them out from magazines. Battered but beloved, this book is still in my shelf alongside all the Marcellas, Moros, Rodens I have amassed over the years. Then, for my eighteenth birthday, my siblings clubbed together and bought me *The Oxford Companion to Literature*, and Elizabeth David's *Summer Cooking*, *French Country Cooking* and *A Book of Mediterranean Food*. An obsession was born.

Over twenty years ago, when I was a junior editor in publishing, I suggested commissioning Jennifer Paterson (later known as one of the 'Two Fat Ladies') to write a cookery book, and was gently let down with the words 'cookery won't sell'. Last Christmas four copies of Jamie Oliver's latest cookbook were gifted around my house, not all of them to me. Looking at the pile of books on the kitchen table, and from them at the couple of hundred of cookery books I own, I began to think about them at a different level from the usual 'what shall we eat tonight?' question.

Thanks to the work of such as Delia and Jamie (so well known now that they, along with Nigella, require only a Christian name – very monarchs of the food glen), the rise in British perception and expectation of good eating has driven the restaurant industry upwards; thirty years ago the best food you could expect outside a major city was a decent gammon egg (or pineapple) and chips in a pub. Now good, not to say outstanding, restaurants can be found even in the wilds of Exmoor.

What is it that now preoccupies the English with food so much that there is a multi-million-pound industry around our efforts to present an acceptable lasagne? There is no doubt that thanks to Jamie and the like we are more likely to be offered a decent dinner at the tables of our friends than we were a generation ago, yet the English are still mocked abroad for their food and when Delia Smith was published in France (*La Cuisine Facile d'aujourd'hui, par Delia*, 2002), the Gallic nation nearly died laughing. Any week of the year the nonfiction bestseller lists are dominated by cookery books. The question is, of course, whether they are read or even used – but even if they are not, the fact that they are sold represents a hunger in the English psyche that is about more than just eating.

And so I began to look further afield. My mother had Mrs Beeton, but her bible was Elizabeth David. Who else was there who had really shaped English eating habits? And why had they cared enough to do so? Why had they not, like my mother, been content with serving delicious food rather than trying to persuade a nation that it could do better than overcooked vegetables and meat?

Ask a foreigner what the English diet involves, and he will say 'roast meat'. This is a perception which was already old hat in the seventeenth century when French travel writer Henri Misson wrote of the English, 'I always heard that they were great flesh eaters and found it to be true.' He noticed that the tables of the English 'who do not keep French cooks are covered only with large dishes of meat'.

Part of the modern obsession with cooking is to do with another modern obsession – health. The very poor do not have the luxury of thinking about *roux* and reductions. The richer a nation becomes the more its people can be creative with food. But health is not such a modern obsession, after all. From Eliza Acton onwards, cooks have been concerned with the freshness of ingredients and indeed Eliza, after her great *Modern Cookery for Private Families*, turned her attention to the bread industry as much out of concern for the poor who were being fed adulterated bread by crooks as out of an interest in baking.

Brillat-Savarin, whose *Physologie du Gout* (1825) is one of the greatest books about our relationship with food ever published, argues fluently for the importance of respecting and appreciating the taste of food. It was he who made clear the difference between the English word 'gluttony' and the French 'gourmand'. 'I remark with pride that coquetry and gourmandism, those two great modifications born of extreme sociability in response to our most pressing needs, are both of French origin,' he wrote – and indeed, despite our much larger vocabulary, no Anglo-Saxon word can quite express those two notions. Even he is insistent on linking gourmandism with health. 'A series of exact and rigorous observations has proved that a succulent, delicate, and well-ordered diet long delays the outward and visible signs of old age.

'It lends new brilliance to the eyes, new bloom to the skin, and new strength to the muscles; and as it is certain, physiologically, that depression is the cause of wrinkles, so it is no less true to say that, other things being equal, those who know how to eat are ten years younger than those to whom the science is a mystery.'

It was not, however, until one of the early greats came into my kitchen that I really began to think seriously about those who have shaped and guided how we cook and eat at home. I found a recipe for rice pudding, credited to Eliza Acton. I had no idea who Eliza Acton was, but once I had eaten that pudding, smoothly spiced, a sweet custard blanket covering the rice, I needed to know more about this paragon of the kitchen.

And thus a second obsession was conceived, and from it this book was born.

INTRODUCTION

'Kissing don't last; cookery do.'

George Meredith

We eat, we think about eating, and we write, and read, about eating. Fashions may change, but there are some things that never can. On the walls of the oldest known tomb of an Egyptian woman are painted pictures of bread-making so detailed that they amount to a recipe. They show us how bread was made four thousand years ago, in another time, another place. They also, by the by, show how important a part of life bread was; it is not a dainty canapé's construction that featured so large in Senet's life, after all.

Through the ages recipes were passed down from mother to daughter by word of mouth, or on scraps of paper. The kitchen was for centuries the woman's domain. In great houses or palaces the cooking might be undertaken by a man, but elsewhere the aprons were stretched tightly over bosoms, not chests. Those great houses valued their cooks, as we know through literature from Livy, who wrote in his *History of Rome* that by around 187BC 'the cook...who had been employed as a slave of low price became dear: what had been nothing but a métier was elevated to an art'. From there we can leap across the ages to Anatole, Bertie Wooster's Aunt Dahlia's cook at Brinkley Court. Many a Wodehousian denouement is come to through the fear of Anatole's leaving.

Although the British can now, in the twenty-first century, eat as well in our great cities as anywhere else in the world, we are still not noted abroad for our own cooking. The French have referred to us as 'rosbif' for two reasons – one being the unappealing colour so many of us go when we meet the sun, but the other being that for centuries we have been known more for offering up slabs of

9

beef than for any fine tuning of our ingredients. It is not, therefore, surprising that none of the Western world's earliest cooking manuscripts come from England, nor that most of our culinary words come from Latin or French, not Old English. (Beef from boeuf for cow meat, pork from porc for pig etc. And the very word 'recipe' is the Latin for 'take', the word that opens so many recipes.)

The first surviving cookery manuscript was, unsurprisingly, from Rome, a collection of 459 recipes called 'De re coquinaria' (on the subject of cooking), which was probably not written by the famous Roman gourmet Apicius in the first century AD, but by someone else of the same name a few centuries later. As with most of the earliest cookery books, these recipes were aimed at the rich, not the housewife kneading her loaf of bread, so include some of the most exotic ingredients of the time, including flamingo.

The earliest cookbook to survive in England was also aimed at the Great Houses of the land. *The Forme of Cury* (nothing to do with our later obsession with chicken tikka masala, but from the Latin 'curare' – to dress food) is a collection of 196 recipes handwritten on calfskin by Richard II's master cooks and physicians. At this time, and for centuries after, cooking and medicine were closely linked and cookbooks would include home remedies. What is of interest about the food that was eaten at that period is that, contrary to what you might expect, garlic and spices were used. In the twelfth century the Crusaders brought them back from their travels, and in many ways our medieval food (in the great houses at least) was surprisingly close to the now fashionable Moroccan cookery.

With the arrival of the printing press in England came the beginning of the more general cookbook. Indeed one of the earliest books printed was a carving manual (the art of carving carried with it a whole lot of class connotations), written by William Caxton's assistant, and early cooking books include the old-fashioned *A No-*

ble Book of Cookery ffor a Pryncis Household (1540) and *A Propre New Boke of Cokerye* (1545). At this time cooking books were very vague as to quantities and instructions. For example, a recipe for 'Chekyns upon soppes' (Chicken served on bread and sauce) does not even mention how to cook the chicken: 'Take sorel sauce a good quantitie and put in Sinamon and suger and lette it boyle and poure it upon the soppes then laie on the chekyns.' Something as vague as that would throw many British housewives, now used to step-by-step instructions for a whole menu (à la Jamie's *30-Minute Meals*) into a frenzy of fear and panic.

By the end of the sixteenth century increasing numbers of little cookbooks began to be printed and, more interestingly, were being aimed at householders rather than professional cooks. Quantities were beginning to be included, as well as some timings; clocks were making their way into homes. The question of the audience a book is aimed at continues to be potentially problematic; when, in 1989, the chef Raymond Blanc wrote *Recipes from Le Manoir aux Quat' Saisons*, it proved far too difficult for the market at which it was officially aimed – the home cook. He acknowledged this by following up with *Cooking For Friends* (1991). 'This book,' he wrote in the introduction, 'has not been written for chefs but for cooks at home.' These, the books which were published for the home cook, are the ones which are dealt with in this book. It is the history of Domestic Cookery Writing which concerns us, not the grand furbelows of the professional chef.

The first really important book aimed at the housewife was the aptly named *The English Huswife, Containing the Inward and Outward Virtues Which Ought to Be in a Complete Woman* by Gervase Markham, published in 1615. Continuing the fashion of including medical recipes, it contains the first ever published recipe for baking bread – only a few thousand years after the paintings on Senet's tomb.

In many ways Markham was the first real ancestor of writers we still know and love, such as Isabella Beeton. Alongside the recipes was advice on what made a 'complete woman'. 'She must bee cleanly both in body and garments, she must have a quick eye, a curious nose, a perfect taste and a ready ear; she must not be butter fingered, sweet toothed nor faint hearted,' he wrote, not so many miles away from Mrs Beeton's 'Cleanliness is also indispensable to Health, and must be studied both in regard to the person and the House, and all that it contains.'

It is through Markham that we really first see what was to become the bedrock of the buyer of cookery books for the future: the careful, aspirational, health and price aware middle-class housewife. And this is partly because at this stage in history – late Elizabethan, early Stuart – the middle class was growing. Not only that, but, with the great Queen Elizabeth at the head of the country, women were being looked at slightly differently. More women were literate, more women ran their households supported by female servants. One of the big differences between then and now was how much more these women were expected to know. Markham's premise was that if you were truly to understand how to cook, a woman had to understand *and be able to grow* her own herbs and vegetables. Two hundred years later Mrs Beeton included facts about vegetables, but there was no gardening advice. In our time, there is beginning to be a slight swing back, with Jamie Oliver's *Jamie at Home* and Nigel Slater's *Tender* books. Both these authors talk about how and what to grow, rather than just how to eat.

Although travellers to England continued to mock the English practice of serving slabs of roast meat, 'made' dishes – i.e. dishes involving putting various ingredients together – began to make their appearance both on the table and therefore in the cookery books. The fricassée, a French dish where meat is served in a sauce

12

made of its own stock or juices, and the hodge-podge, from the Spanish stew olla podrida, both arrived in England at this time. The fricassée has survived. The hodge-podge, despite its delightful name, has not. As it seems to have been the culinary equivalent to Noah's Ark, with almost every walking and flying thing along with an entire vegetable garden all boiled up together, this is probably for the best.

With a dip during the troubled times of the Civil War, cookery books continued to be produced. Sometimes, in modern 'celebrity endorsement' style, by aristocrats willing to share their (or their cooks') secrets. Lord Ruthven's *Ladies' Cabinet Opened*, published in 1639, was successful enough to call for a revised edition in 1654. This book followed the fashion of producing a mixture of recipes for food, sweets and medicine. Shortly after that came the first real innovation for some time with the publication of a professional cook's book. Robert May's *The Accomplisht Cook, or the Art and Mystery of Cooking* was published in 1660 and reprinted several times. It was the first cookery book to use illustrations and really the first major recipe book published. It is a book that crosses the medieval world with the new; recipes from the middle ages go side by side with modern French and Spanish recipes.

May also established the tradition of addressing his readers almost personally, and as though he has a moral duty to share his knowledge: 'To all honest and well-intended persons of my profession, and others, this book can not but be acceptable, as it plainly and profitably discovers the mystery of the whole art; for which, though I may be envied by some, that only value their private interests above posterity and the public good; yet God and my own conscience would not permit me to bury these, my experiences, with my silver hair in the grave.' However important May's *Accomplisht Cook* is in the development of the cookery book, it was aimed at others like him – the professional chefs of large houses, and as such did not forward the skills of the middle-class housewife. May saw himself as an Artist, and had no time or patience for any restraints of purse. 'To be confined and limited to the narrowness of a Purse is to want the materials from which the Artist must gain his knowledge,' he wrote. This is not what the housewife, faced with the remains of a leg of lamb and four hungry children, needed to be told.

These then are the ancestors of the cookery books which now take up so many shelves in the bookshop and indeed in my own kitchen. Publishing has changed, and so have fashions, but from Hannah Woolley on one strand has remained consistent: we look to cookery books for advice as much as inspiration, for security as much as greed. Whether we are using Delia or *The French Laundry Cookbook*, we are hoping that the recipes given us will be easy to follow and not beyond our purse. (We may well be disappointed in both if we've chosen *French Laundry*.)

In keeping with this aim, the recipes I have chosen are ones which I feel still have resonance today. They were worth cooking then; they are worth cooking now. They will not cost the earth, and although some of them might include ingredients that are not in fashion now, they are all easy to find.

PART ONE

THE WRITERS

HANNAH WOOLLEY
1622–1675

THE COOKS GUIDE (1664)

Hannah Woolley, the first woman who wrote with a straightforward commercial aim, knew exactly what the housewife needed to be told.

After the jumble of the Civil War, society was on the move. There were women whose families had lost their fortunes, and those who had made them. Those on the up and those on the down both had a lot to learn about how to run a household. Eliza Acton is credited with being the 'real', or at any rate first, Mrs Beeton, but it is Hannah Woolley who can really lay claim to that title. As with Mrs Beeton, Hannah Woolley's books not only include recipes, but also give advice on marketing, menus and how to behave. Unlike Mrs Beeton's, Woolley's books are addressed as much to the cook and the kitchen maids as to the lady of the house.

Where her writing is similar to Mrs Beeton's is in two ways: firstly in that her first book, *The Ladies Directory* (published in 1661), was written with a very simple aim in mind – Hannah Woolley needed to make money – and secondly in that her books dealt with a great deal more than 'mere' cooking.

There are conflicting theories about Woolley's life. Going against the customs of the time (women writers barely existed and certainly did not publicise themselves) Woolley was happy to write about her life, but there is some dispute as to whether her last book, *The Gentlewomans Companion*, in which some biographical detail is included, was entirely her work. Some scholars believe that by then her success was enough that the publishers hired a hack to write the book and Woolley just passed the proofs and made additions and corrections at the end. Be that as it may, some facts are undisputed.

17

Woolley (maiden name unknown) was orphaned at fourteen. According to *The Gentlewomans Companion*, she then, unlike most penniless girls at the time, gained employment as a teacher and 'began to consider how I might improve my time to the best advantage, not knowing at that age anything but what reason and fancy dictated me'. Even at this early age Hannah was clearly a girl with energy and ambition. At seventeen she was taken up by a noble lady who recognised a 'perfect treasure' in the making and encouraged her education. *The Gentlewomans Companion* suggests that Woolley then taught, but *The Queen-Like Closet* has her staying with 'the noble lady' until her 1647 marriage to Benjamin Woolley.

Woolley was a grammar school boy made good, now Master of the Grammar School at Newport Pond in Essex. Hannah's experience, especially with medicine, made her an invaluable wife, and in 1655 the couple set up a school in Hackney outside London. The marriage was a happy one, with at least four surviving sons to its name, one of whom Hannah lived with in her final years.

In 1661 Woolley was widowed. It is thought that at this time she worked for a Lady (Anne) Wroth, whose husband Henry had been knighted by Charles I for loyalty to the Crown. Her second book, *The Cooks Guide*, was dedicated to Lady Wroth's daughter Mary. More significantly, it was during her first widowhood that she decided to self-publish. Woolley is important not only to the history of cookery writing, but also to the history of writing itself; she is the first woman in England to have put her name to a book, and to have made a living from books. Woolley was never behind-hand in blowing her own trumpet, so when she writes of her reasons for her career she cannot help but point out her success: 'It is no ambitious design of gaining a Name in print (a thing as rare for a Woman to endeavour, as obtain) that put me on this bold undertaking; but the meer pity I have entertain'd for such Ladies, Gentlewomen, and others, as have not received the benefits of the tythe of the ensuing Accomplishments.' This is pure disingenuity; she definitely had the accomplishments, but she also needed an income.

The Ladies Directory dealt mostly with medicine and confectionary, and was not cheap at six shillings, but with her usual chutzpah and self-promotion she wrote, 'I beseech you, grudge it [the cost] not, since there is in it, many Pounds worth of Skill imparted to you.' The public clearly did not begrudge the six shillings as within a few years she had to reprint the book, and her next, *The Cooks Guide* (dedicated to Anne Wroth), was paid for by a publisher.

Woolley married again in 1666 to a widower, Francis Challinor. There was a brief period of silence from her, but on his death (which was before 1699) she began to write again, not without a mention of her two husbands: 'I have been married to two Worthy, Eminent and brave persons.'

In 1670 she published *The Queen-Like Closet* 'OR RICH CABINET: Stored with all manner of RARE RECEIPTS FOR *Preserving, Candying, and Cookery*. Very Pleasant and Beneficial to all Ingenious Persons of the *Female Sex*'. She promised the reader that 'it is worthy of the title it bears, for the very precious things you will find in it.' This ran to five editions. Her next book, *The Accomplish'd Lady's Delight* (1672), was a cunning revision of the first two in one volume. In the preface she continues in her work of self-promotion. She tells the reader that the book 'containeth more than all the Books that ever I saw Printed in this Nature, they being rather Confounders, than Instructors'. She also set forth her stall for being remembered, writing 'I would not willingly dye while I live nor be forgotten when I am dead.'

After her second widowhood, Woolley lived in London with her son Richard. She continued to work, making a living selling medicines and advice and she also ran what might well have been the first domestic employment agency. Using her vast experience, she trained up servants as well as finding them places. Hannah Woolley is no longer a household name, but hers is a name that fits in the pantheon both of great food writers and of early feminists.

THE BOOK

After the success of *The Ladies Directory*, Woolley knew the direction in which she needed to travel next. *The Ladies Directory* was mostly about medicine, confectionary and preserving fruit and vegetables (clearly an important skill in a pre-fridge, pre-canning, pre-freezer world); *The Cooks Guide* (1664), written to complement it, was more recipe based. Although aimed at employees, there was also the awareness that as many servants still could not read, the employers might themselves need a bit of a hand. 'It is a miserable thing for any woman,' she wrote in a letter to Anne Wroth's daughter, printed in *The Cooks Guide*, 'though never so great, not to be able to teach her servants.'

Woolley's works reveal a great deal about the accomplishments it was thought a seventeenth-century woman, or at any rate 'lady', needed. As well as the presumably ladylike, but also useful, arts of preserving flowers and fruit, she was expected to make jams and pickles. She should have some knowledge of basic medicine, and some ideas as to how to cure more advanced illnesses. Her cure for breast cancer ('Take the Dung of a Goose, and the Juice of Celandine, and bray them well in a mortar together, and lay it to the Sore, and this will stay the Cancer, and heal it') might explain why scientists are still working on this problem. Her grasp of wrinkle cures and cosmetics 'some Rare Beautifying Waters, Oyls,

Oyntments, and Powders, for Adornment of the Face and Body, and to cleanse it from all Deformities that may render Persons Unlovely' is probably more efficacious.

Another surprising element in *The Accomplish'd Ladies Delight* is a section giving tips on Angling, which she stresses is not 'improper in a Book of this Nature'.

Last, but by no means least, is a 'Guide to all manner of Cookery, both in the English and French Mode', and it is this area which is of course our special interest.

Her final book, or however much of it was in fact hers, was *The Gentlewomans Companion*. It is a fantastic work, aimed at every woman 'from the Lady at the Court, to the Cookmaid in the Country'. As was the way then, the books include medical advice 'a most incomparable broth or drink for a sick person' (basically chicken broth) and 'an excellent restorative for a weak back' (dates, catmint, 'the pith of an ox', eggs, etc.), among others, but Woolley is both of her time, and surprisingly ahead of it. She writes with passion about the right of girls to be educated – 'I cannot but complain of, and must condemn the great negligence of Parents, in letting the fertile ground of their Daughters lie fallow, yet send the barren Noddles of their sons to the University, where they stay for no other purpose than to fil their empty Sconces with idle notions,' pointing out that 'had we the same Literature, he [man] would find our brains as fruitful as our bodies.' She writes wryly of fashion, suggesting that the 'Farthingals of old, were politickly invented to hide the shame of great Bellies unlawfully puft up'; she is not against adornment, but very anti 'paint'. She gives instructions as to good manners, health, hygiene, diet and medicine. She even, like Mrs Beeton so many years later, gives advice on how to keep a husband from the pub: 'Let whatever you provide be so neatly and cleanly drest that his fare, though ordinary, may engage his appetite, and disingage his fancy from taverns, which many are compell'd to make use of by reason of the continual and daily dissatisfaction they find at home.'

A great deal of the interest of this book comes from the light it throws on the manners and mores of the time. She counsels children on how to treat their parents and vice versa, but does not insist on all reading being pious, encouraging the reading of 'Romances which treat of Generosity, Gallantry, and Virtue.' Of course she insists on moral books – 'Books are the true discoverers of the mind's imperfections...In perswading you to read, I do not advise you should read all Books; advise with persons of understanding... and fancy not their quantity but quality.'

For a woman writing in the seventeenth century, a lot of what she says is refreshing and modern. Perhaps her only rule with which one would entirely disagree today is her opening advice on the subject of Marriage: 'There are these two Essentials in Marriage, Superiority and Inferiority. Undoubtedly the Husband hath power over the Wife, and the Wife ought to be subject to her Husband in all things.' Like her intellectual descendant, Isabella Beeton, Hannah Woolley is pleased to back up her advice with scholarly allusions to Classical history and myth. This may show off her learning (considerable for a woman of her time) but does not entirely advance her case. But, also like Mrs Beeton, Woolley is keen to encourage women, however learned they may be, to take pride in being good housewives: 'To govern an House is an excellent and profitable employment; there is nothing more beautiful than an Houshold well and peaceably governed; it is a profession that is not difficult; for she that is not capable of any thing else, may be capable of this.'

Her rules for table manners would apply as well today; it is that she needs to point them out that makes us wonder about how many women must have behaved at table: 'Fill not your mouth so full, that your cheeks shall swell like a pair of Scotch bag-pipes… Gnaw no bones with your Teeth, nor suck them to come at the marrow…It is very uncivil to criticize or find fault with any dish of meat or sauce during the repast…or to ask what such a Joint or such a Fowl cost…it is uncivil to rub your teeth in company, or to pick them at or after meals, with your knife…' and so on.

Woolley's cookery writing represents the ranks of the middle classes who wanted good honest English traditions respected and veered away from the 'fancy' French food of writers such as the French Francois de la Varenne, whose *Le cuisinier francois*, published in France in 1651 and translated into English in 1653, raised the profile of French food. On the return to the throne of Charles II in 1660, from an exile partly spent in France, things French – including and perhaps especially cooking – became very much the fashion. Of course many of our culinary words come from the French, but it is interesting to see in Woolley's writing the beginnings of a pride in English food and English terminology. One of her recipes tells her readers how 'to Farce, or stuff, a Fillet of Veal'. 'Farce' may still be the more familiar word to housewives, but Woolley is fighting back with a good English word. Look forward a few centuries to the craze for nouvelle cuisine which took over English food, and remember Gary Rhodes's down to earth riposte of English cooking, and you will realise that nothing changes. Woolley cared – and knew that her readers would care – about practicality and economy. She included recipes using up leftovers, turning them into 'handsome and toothsome dishes again' but because she knew that the food you cook announces your social status, she also included some of the more 'modern' flavours such as anchovies, wine and cream.

For our purposes, it is Woolley's cooking that is most important, and by her own writing we know that this was the case with her, too: 'As to your divertissements, none carries in it more profit than Cookery.' She refers to cookery as a 'commendable art', and this very word 'art' gives the housewife turning to the recipes a sense not just of purpose, but of creativity.

To the modern reader, Woolley's recipes are a little confusing. They are ordered any old how which suggests that the book was just a transcription of a manuscript of collected recipes. At the beginning of the eighteenth century there had been a passing fashion for ordering cookbooks alphabetically, but Woolley did not go for that, although there is an index. She rarely gives quantities, cooking times and of course never listed the ingredients at the beginning of the recipe (this did not regularly happen until Beeton). Remember, though, that with most of the cooking done on an open fire, or directly onto charcoal, cooking times were bound to be more varied than now with our thermostated ovens. Her instructions as to sizing are also vague; in one recipe she says to cut bread in slices 'about the bigness of a groat, and as thin as Wafers'. Elsewhere we are told to cut meat the size of a pullet's egg. But even now, we can use our imagination and intuition to understand what she means.

Woolley was trying to make a living; she had to appeal to as wide an audience as possible. So while the (male) French chefs were writing recipes for fancy feasts, Woolley was trying to adapt their fashions to humbler, English tastes – and smaller pockets. While using modern French tastes regularly, she does not let go of the older ingredients – verjuice, and of course sugar. The French were beginning to separate sweet ingredients from savoury, and Woolley did begin to follow their lead, but not entirely. To us, Woolley's use of sugar with almost everything would seem (never

24

mind unhealthy) almost disgusting. A leg of lamb stewed with nutmeg, raisins and gooseberries might be delicious, but do we really want sugar in the stew, and yet more sprinkled on it when served? I think not. But the recipe shows that the Englishman's love of sugar, which led to Elizabethan English being famed for their rotten teeth and bad breath, still had a hold in the seventeenth century. By the 1680s, when Woolley began to go out of fashion and was no longer reprinted, the reason was mostly to do with the sweetness of her cooking.

Another much-used ingredient in Woolley's kitchen is butter, using much more than our modern, health conscious cooks do. Her recipe for scrambled, or buttered, eggs involves twenty eggs and more than a pound of butter.

We are also unlikely to bother with boiling a cod's head, nor with mincing a chicken's brain to add to a fricassée. We could not find enough 'Sparrows, Larks or other small Birds' to feed a family, although the recipe does sound rather good. Other recipes, though, have recognisable descendants in our kitchens (such as poached chicken with asparagus) and others, less familiar, stand the test of time, even if they use ingredients that we have more or less forgotten, or use very rarely. (How many of us have a once-used jar of mace in our cupboards?)

Some of the ingredients that come up again and again might surprise us; those of us that imagine Elizabeth David opened our eyes to Mediterranean ingredients would not expect anchovies and capers to be used as often as they are in *The Cooks Guide*. Nutmeg, mace and cinnamon, spices which first came to England in the Middle Ages, are all used for both sweet and savoury dishes.

There are also recipes that are of historical, rather than gastronomical, interest. Who can forget the furmity laced with rum that caused Michael Henchard to sell his wife before he became Mayor of Casterbridge? Hardy calls this drink 'antiquated slop', but looking at the recipe (without the rum) you can see it is a wholesome and cheap combination of a soup and a drink for the poor: barley, cream, ginger, mace and nutmeg for taste, eggs to thicken and (of course) sugar. Less wholesome-sounding is a recipe for 'Water-gruel' which must be the ancestor to poor Oliver Twist's fare – a handful of 'great Oatmeal' boiled in water with a few herbs and currants.

Another recipe which brings a common saying to life is Umble Pie. The umbles were the offal, usually of a deer, given to the servants or keepers. Nutritious, and possibly delicious, the umbles were diced and made into a pie with bacon and suet. Woolley uses the umbles more than once, including in a recipe for white pudding, where she refers to them as 'humbles', in this case of a hog. Nowadays you could certainly 'source' your umbles after a hunt on Exmoor – hunt followers are still given the heart and liver, with the rest going to the hounds. However I've not yet found a follower who admits to making an umble pie. Although to us the seventeenth century is modern history, in terms of its cooking there are more links to the medieval past than to our present.

Woolley closes the first part of *The Gentlewomans Companion* with a list of points by which a housewife should live; they are about food, not manners, and as apposite today as they were in 1675:

> The principal precepts that belong to the frugal ordering and disposing Houshold-affairs may be compremis'd under these heads.
> First to buy and sell all things at the best times and seasons.
> Secondly, to take an especial care that the goods in the house be not spoiled by negligence...
> Let me counsel you not only to avoid unnecessary or immoderate charges, but also with a little cost make a great shew; but above all suffer not your expence to exceed the receipt of your Husbands income.

Solid advice from then, through Dickens's Mr Micawber – 'Annual income twenty pounds, annual expenditure nineteen [pounds] nineteen [shillings] and six [pence], result happiness. Annual income twenty pounds, annual expenditure twenty pounds ought and six, result misery' – to now, when writers are publishing titles such as *Feast for a Fiver* (Sophie Grigson) and *Frugal Food* (Delia Smith).

HANNAH GLASSE
1708–1770

THE ART OF COOKERY MADE PLAIN AND EASY (1747)

'First catch your hare' is reputedly the opening to one of Hannah Glasse's recipes. With an instruction like that it is a wonder that her book, *The Art of Cookery*, ever became the smash bestseller that it was for over a hundred years. Unfortunately (or otherwise) the story is a mish-mash of truth and misunderstanding. The recipe in fact begins 'take your hare when it is cased and make a pudding...' 'Casing' a hare is the skinning of it, and a reasonable instruction in a cookery book. It is sad that Hannah Glasse, one of our earliest great domestic cookery writers, is often only misremembered with a snigger.

At the time of first publication, even after the fourth edition came out in which she identified herself, many did not believe that a woman could have written such a successful cookery book. Boswell, in his *Life of Johnson*, tells of a conversation about the *Art of Cookery* in which Johnson not only said the book could not have been written by a woman, but added 'I could write a better book of cookery than any that has yet been written.' Another guest remarked 'That would be Hercules with the distaff, indeed.' 'No, madam,' Johnson retorted. 'Women can spin very well; but they cannot make a good cookery book.'

The Hannah who reaches across the centuries is in some ways a very modern woman. She is doing her best with a large family, endless financial difficulties and a fairly feeble husband. That one of her ventures was a huge success seems almost to be by chance, when you look at the varied enterprises to which she put her hand in an effort to survive.

She was born in London in 1707, the illegitimate daughter of a Northumbrian gentleman, Isaac Allgood, and Hannah Reynolds, a widow, who Glasse referred to later as a 'wicked wretch'. Isaac Allgood's wife, another Hannah, had a son, Lancelot, with whom Hannah was brought up near Hexham. Her childhood was fairly affluent, unlike her later life. Her father, reputedly something of a drunk, died young in 1725, but by then Hannah was already married to John Glasse. At the time of their marriage (which was secret, raising various questions both about the man and the parents) Glasse was a junior officer in the British army. Later (1728–32) he and Hannah worked in service together for the 4th Earl of Donegall in Essex.

Hannah's father had left her £30 a year, but in such a way that her husband could not come near it. His wife had tricked him into signing over his estate to her, and Hannah's money did not come to her until 1740. Her half brother, Lancelot, a thoroughly respectable member of Northumbrian society, had intervened to put the wrong right. His involvement speaks well for their relationship, and Hannah and her children were clearly proud of the connection, referring to it in the death notice. Lancelot was a much more successful man than his father, serving both as Sheriff and later as MP for Northumberland.

One area in which John Glasse (who died in 1747) was not feeble was in fathering children; he and Hannah had eleven children, of which five survived to adulthood.

It is in 1746 that we find the first reference to what would become *The Art of Cookery*. In a letter to a Northumbrian aunt Margaret, Glasse writes that she has begun work on the book. She had already tried to make money through a 'medicine', which had failed (clear quackery, but remember how food and medicine were closely linked), and through weaving, which was equally unsuccessful. As was common in those days, the book was originally published by subscription, with only two hundred and two copies printed. As was also common in the eighteenth century, Hannah's name did not appear on the book, instead being credited simply 'By A Lady'. It was not until 1746, after huge success and many reprints (the first in the first year of its publication), that she claimed the book as her own, registering it as her work at Stationer's Hall.

Her husband having died in the same year as the publication of her most successful work, Glasse took up another job, setting herself and her eldest daughter Margaret up as habitmakers in Tavistock Street, Covent Garden. She was clearly proud of this business, as in the fourth edition of her book (the first time she identifies herself by name) she mentions that she is 'Habit Maker to her Royal Highness the Princess of Wales'. (This was of course also by way of drumming up customers for the business.) Despite the royal patronage this venture fared no better than had the weaving and 'elixir'. In 1754 Glasse became bankrupt, leading to a terrible loss; she had to sell her most valuable property, the copyright of *The Art of Cookery*. For a while she seems to have recouped her position, and was discharged from bankruptcy by the end of the year, but matters deteriorated again and in 1757 she was committed to debtors' jail at the Marshalsea. Anyone who has read *Little Dorrit* will have a picture of the grim life led by debtors in that prison. However she was only there a month, after which she was transferred to Fleet Prison, from which she was released by the end of the year.

Glasse did not lose heart. Her next venture was a book on household management, *The Servants Directory*. It did not mimic the success of *The Art of Cookery*. Neither did her final book, *The Compleat Confectioner*, published in 1760.

After that work, Hannah Glasse disappears from history until the brief announcement of her death in the *London Gazette*.

THE BOOK

So what was it about *The Art of Cookery* that made the book such a runaway success after its humble two hundred and two copy print run? Part of the answer lies in the full title: *The Art of Cookery Made Plain and Easy, Which far Exceeds any Thing of the kind ever yet Printed.* This is a big boast, but every part of it is true. Until *The Art of Cookery* recipe books were, as we have seen, for the most part written by chefs in charge of huge kitchens. Those were of no use to the worried housewife, particularly those on the make.

The introduction to the book is already encouraging to the faint-hearted:

> I Believe I have attempted a branch of Cookery which nobody has yet thought worth their while to write upon: but as I have both seen, and found by experience, that the generality of Servants are greatly wanting in that point, I therefore have taken upon me to instruct them in the best manner I am capable; and, I dare say, that every Servant who can but read, will be capable of making a tolerable good Cook; and those who have the least notion of Cookery, cannot miss of being very good ones.

Part of the joy of the book is Glasse's unpretentious style, and her determination to push English food and ideas over French ones. She makes clear that this is her plan from the outset:

> If I have not wrote in the high polite style, I hope I shall be forgiven; for my intention is to instruct the lower sort, and therefore must treat them in their own way. For example: when I bid them lard a fowl, if I should bid them lard with large lardoons, they would not know what I meant; but when I say they must lard with little pieces of bacon, they know what I mean. So, in many other things in Cookery, the great cooks have such a high way of expressing themselves, that the *poor* girls are at a loss to

know what they mean; and in all *Receipt Books* yet printed, there are such an odd jumble of things as would quite spoil a good dish; and indeed some things so extravagant, that it would be almost a shame to make use of them, when a dish can be made full as good, or better without them.

Glasse understood, as did later domestic cookery writers, that her readers needed confidence not just in cooking, but in shopping, and that for many of them prices were important; she saves much of her scorn for those who stick to the French way of cooking: 'If gentlemen will have French cooks, they must pay for French tricks...So much is the blind folly of this age, that they would rather be imposed on by a French booby, than give encouragement to a good English cook!' The very use of the word 'tricks' shows her scorn and her feeling that French cooking was no more than show.

Early cookbooks dealt with huge showpieces which might interest other chefs but would be useless to the domestic cook. One of the reasons Glasse's book was so successful at the time, and why her name has remained high in the memory of those interested in domestic cookery, is that she was one of the very first to produce a book designed for everyday living:

> I do not pretend to teach professed Cooks, my design being to instruct the ignorant and unlearned (which will likewise be of use in all private families) and that in so full and plain a manner, that the most ignorant Person, who can but read, will know how to do Cookery well.

Setting out her stall like this, she cleverly creates an audience of both mistress and servants; *Household Management* was aimed just at the mistress, and it was only in later editions that her husband, publisher Sam Beeton, realised he could widen the market up and down the social scale. Although some critics at the time commented that Mrs Glasse's style was rough and ready, rather than the writing of someone of education, she approached this head-on in her introduction: when she refers to 'the lower sort', she is not intending to be patronising, more to ease any worries of her prospective audience.

Glasse realised that the truly inexperienced would be nervous of the very first basics of cooking – how to choose the produce. Nowadays you have to try fairly hard to buy food that is 'off'. Imagine how much more daunting the markets and traders of the eighteenth century were to the new housewife. The glory of this part of the book is that it is as relevant now as two hundred and fifty years ago. Cheese that is too wet might have maggots, too dry and it might have mites. (I did once eat a mouthful of Brie only to realise that the maggots were running all over the cracker. I finished the mouthful before telling my hostess; my then husband thought it was ill-mannered of me to point it out at all.) You can tell the age of venison by its hooves – as the deer ages the clefts become wider apart and rougher. The first place a carcass will begin to go off is by the kidneys. We may not shop in that way any longer, but let's not pretend we don't sometimes have something potentially dodgy in the fridge. Not maybe a lamb's head ('mind the eyes; if they be sunk or wrinkled, it is stale, if plump and lively it is new and sweet') but the fat on meat might well bear inspecting for colour.

Anyone new to cooking could do worse than read Hannah Glasse's book. Not just the recipes, but the general facts before she begins the body of the book. I am amazed by the number of people who do not know that if you put salt on beef before roasting it, it draws out the gravy and dries it up. Hannah would have told them. She also advises on the freshness of an egg – put it into water and see if it sinks (fresh) or floats (stale). It is little tips of that nature that, reading it even now, make clear why women seized so avidly on the book. The writing, too, is very accessible. In the same way that Delia and Nigella write in a cosy, chatty style, Hannah Glasse's voice also comes through. She will often, mid-recipe, give a little personal aside, such as 'this is the best sauce; but you may make what you please'. Less of a 'teacher' than Eliza Acton, more of a 'person' than Isabella Beeton, a tentative cook would feel safe in Hannah Glasse's hands. Her recipes for different sauces for pig begins thus: 'Now you are to observe there are several ways of making sauce for a pig. Some do not love any sage in the pig, only a crust of bread; but then you should have a little dryed sage rubbed and mixed with the gravy and butter.' She runs through various sauces that might be good with pig (including, oddly to our tastes, bread sauce) and then writes, 'Some love a few currants boiled in it, a glass of wine, and a little sugar, but that you must do just as you like it.' While she's not giving up on the sage, she (like Elizabeth David so many years later) throws out culinary ideas at the same time as setting out recipes and giving tips. How to make the crackling crisp? Flour the pig all over and 'keep flouring it till the eyes drop out, or you find the crackling hard'. Her main recipe for good gravy is to add butter to the gravy from the animal, 'boil it, and pour it into the dish with the brains bruised fine, and the sage mixed all together, and then send it to table'.

Of course much about the book is dated, but at the time it was a book which moved the way the English ate forward. The fashion for the overpowering sweetness of the seventeenth century (as seen in Woolley's book) was on the wane. The puddings Glasse copied from other writers are unchanged, whereas savoury dishes are adapted to more modern tastes.

The modes of cooking are of course still completely alien to us. Most cooking would have been on an open fire. Roasting would

34

have been on a spit, with a huge metal basting dish underneath to catch the fat and juices. Never mind the ease we have in the way of blenders and choppers, the cook's first task would be to ensure the fire was burning at the right heat and to keep it at that level. Other recipes, which seem obvious to us, were in fact new at the time; she was the first to suggest frying potatoes in butter till brown, and hers was the first printed recipe for 'Currey the India way' (in which she suggests adding browned and ground coriander seeds to an onion or rabbit stew). For the fifth edition of *The Art of Cookery* (1755) she gave a recipe for raspberry and cream ice, a new fashion which ten years later had become almost the norm ('ice cream is a thing to be used in all desserts'). She also advocated vegetables *al dente* long before Elizabeth David. 'Most people,' she wrote, 'spoil garden Things by over boiling them; All things that are Green should have a little Crispness for if they are over boil'd they neighte have any wetness or beauty.' In fact it is surprising to notice that the French (nowadays at any rate) often over-boil their vegetables, producing green beans that are cooked almost to the point of greyness.

The order of the book might well confuse a modern housewife: there is a chapter on food for a 'fast-supper', i.e. in Lent. In this chapter come many (indeed most) of her fish recipes, as well as those for vegetables, vegetable soups, puddings and eggs. Other chapters which you would not find nowadays are 'directions for the sick' (simple broths rather than medicines) and 'for Captains of ships'. Perhaps most amusing, even for a confirmed Francophile, is Chapter III. Its title is: 'Read this Chapter, and you will find how expensive a French cook's sauce is.'

Before Glasse, cooking and medicine were very closely linked; both, after all, used ingredients from nature. But Glasse was an innovator with a clear idea of her purpose. Not for her a mishmash

35

of economy, fashion advice and home management. Glasse's only medical recipes are for the 'certain cure for the bite of a mad dog', a recipe against plague, and one to clear a room of bugs ('First take out of your room all silver and gold lace'). 'Nor,' she says, will [I] 'take upon me to direct a lady in the economy of her family…I shall not fill my Book with nonsense of that kind, which I am very well assured none will have regard to.' Indeed the only instruction for matters of the household (aside from shopping for food) is a brief direction to the housemaid to throw a little wet sand to the floor before sweeping a room. That, combined with the words 'nonsense of that kind' imply simply that Mrs Glasse was, like so many other women before and since, happier in the kitchen than behind a broom.

The key to Glasse's success, apart from her style, lies in her realisation that simplicity is all. Her recipes are easy to read and easy to cook, her advice sound and not patronising. Neither (on the whole) are the recipes extravagant – this was not a book written by a chef for chefs, but written by a woman for women.

ELIZA ACTON
1799–1859

MODERN COOKERY FOR PRIVATE FAMILIES (1845)

Eliza Acton was not a woman of her time. In an era when women without a husband were nothing, when women writers often chose to write under a male pseudonym, coy initials, or the even more coy 'By A Lady', Acton put her own name on her books with no shame.

She was born in Battle, Sussex in 1799, the oldest child of John Acton (who later took great pride in the acquisition of the title 'Gentleman'). Shortly after her birth the family moved to Ipswich, where John worked as the business manager of a company of brewers, Trotman, Studd and Halliday. Eliza was the first of nine surviving children, the youngest born in 1815 so, like the later Isabella Beeton, was part of a large family.

The family was affluent; in 1811, after the death of Trotman, John became a partner in the brewery, and although buying in to the partnership must have cost him dear it was clearly worth the investment. The most interesting piece of information to be found about Acton's childhood was the death of her sister Lucy, born in 1812. Lucy's nursemaid overdosed her with laudanum (given to soothe colicky babies) and the child died. Eliza, aged twelve, would certainly have been aware of the death of the child, and of the trial which was held in their own house. Although the nurse was let off on the charge of misadventure rather than murder, history does not relate whether she was allowed to keep her job.

Acton was clearly a young woman of drive. Although of course women had to have something in their bag in case they didn't find themselves a husband, her independence began early. Still only aged seventeen, in 1816 she and a 'Miss Nicholson' placed a notice in the *Ipswich Chronicle* stating that they were to open a boarding school for Young Ladies. Three years later, in 1819, there is another advertisement in the same paper saying that the Misses Acton were to open a boarding school for Young Ladies in Great Bealings, a village outside Woodbridge. It is not known which, or how many, of her six sisters were in cahoots with this scheme, but a year after the new school opened Miss Nicholson's closed and in 1822 the Acton school moved from the village to more upmarket (and therefore expensive) premises in Woodbridge.

Meanwhile Eliza was beginning to write poetry. Read now, much of it seems facile and derivative, but some of it speaks with real energy and passion, a passion which was later directed into her fight for unadulterated food and healthy eating. (Rather bizarrely, re her love of poetry, she includes a poetic recipe for salad in her book.)

Much of the detail of Eliza's youth is lost in the mists of time. Even when we know she undertook some action, we don't know why. She went to Europe in 1823, just after her school had moved premises. Like most English families, the Actons were feeling the economic squeeze after the end of the Napoleonic Wars and were not quite as well off as they had been. With such a vast family John Acton was unlikely to be footing the bill for pleasure trips so far afield, so it is possible that Eliza travelled as a lady's companion, or a governess. She could also have been travelling for health reasons; she certainly became a woman very preoccupied with her health. The best we can do is make educated guesses.

Even more interesting are the possibilities around her visit to France in May 1826. We know she went, and we know from her poetry that part of her was expecting to die:

I HAVE but left my pleasant home
And native vales, to die!—
… My Mother !--thou wilt hope in vain
Thy wandering one's return:--
… But sever'd thus by land, and wave,
    From tenderness, and thee,
And all whose love, might sooth, or save,
I perish here-and ev'n my grave
    In stranger-earth must be !

Well she didn't die, but one theory is that she had an illegitimate baby, which was then integrated into her family and passed off as her married older sister's child. The child, Susannah, certainly believed herself to be Eliza's, kissing a portrait of her every night and referring to her as her 'real mother', and Susannah's daughter Mary used also to refer to 'my grandmother', swiftly correcting herself each time. The father of the child is of course unknown, but a clue could be in the first poem of her collection, 'On the Death of Major Whitefoord, December 15th 1825'. The poor Major shot himself with a fowling piece in an accident while out shooting game. Whether it was in despair at having impregnated his neighbour's daughter, or a genuine accident 'while pursuing the sports of the field', is anyone's guess, but Eliza certainly took his death hard:

LIKE blighted leaves, around us fall
    The young, the gifted, and the brave;
And still the most belov'd of all
    Seem earliest fated to the grave.

The timing certainly works; the Major died in 1825 and in 1826 Eliza was setting off for France and writing mournful poetry about death.

Her poetry also reveals another love affair, presumed to be with a French soldier. She loved and lost a handsome man with dark curly hair. Writing a poem called 'L'Abandonée', she tells of her betrayal. 'They said the words I loved to hear/Were whispered in another's ear.' 'Take back thy ring!' she shouts (poetically) and declares that there is more to her rage than his faithlessness:

> But never shall my fate be twin'd
> With that of one, whose fame is blasted;
> Whose word is as the idle wind;
> Whose days in servile guilt are wasted!

There are other clues to the man's shame, but alas no hard facts. She talks of a 'dark tale' which 'links [his] name/To perfidy and deepest shame' and she 'shudder[s]' even to remember that she ever loved him. 'Forgive thee! – Yes' she writes in another poem, but then it's all a little in her future, as the forgiveness will only come 'when ev'ry chord/which binds my soul to earth, is broken'. It's all wonderfully Wilkie Collins, but without the explanatory denouement.

Be that as it may, in October of 1826, not long after her possibly childbearing trip to France, Eliza published her volume of poetry – sixty-three poems in all, with a subscription list of 328 names. So successful was it that it was reprinted within a month. Any money that came to her would have been more than useful, as by then the Actons were in big financial trouble. In 1827 John Acton was declared bankrupt and all his household furniture was sold. He fled to France to avoid his debtors (and perhaps a Dorritt-like incarceration) and Mrs Acton moved to Tonbridge where she established a boarding house.

The story goes that in 1835 Eliza went to London to see Longman, her publishers, about another book of poetry. Always with an eye to the main chance and on the lookout for a new

Maria Rundell, they told Eliza that rather than write more poetry she should write a cookery book. Maria Rundell's *A New System of Domestic Cookery* (subtitled at length *Formed Upon Principles of Economy; and Adapted to the Use of Private Families*) was a short collection of recipes published by John Murray in 1806. It had had great success; Longman had made an unsuccessful effort to poach the author and was now retaliating.

Acton, not a woman to do things by halves, spent ten years researching, writing and above all *cooking* for the book. Unlike Isabella Beeton Eliza, aided by her live-in servant Ann Kirby, tested every single recipe. Not all the recipes were originally her own; Acton wrote to current 'celebrities' asking for recipes. She also wrote to authors asking about dishes which appeared in their works, but, again unlike Isabella Beeton, made sure to credit every recipe she borrowed. Acton's book put Rundell's for ever in the shade.

Acton's honesty about her sources was something very dear to her heart. In the ten-year gap between the publication of the first and second editions of *Modern Cookery* twenty-five new cookery books were published, and in the preface to the second edition Eliza writes crossly about the theft of her recipes by other authors: 'At the risk of appearing extremely egotistic, I have appended "Author's Receipt" and "Author's Original Receipt" to many of the contents of the following pages; but I have done it solely in self-defence, in consequence of the unscrupulous manner in which large portions of my volume have been appropriated by contemporary authors, without the slightest acknowledgement of the source from which they have been derived.' She died before the publication of Mrs Beeton's book, which is probably just as well as had she not she would probably have expired of an apoplexy.

There is no doubt that even if Acton were pushed into food writing by her publishers and economic necessity, in doing so she discovered a new passion. She did not just take on a job and do it well, she cared deeply for the tenets that drove her work. She minded about good food, good cooking, and economy. She could not bear fancy food for fancy food's sake, nor could she bear waste. She will not have it that poor people cannot eat as well as the rich, and includes many economical and healthy dishes. Later, in her *English Bread Book* (1857) she took on the corrupt bakers who sold adulterated bread. Adulterated and processed food became her bête noir, and she worked with the energy that ultimately wore her out and brought about her early death to expose the scams that were giving the poor an even more unhealthy diet.

With her increasing success in, and passion for, food writing, Eliza's poetic output decreased. Just as well, if her last known poem (an ode on behalf of the Scots greeting the visit of Queen Victoria in 1852) is anything to go by.

Eliza Acton died in Hampstead on 13th February 1859, two years after the publication of her bread book. 'Premature old age' is entered on her death certificate as cause of death, which raises as many questions as it answers. It is thought that Eliza, for so long a vigorous, thinking, hardworking and independent woman, suffered from dementia. 'Old age' itself was not allowed to be entered on a death certificate, so the word 'premature' might well indicate early senility. In any event her legacy shows a woman of a stern and passionate mind, and it is for that that she will be remembered.

THE BOOK

Like all the best teachers, and indeed writers, Acton had a passion for her subject. Whether that passion existed before Longman sent her off with her commission to write a cookery book, or whether she developed it over the hours she spent in the hot kitchen with Ann Kirby, is irrelevant. You cannot read *Modern Cookery* without being aware that here is a writer who cares.

The book is dedicated 'to the young housekeepers of England', and this points out one of the key aims of the book. In an age where most cookery books were written by top chefs, rather than cooks, Acton made it clear that her goal was to help women (men were the chefs, women the cooks) provide good, economical and healthy meals for their families. In the preface to the first edition, Eliza observes that she has never yet found a cookery book 'quite intended for, or entirely suited to the need of the totally inexperienced', and it was this fault which she was trying to redress.

Aimed as it was at readers with little or no experience, Acton recognised that clarity was all, and she devised an entirely new way of laying out recipes. First came the method, then the ingredients and quantites, and then 'the precise time required to dress the whole', broken down into parts. This is not what we are used to now – Beeton popularised (but did not invent) the inversion of the order, with ingredients coming first – but is a very pleasing way in which to read the recipes. After all, it is not the ingredients but what is done with them that brings out the taste, so if you read the method first you can imagine the end product, and only then need to write your shopping list.

By the time the second edition was brought out, in 1855, Eliza had seriously taken up the cause of nutrition, especially for poorer families. 'The influence of diet upon health is indeed a subject of far deeper importance than it would usually appear to be considered, if we may judge by the profound indifference with which it is commonly treated.' Working from the second edition (because, unlike all the subsequent editions of Mrs Beeton's *Book of Household Management*, the author herself updated the book), it is easy to see how influenced Eliza Acton has been by scientific ideas about nutrition, especially the German Baron Liebig. However Eliza's research does not turn her into some crazy, you are what you eat, faddist. If anything it just underscores what she believed in already: 'It may safely be averred that good cookery is the best and truest economy, turning to full account every wholesome article of food, and converting into palatable meals, what the ignorant either render uneatable, or throw away in disdain. It is a popular error to imagine that what is called good cookery is adapted only to the establishments of the wealthy, and that it is beyond the reach of those who are not affluent.' Eliza defends her expensively meat-laden beef soup by pointing out that doctors and medicine will be much more expensive than a well-made beef tea and that therefore it is in the end economical to make. Why then, is it the poorest people (in the Western world) who are the fattest? A Big Mac may be cheap and (briefly) filling, but it is no cheaper nor more satisfying than a good homemade soup or stew, or plate of pasta with tomato sauce. 'Cheap, and very wholesome' are words which often occur at the beginning of an Acton recipe, to entice her poorer reader towards good food.

It is with this same end in view – that of helping people cook good and economical meals – that Eliza has 'occupied [myself] but little with the elegant superfluities or luxurious novelties with which I might perhaps more attractively, though not more usefully, have filled my pages'. Isabella Beeton, following closely after Eliza Acton, gave recipes for dished up hashes from old joints, but also included some extravagant and exhausting-looking dishes, which were avoided by Eliza.

Modern Cookery is incredibly readable, in the way that Elizabeth David later managed (indeed David thought that *Modern Cookery* was 'to my mind unquestionably the finest cookery book ever written in the English language'). It is also full of interesting surprises. Bottled sauces were beginning to appear and Acton will suddenly make a comment that could be made by a woman in Waitrose now, for instance praising Maldon salt for its superior strength and 'other qualities' over fine common salt.

Eliza Acton would not have agreed with Brillat-Savarin's enjoyment of eating for the sake of taste, though: '"Eat, – to live" should be the motto, by the spirit of which all writers [of any work on cookery] should be guided.' In fact she was naturally suspicious of the French way of cooking, preferring to rely on 'plain English dishes'. She is not too closed-minded not to give credit where it is due, however, asking 'why should the English, as a people, remain more ignorant than their continental neighbours of so simple a matter as that of preparing [nourishing food] for themselves?' and reporting that 'French vinegar is so infinitely superior to English in strength, purity, and flavour, that we cannot forbear to recommend it in preference for the use of the table.' It is in her recipe for mayonnaise that she perhaps most pointedly shows what she feels to be the difference between her cooking and the French: 'This receipt was derived originally from an admirable French cook [Carême] who stood quite at the head of his profession: but as he was accustomed to purvey for the tables of kings and emperors, his directions require some curtailment and simplifying to adapt them to the resources of common English life.'

Writing bossily was perhaps one way in which she asserted her knowledge; it could also have been another way in which young cooks were reassured. 'As this salad is the result of great experience and reflection,' she notes after one recipe, 'it is hoped young salad makers will not attempt to make any improvement upon it.'

These days, when cookery books are so ubiquitous, we might well remember Acton's stricture: 'It is not, in fact, cookery-books that we need half so much as cooks really trained to a knowledge of their duties.' By 'cooks' now we mean the domestic cook in her or his own house, rather than a servant, but the same message applies. So many people leave home and school without the faintest idea how to cook the very basics on which we survive; you need to know how to poach a fish before you need to know how to make the hollandaise for its aggrandisement.

ISABELLA BEETON
1836–1865

THE BOOK OF HOUSEHOLD MANAGEMENT (1861)

'What moved me, in the first instance, to attempt a work like this,' wrote Isabella Beeton in her Preface to the first edition of her monumental *Book of Household Management*, 'was the discomfort and suffering which I had seen brought upon men and women by household mismanagement.' This statement, while disingenuous in the extreme, nevertheless was the first of many in her book which were designed to comfort the confused housewife in need of help. With words like that, and 2,751 numbered paragraphs of guidance, the book was launched (firstly in parts as a forty-eight-page supplement to her husband's *Englishwoman's Domestic Magazine*) in a single volume in 1861 and became the standard handbook for housewives for the next hundred years.

Mrs Beeton as a brand needs no introduction: no household with any cookery books at all will be without either the *Book of Household Management* or one of its many bastard offshoots. Mrs Beeton's name appears on tea towels and biscuits, cakes and pies. But who was Mrs Beeton and how did her work come to stand in many ways for the spirit of the Victorian age?

I called her early words 'disingenuous'. In them she implies that her work grew out of some sort of philanthropic urge after a lifetime spent in the hurly burly of badly organised dinners watching miserable husbands starve and desperate wives fret their marriages away. The words suggest that 'Mrs Beeton' is a well-upholstered matron, adept at preserving and pickling, with experience of running a considerable household. In fact Mrs Beeton was little

47

more than a bride, married to a feckless but passionate publisher. She was also, perhaps to her surprise and certainly to her family's disapproval, a working journalist every bit as much as she was a wife and home-maker.

Isabella was born in March 1836 to Benjamin and Elizabeth Mayson. Elizabeth's parents, Isaac and Mary Jerrom, were servants until Isaac started his own business running a livery stable while his wife ran a boarding house. Their business sense and understanding of how to spot and use an opportunity brought them considerable success, but the changes in their circumstances were as nothing compared to the changes their daughter Elizabeth would see in her lifetime. Elizabeth Jerrom/Mayson/Dorling was a fine example of nineteenth-century social mobility, and Isabella Mayson/Beeton became a fine example of how to use that mobility to her business advantage.

Benjamin's father John Mayson was a not very successful Cumbrian clergyman (he did not make vicar until he was sixty-four) and his mother, Isabella Trimble, was the daughter of a successful brewer. Benjamin Mayson, as second son of a barely comfortable family, went to London to make his own way, and there he became a linen wholesaler in northwest London; the boy did well. The Jerroms would have seen the businessman with a vicar for a father as a good catch for their daughter.

Shortly after Isabella was born, the first of four children, the family moved to Benjamin's business premises in the City of London. This was the first of many moves for Isabella in the first few years of her life. Were we to play the game of pop psychology we could assert that Isabella's later dedication to showing the way towards a stable home had something to do with her desperate need for stability after an unsettled childhood; this would be nonsense. Her way was motivated by business, not emotion.

Isabella's childhood was fractured – as so many children's were in those days of early mortality – by the death of her father in 1840. Benjamin and Elizabeth had had two more children by then, Elizabeth Anne (Bessie) in 1838 and John in 1839. Seven months after Benjamin's sudden death from the usefully vague 'apoplexy', a final child, Esther, was born in February 1841. If the row of new children and the sudden death of her father were not enough to confuse the five-year-old girl, her mother now sent her, alone, to Cumbria to be looked after by her widowed grandfather, the seventy-nine-year-old vicar.

Isabella later returned home, but two years after her father's death there came about another change. Elizabeth Mayson married again. This time it was to Henry Dorling, a printer. Dorling was also widowed. Not only that, but his four children pretty much matched the four Maysons in age (the oldest Dorling, Henry, was born in 1834, the youngest in 1840). Who can say whether it was a marriage of affection, love, friendship, convenience or a mixture of it all? What can be said is that Dorling proved a more than fair stepfather to the four Maysons, treating them absolutely the same as he did his first four, and the further thirteen that Elizabeth and he had together.

On the marriage Elizabeth gave up the warehouse business she had been running since her husband's death and moved her family, including her very useful mother, to Henry's business in Epsom High Street.

Epsom was, and still probably is, most famous as the home of the Derby. Epsom salts says something to me, but it is mostly to do with soothing baths and therefore probably loosely connected with a long day at the races. Frith's great painting 'Derby Day', painted in 1858, shows the big day in all its glory and horror. When the races were on, Epsom was open to the world, and the world came to it. In 1843 it is thought 127,500 people came into the town on Derby Day, bringing with them drink, prostitutes, horsemen, gamblers, gypsies, acrobats, beer and wine sellers and a cross section of the world in general. And Henry Dorling, Isabella's stepfather, was a man determined to take advantage of it all.

Dorling's father William was already a somebody in Epsom at the time of his son's marriage. He owned the first printing press in the town, and printed (among other things) race cards, carrying as much information as possible about the horses and riders. These cards were the beginning of imposing some sort of sense on the chaos of the racing world, but Dorling had yet grander ideas, one of which was later to have a large impact on his step-granddaughter Isabella's young life.

He had bought shares in the Epsom Grandstand (which looms over Frith's depiction of the racing crowds), opened in 1830, and he and his son gradually acquired more and more until Henry became the largest shareholder. The Grandstand had been built to encourage a more respectable element to the races, making room for five thousand spectators and including (behind the stands) various reception rooms, a betting room and 'retiring rooms for ladies'. There was a billiard room, a thirty-yard saloon, refreshment rooms, committee rooms and public rooms. And above all, in terms of who Isabella Mayson later became, there was a huge kitchen which could dish up food for thousands of people a day. When Charles Dickens visited the Grandstand and was shown around by Dorling he commented in some amazement on the fact that 'eight hundred eggs have to be boiled for the pigeon pies and salads alone'. (Paragraph 975 of the *Book of Household Management* is the Epsom Grandstand recipe for Pigeon Pie which is decorated by pigeon feet that appear to be fighting their way out of the pie.)

All in all Henry, with control of the Grandstand and the title Clerk of the Course since 1839, was an important figure in the racing world of Epsom. But the Grandstand was only in full use a week of the year. And meanwhile, in the Dorling High Street establishment, more and more babies were being born. Even though the Dorlings had, by 1851, moved to a more distinguished address in Epsom, there was still not room enough for the ever growing family. The answer seemed simple enough. Granny Jerrom and Isabella (the eldest daughter on both sides of the family) were moved into the Grandstand with a posse of young Dorlings. Between weaning and teaching, the children ran riot in rooms built for hundreds, a kitchen built for thousands, with their eldest sister and grandmother in charge. It cannot have been too uncomfortable; in 1840 the young Queen Victoria visited the races and the whole place was of course done up for her, with new wallpapers and carpets. The children slept in rows on truckle beds that could be folded up and hidden away if visitors appeared and before long Henry, who had moved his business to the Grandstand, dropped in on the children every day. When there was a race meeting they were brought down into Epsom and scattered around the town: 'I am going to the Stand this afternoon to assist in bringing down that living cargo of children into the town, where they will remain ten days,' Isabella once wrote.

Beeton does not suggest, in her chapters on child rearing, that the ideal way is to ferry your children to the other end of town and let them run riot in a building as big as a small ship. In fact she has strong views on how a mother should be: 'It ought…to enter into the domestic policy of every parent, to make her children feel that home is the happiest place in the world; that to imbue them with this delicious home-feeling is one of the choicest gifts a parent can bestow.' She does, however, refer to circumstances in which 'the mother is either physically or socially incapacitated from undertaking these most pleasing duties [of childrearing] herself...

where, consequently, she is compelled to trust to adventitious aid for those natural benefits which are at once the mother's pride and delight to render to her child.' Whether, in writing this, Mrs Beeton thought of her young self as an 'adventitious aid' to her mother cannot be known, but what she has done here is make it *all right* to have help in the nursery. She admits that 'every woman is not gifted with the same physical ability for the harassing duties of a mother' (and very few can be gifted with the physical ability to do it for twenty-one as Elizabeth Dorling had to do) so, once again, with her eye to the main market, Mrs Beeton is encouraging the young and confused mother to reach for her book. Although the idea of Isabella as a calm figure, marooned in the Grandstand in the middle of a storm of ever-changing younger siblings is a charming one, it cannot have taken up more than a couple of years of her youth, and she was not in any event banished full time to the Grandstand. There was constant movement between there and Ormond House.

Meanwhile Dorling was becoming increasingly successful and with success came ambition for his children. Isabella and Jane Dorling (Henry's oldest daughter) were sent together to finish their education at the Heidel Institute, run by three sisters and a brother, in Heidelberg. At the Institute Isabella and Jane, along with a family of girls called Beeton, were taught French and German, maths, history, geography and needlework – but not cooking. The closest Isabella came to cooking was to learn pastry-making, and her interest in this was such that when she returned to England she asked her parents for further lessons in the art from a local baker, William Barnard. That, and the excellent French and German with which she returned to England were perhaps the most useful lessons of her life before marriage; her ability with languages was to hold her in good stead later when she travelled with her husband to do business in Paris.

The Beeton family, whose daughters were educated in Germany with Jane and Isabella, was not unknown to the Maysons. Before the move to Epsom both families had lived in Milk Street, where two Samuel Beetons (grandfather and father of Sam, Isabella's future husband) owned a pub called the Dolphin.

So in 1854 Isabella returned to Epsom, the oldest girl of an increasingly huge family, learned baking, helped out with the children, gossiped with her Granny Jerrom and, thanks again to Dorling's generosity and his recognition of her genuine musical talent, went once a week to London for piano lessons, and somehow fell in love with Sam Beeton. Before a year was out they were engaged, with her parents' consent but without much joy on their part.

Sam Beeton was in many ways different from Isabella. While she had had to be calm and phlegmatic – the eldest daughter of a huge family, trusted with the care of the children – he, the eldest son of a successful publican, sure to inherit a good business, had been allowed to go his own way. He turned his back on the pub business and went into the paper trade. Brought up in part by his grandmother Lucy and, when back in Milk Street, surrounded by his younger half sisters, Sam was used to and respected women. His and Isabella's marriage was a love match, and grew into one of real friendship and partnership. The engagement, however, was not smooth. The Dorlings's dislike of Sam grew and Isabella, under her parents' thumb, did not stand up to them. Sam came down to Epsom less and less often, making excuses to avoid seeing his future parents-in-law. Isabella wrote needy letters, busy Sam dashed off replies which barely satisfied her, although occasionally he showed signs of awareness that she was not having an easy time: 'I trust you will not have been much tortured with many catechizings?' he wrote to her in April 1856, and then not long before the wedding, 'I fear you are made very miserable oftentimes on my poor account.'

Sam, bright young entrepreneur, trying to launch the *Boy's Own Journal*, a magazine aimed at working-class boys who needed new reading material, had every business excuse he needed, but at this stage Isabella seemed less interested in his business than in his emotions. While his letters could be extravagantly emotional – 'Shall I nauseate you with too much loving you, shall I not intrude too far upon your leisure and make you exclaim in your own most practical way – "Sam I wish you would leave me alone, and allow me to continue my preparations in peace and quiet"' – he was also more than capable of not answering at all, let alone visiting. Isabella, varying between pleading and haughtiness, began to realise that she was going to have to break away from her parents, and wrote to him 'in a very short time you will have the entire management of me and I can assure you that you will find in me a most docile and willing pupil'. If she sounded in this letter like the average Victorian miss, Sam's reply is much more modern: 'I don't desire, I assure you, to *manage* you – *you* can do that quite well yourself – my only desire, my sweetest darling, is that *no one else* should manage you. You, as you know, can do anything with me – any one else, in your account, nothing!'

At the point of their engagement Sam had, since his beginnings in the paper trade, had some great successes, and some equally great failures. Beginning as a stationery seller, Sam bought into partnership with the publishers Salisbury & Clarke. He wanted to publish for the rising lower middle classes, particularly boys – throughout his publishing career this was his real ambition, and it was not just to do with money. The tide of aspiration was rising, and Sam was there both to encourage and to profit from it.

At the right place at the right time, Sam made an early strike into success with the publication of *Uncle Tom's Cabin*, the slaving story that swept first America and then England. An even more important venture was the launch of a new magazine which was to prove his most lasting success – the *Englishwoman's Domestic Magazine*. This, a careful mix of ladies' and family magazines, was to last for twenty-five years, outliving the young woman Sam had not yet even married.

Sam's introduction to the first edition foreshadows the concerns and aims of his future wife's *Book of Household Management*. 'If there is one thing of which an Englishman has just reason to be proud, it is of the moral and domestic character of his countrywomen,' he wrote. Aiming the magazine at women of all levels of domesticity, he goes on to say that it will 'doubtless be found an encouraging friend to those of our countrywomen already initiated in the secret of making "home happy"; and to the uninitiated who, sometimes from carelessness, but oftener from the want of a guiding monitor, have failed in this great particular, we shall offer hints and advice by which they may overcome every difficulty and acquire the art of rendering their efforts successful and their homes attractive'.

However, there was more to the magazine than a collection of top tips for housewives – as there was later more to the *Book of Household Management* than recipes and advice on which colours brunettes should wear ('silks of a grave hue'). The first edition included an article on female education, which shows that Sam shared the views of both his step-mother and the Dorlings when it came to education. A girl was worth more than a second-rate schooling involving watercolours and needlework. 'It must be the aim of a sound system of education to cultivate those sterling qualities which will make a good wife, instead of imparting that superficial polish which only gives the *appearances* of one.' Hardly hard-line feminism, but Sam – along, later, with his wife – was sufficiently grounded in Victorian thinking still to suppose that a woman's first aim was to marry and care for her family. Nevertheless his magazine also espoused a woman's right to divorce, and her right to a decent and decently paid job. Sam showed some real editorial bravery in the decisions he made for the magazine; he included 'Cupid's Bag', a very early form of the Agony Aunt who still figures in women's magazines today. He also took the risk of serialising *The Scarlet Letter*, Hawthorne's tale of adultery in Puritan America, which many thought too strong for Victorian tastes. He ran writing competitions – a cheap way to raise sales and fill pages – on subjects which were at first modest ('the Duke of Wellington's Funeral') but became increasingly risqué: 'Do Married Rakes make the Best Husbands?'

Sam's magazine was not enough to earn his father-in-law's respect. Some of the Beetons had been too shady, and Dorling thought that Isabella, as the daughter of an increasingly successful man, could do better. Nevertheless on 10th July 1856 Sam and Isabella married, and after a wedding breakfast at the Grandstand they set off on a honeymoon of a tour of France before returning to their new home, 2 Chandos Villas in Pinner. Isabella became pregnant almost immediately, and their son, Sam Orchart, was born ten months after the wedding, in May 1857.

Isabella was only just twenty when she married, a young girl pretty much out of the schoolroom who may have been sent abroad to school, and been made to grow up young with so many younger siblings, but with very little experience of the world. However little experience she had, there was no doubt that she had energy. Before little Sam was born she had already begun to contribute to the *Englishwoman's Domestic Magazine*. She started by using her skill with languages, translating French and German fiction. Before long that was not enough. In March 1857 Isabella began to write a cookery column for the magazine, with plans for a second column 'The Nursery'. In her April column Isabella made clear what she was trying to do – 'A daily supply is a daily waste,' she wrote, impressing on her readers, not the idea of fancy or even delicious food, but on the need to establish a system that was economical. And already the idea of writing a cookery book had been born.

When Isabella wrote to her friend Henrietta English, thanking her for the congratulations on Sam's birth, she mentioned that she was considering writing a cookery book. She might have supposed that Mrs English, a Frenchwoman with a good inside knowledge of the cooks of some of the greatest aristocratic houses in England, would be delighted to give advice on such a project but Mrs English's response was not at all warm. Despite this it was, in a roundabout way, incredibly helpful.

My Dear Mrs Beeton

...As regards yours of the 18 I see difficulties in your way as regards publishing a Book on Cookery. Cookery is a Science that is only learnt by Long Experience and years of study which of course you have not had. Therefore my advice would be compile a book from receipts from a Variety of the Best Books published on Cookery and Heaven knows there is a great variety for you to choose from. One of our best Woman Cooks who is now retired recently told me one of the Best and Most Useful books is

SIMPSON'S COOKERY

REVISED AND MODERNISED

Published by Baldwin and Craddock, Longman and Co... She is a good authority for I consider her one of the best woman cooks in England... I had her and her Husband Lately on a visit with me and showed her several books I had but she Preferred Simpson's.

And is your *intended* book meant for the Larger or the Higher Classes or the Middle Class? The latter is one I should recommend you...

Yours v sincerely

H English

In some ways this letter reads like a put-down – the dismissal of Isabella's experience, and the stress on 'intended'. But Mrs English did offer some help. She introduced Isabella to the Duke of Portland's cook Mr Orpwood, saying 'he is a very clever little fellow in his profession and a great economist, and very minute and cleanly in his kitchen'. Within the letter are two of the most important strands of the book Isabella was to go on to write. First of all, the suggestion that she use other people's recipe books, and second the question about the audience at which the book was to be aimed. Although Isabella of course tried to stretch her potential audience as widely as possible, most of the success of the *Book of Household Management* was due to the fact that it was basically aimed at the aspiring middle classes and the growing army of married, non-working women. In 1851 one in four married women was employed. Elizabeth Dorling had taken over her husband's work, Sam Beeton's stepmother ran his business; contrary to modern imaginings a fair proportion of Victorian women did work. By 1911 this ratio had dropped to one in ten married women working. So nine in ten were at home, running the house. And a lot of them were unsure as to how to do this. Isabella Beeton tapped into those women's anxieties and in doing so made her name.

Isabella, no faintheart, did not allow Mrs English's dampening letter to have any effect on her determination. Throughout her pregnancy she worked on her columns, and while work could not stop labour and birth, it did seem to get in the way of the child ever being registered. Although both she and the baby were weak and ill after the birth, Sam and Isabella went to visit the Englishes at Newmarket in August, perhaps further to pick Mrs English's brain about cookery books. While there young Sam, who had seemed to be gaining strength, sickened and died, aged only three months.

Poor Isabella, remembered for over a century as the great English advisor on homemaking, failed, through no fault of her own, to create her own family. Although, after Sam's death, she dropped 'the Nursery' column in the *Englishwoman's Domestic Magazine*, there is a chapter on the 'Duties of the Nursemaid', and another on 'Rearing etc of Children'. Her youth with the siblings would have given her much more experience to draw upon when writing these chapters than she had in cooking.

Sam Beeton, young man about town, almost certainly visited prostitutes before his marriage to Isabella. It was the entirely accepted way for young men to keep themselves satisfied until they were in a position to marry. Isabella would not be the first, nor the last, Victorian bride infected by her husband, and part of the disease in women was the effect it would have on their childbearing. Sam was quickly conceived, went to term and lived, a sickly boy, for a few months. It took two more years before another child was born to term, in June 1859, and family history suggests that Isabella had many miscarriages in between. The second Sam Orchart Beeton lasted longer than his elder brother, but died aged three and a half. All of this – the miscarriages, the weak children – suggest that Isabella had been infected with syphilis. It was not until December 1863 that the Beetons had a child – another son, this time without the Sam, but still Orchart, who lived to adulthood (in fact to a ripe age, dying in 1947). Their fourth child, Mayson Beeton, was born in January 1865.

Isabella began working properly on the first part of the *Book of Household Management* in the autumn of 1857, not long after young Sam's death. The first instalment was published in September 1859. By 1860 Isabella, now officially 'Editress' of the magazine, with Sam still Editor, continued her work on *Household Management*. Meanwhile, before it had even been published as a book, other publishers were copying the idea and bringing out their own versions.

In the next year, 1861, the indefatigable Sam founded *Queen* – later half of *Harpers and Queen* – and Isabella became its first fashion editor. This too was the year of the publication of her great work.

However, Sam's ups and downs – of which Isabella had had fair warning before their marriage, although at that stage she was more interested in love than business – never really came to an end. After only a year he was forced to sell *Queen*, and, probably more distressing for Isabella, the family had to leave Chandos Villas, their home throughout their marriage, a year before the lease was up. Isabella and Sam and baby Sam moved into the Strand, where S.O. Beeton's offices were. Isabella might not have been the world's best cook, but she was probably one of the world's most loyal wives. Although the Dorlings continued in their animosity to Sam, Isabella continued to support him. Her calmness and efficiency counterbalanced his passion and emotion throughout their marriage and work together.

That Christmas the Beeton family left the Strand for the Sussex Hotel in Hove. It was there, again away from home as had happened with the first Sam Orchart, that the second child died, on 31st December.

Sam did not allow the single volume publication of the *Book of Household Management* to mean the end of it. He soon realised that the main draw of the book was the cookery section (how many of us nowadays have actually read the household management parts of the book, or the dissertations on the scientific background of various plants?) and soon began releasing parts of the book in different formats and, cleverly, at different prices for different audiences.

At last, in spring 1864, they managed to move out of London to a rented farm in Greenhithe. Isabella was working in Greenhithe on the proofs of *The Dictionary of Every-Day Cookery* when she went into labour with her fourth child on 29th January 1865. Mayson was safely born that day, but the next day Isabella became sick. Sam, whose financial worries were deepening daily, still needed her, and although (according to their maid) he 'was told not to worry her anymore, *by the doctor*...he went into her room and told her all his latest troubles (as he always used) – something to do with banking – and she turned her face to the wall'.

There is something unbearably poignant in this account. Sam, flapping and emotional, turning as ever to his wife for her calm and sound advice, and she, weak and dying, for the first time turning away from him both physically and emotionally.

On 6th February she died of 'Peritonitis 2 days Puerperal Fever 6 days' and was buried five days later at Norwood cemetery along with her second baby. Soon after that the bailiffs began to remove furniture from Mount Pleasant.

Most of Sam's life after Isabella's death need not concern us here. The two last boys survived to adulthood, brought up by Sam and his 'friend' Mrs (Myra) Browne who in more ways than mothering the boys took Isabella's place in Sam's life. She and her husband lived with the Beetons and she too became closely involved with his work. A son, born very late in her long marriage, was possibly Sam's.

As far as his career, let it just be said that he continued as he always had, up and down with debt, and endlessly relying on the *Book of Household Management* and his wife's name to shore up his increasingly untenable position. In 1866 he sold everything to Ward Lock and Tyler, a company only really interested in the

Englishwoman's Domestic Magazine, *Boy's Own Magazine* and *Book of Household Management*, with Sam keeping some editorial input. With syphilitic dementia creeping up on him, the last few years of his life passed in a whirl of litigation and abuse. He died of consumption in June 1877.

Isabella's husband's life may have ended in sickness, grief and shame, but there was much in the early part of it which is to be applauded. He was passionate in his publishing; he loved and respected his wife and gave her an equal place in his enterprises that she might well never have been given by another husband. The book was originally called 'Beeton's', not 'Mrs Beeton's', book, a point their son Mayson rather boringly fought on about for another generation. But Mayson did have a point; Sam and Isabella were a pair, and it should still be remembered that it was a partnership that brought about one of the world's most enduring cookery books.

Perhaps Sam's most moving piece of work was an introduction to the *Dictionary*, the book on whose proofs Isabella had been working before her death. He just had time to add this to the first edition (although he removed it from later ones, to keep up the pretence that she was still alive and working):

USQUE AD FINEM

Her hand has lost its cunning – the firm true hand that wrote these formulae and penned the information contained in this little book. Cold in the silent tomb lie the once nimble, useful fingers – now nerveless, unable for anything and ne'er to do work more in this world. Exquisite palate, unerring judgement, sound commonsense, refined tastes – all these had this dear lady who has gone 'ere her youth had scarcely come. But four times seven years were all she passed in this world; and since the day she became wedded wife – now nearly nine years passed – her greatest, chiefest aims were to provide for the comfort and pleasure of those she loved and had around her, and to employ her best faculties for the use of her sisters, Englishwomen generally. Her surpassing affection and devotion led her to find happiness in aiding, with all her heart and soul, the Husband whom she richly blessed and honoured with her abounding love.

Her Works speak for themselves; and, although taken from this world in the very height of health and strength, and in the early days of womanhood, she felt that satisfaction – so great to all who strive with good intent and warm will – of knowing herself regarded with respect and gratitude.

Her labours are ended here; in purer atmosphere she dwells; and maybe in the land beyond the skies, she has a nobler work to accomplish. Her plans for the future cannot be wholly carried out; her husband knew them all, and will diligently devote himself to their execution, as far as may be. The remembrance of her wishes – always for the private and public welfare – and the companionship of her two little boys – too young to know the virtues of their good Mother – this memory, this presence, will nerve the Father, left alone, to continue to do his duty; in which he will follow the example of his Wife, for her duty no woman has ever better accomplished than the late

ISABELLA MARY BEETON

THE BOOK

Both writers and cooks have in the past attacked Mrs Beeton for not being one of them; the point is that she never claimed to be. Wife of a publisher of Dictionaries and Encyclopaedias, Isabella Beeton was a journalist, Queen of the Cut and Paste, Empress of the Secondary Source. Her *Book of Household Management* was a 'how-to' book.

In varying degrees Mrs Beeton used the successful recipe books of the preceding hundred years, and in varying degrees she acknowledged the usage. Was that not, after all, the very advice her friend Henrietta English had first given her when the idea of a cooking book was first mooted? As well as using past, published work, the 'Housewives of Great Britain' were directly appealed to, through the *Englishwoman's Domestic Magazine*, in the search for recipes. 'We shall be exceedingly obliged to any lady who will spare us a few minutes to write out for us some of her choice recipes and thus make the *E.D.M.* a means whereby her knowledge and skill may be communicated to the world for the benefit of all.' The response was enormous, but in thanking the senders Sam made clear there was always room for more: 'We hope also to secure many more of these communications so that, by means of the *E.D.M.* the knowledge and skill of a few may be acquired by thousands...' And in the Preface to the first edition, Mrs Beeton gives credit where it is due in giving thanks to 'many correspondents of the "Englishwoman's Domestic Magazine"' as well as to 'a large private circle'. Her old headmistress at Heidelberg sent her a book of German recipes, some of which she reproduced, and family friends such as Baroness de Tessier from Epsom also contributed ('Baroness Pudding'). She also, and perhaps more importantly, says that 'a diligent study of the works of the best modern writers on cookery was also necessary to the faithful fulfilment of my task'.

This is where those who point accusatory fingers, hissing 'plagiarist', have the most fun. Because yes, Isabella Beeton did take Mrs English's advice and scour the successful recipe books of the past. She used both the grand court chefs' books (the *patissier* Antonin Carême, Ude, Francatelli and Simpson), the great Soyer of the Reform, and the cookery books aimed more or less at her same market. Glasse, Raffald, Rundell and Acton were all sucked into *Household Management*. You could argue that all Isabella Beeton was doing was following her own advice, and turning to those she trusted to make herself at ease with her material.

To be brutally honest, apart from the fact that it was the first cooking book to use colour plates, nothing about *Household Management* was entirely original or innovative. Beeton has been given credit for inverting Eliza Acton's layout by putting the ingredients at the beginning of the recipe, but Mrs Parkes (a writer who contributed to Webster's *Encyclopaedia of Domestic Economy*) had already used this format. Nor was Beeton the first to put an analytical index at the front of the book – this had previously been done in Philp's *Practical Housewife* of 1855. Philp's admittedly much shorter book had the same aim as Beeton's – to help middle to lower middle-class women organise their homes. Mrs Beeton was not, nor did she aim to be, an innovator. She explained the fashion, the way to do things, rather than trailing a blaze for a new fashion.

At the time of her writing, the way dinner was served in England was undergoing a huge transformation. It was at about this time that our modern way of serving food came into being. Where before, huge amounts of food were all laid out on the table at the same time, with everyone leaning across or asking for things to be passed (*service à la Francaise*), the shift was happening towards what was (confusingly) called *service à la Russe*. Now the food was laid out on the sideboard and was served a course at a time. Although this was becoming the fashion, Beeton only gave very few menus for *service à la Russe*. This was quite simply because the middle-class women at whom she was aiming her writing would have been thrown into a terrible panic by it. 'Dinners à la Russe are scarcely suitable for small establishments; a large number of servants being required to carve, and to help the guests; besides there being a necessity for more plates, dishes, knives, forks, and spoons, than are usually to be found in any other than a very large establishment. Where, however, a service à la Russe is practicable, there is, perhaps, no mode of serving a dinner so enjoyable as this.'

While the primary tone of *Household Management* is one of comforting reassurance, Isabella Beeton's voice does come through the lists of ingredients and wise advice in other ways. She writes that 'in the department belonging to the Cook I have striven, too, to make my work something more than a Cookery Book', and there is often a sense of 'striving'. In the 'Natural History' and 'General Observation' chapters she often comes across as an eager schoolgirl, keen to please, longing for praise, showing off her hard work and hard-acquired knowledge. She is clever, and wants you to know it. Whether her audience, who wanted to know how to lay a table and what to do with a box of chocolate ('This is served in an ornamental box, placed on a glass plate or dish. *Seasonable.* – May be purchased at any time.') also needed to know that 'among themselves, turkeys are extremely furious, whilst amongst other animals they are usually both weak and cowardly' is questionable, but it is these asides that really make Isabella Beeton come alive. Sometimes her 'learned' comments are totally pointless – 'Fish are either solitary or gregarious' – at other times she cannot resist either putting in a classical reference, or adding her own comments. 'The love of fish among the ancient Romans rose to a real mania… Hortensius, the orator, wept over the death of a turbot which he had fed with his own hands; and the daughter of Druses adorned one that she had, with rings of gold. These were, surely, instances of misplaced affection; but there is no accounting for tastes.' The reader is left in no doubt that loving fishes would not be of much use in a smooth-running household, nor does she have much time for modern Italians 'who, with the exception of macaroni, have no specially characteristic article of food'. Her view of French food is not much more mellow: 'The French long enjoyed a European reputation for their skill and refinement in the preparing of food. In place of plain joints, French cookery delights in the marvels of what are called made dishes, ragouts, stews and fricassees, in which no trace of the original materials of which they are compounded is to be found.' Although Beeton's voice sometimes jars to our ears ('Strict, however, as the law was respecting the cud-chewing and hoof-divided animals, the Jews, with their usual perversity and violation of the divine commands, seem afterwards to have ignored the prohibition; for unless they ate pork, it is difficult to conceive for what purpose they kept droves of swine') and some of her views can really have been of no use to the housewives for which she wrote ('From the grossness of his feeding, the large amount of aliment he consumes, his gluttonous way of eating it, from his slothful habits, laziness, and indulgence in sleep, the pig is particularly liable to disease, and especially indigestion, heartburn, and affections of the skin') it is in these excerpts that we really hear the voice of the eager young woman. We hear it too sometimes in the anecdotes she cannot help but add to her recipes. A particularly wonderful story relates to the invention of crackling, when a 'primitive' man accidentally burnt his pig-house down. 'In going over the debris on the following day...the proprietor touched something unusually or unexpectedly hot, which caused him...to clap the tips of his suffering fingers to his mouth. The...result was wonderful. He rolled his eyes in ecstatic pleasure, his frame distended, and conscious of a celestial odour, his nostrils widened and, while drawing in deep inspirations of the ravishing perfume, he sucked his fingers with a gusto he had never, in his most hungry moments, conceived.' Stooping to find a burnt pig he picks up a piece of its skin. 'Ye gods! The felicity he then enjoyed, no pen can chronicle! Then it was that he – the world – first tasted crackling.' The man then goes on to starve until, unable to bear it any longer, he sets fire to his next pig-house so he can taste the delicious morsel again. In passages such as these, Beeton writes almost like a modern food writer – Elizabeth David, say, or Nigel Slater, who do not restrict themselves to writing about weights and measures but show a real enjoyment for the food itself.

In a world where fewer and fewer families actually eat together, where fast food and grazing out of the fridge seem to be the norm, Beeton's views on dining may seem old-fashioned, but should be taken seriously. Although her message was as much to do with social behaviour and aspiration as food itself, it also says a great deal more about society than might at first appear. 'Dine we must,' she writes, 'and we may as well dine elegantly as well as wholesomely.' As shown in her chapter 'Dinners and Dining', she is talking only in part about how the table is laid.

'Man, it has been said, is a dining animal. Creatures of the inferior races eat and drink; man only dines…It is equally true that some races of men do not dine any more than the tiger or the vulture…Dining is the privilege of civilisation. The rank which a people occupy in the grand scale may be measured by their way of taking their meals, as well as by their way of treating their women. The nation which knows how to dine has learnt the leading lesson of progress. It implies both the will and the skill to reduce to order, and surround with idealisms and graces, the more material conditions of human existence; and wherever that will and that skill exist, life cannot be wholly ignoble.' Her sentiments echo those of the genius Brillat-Savarin, whose *Physiologie du Gout* (1825), a collection of essays on gourmandism raised public interest in the subject. 'Beasts feed: man eats: the man of intellect alone knows how to eat,' he wrote in the opening aphorisms of the book.

Although we are primarily dealing with domestic cooking books, *Household Management*'s recipes cannot be taken out of the context of the whole – a book designed to guide and, perhaps more importantly, reassure, the flustered mistress of a house. Nigella

Lawson's second book ironically claimed to guide you towards becoming a 'Domestic Goddess' (2000), but it is Delia Smith whose calm, reassuring tone is closest in its aim to Mrs Beeton's. Not only did Mrs Beeton aim to show the woman of the house how to run her domain, she also aimed to make her feel that her work was of value. She may have chosen very non-feminist quotations to introduce her work – 'Nothing lovelier can be found/In Woman, than to study household good' (Milton) and Proverb xxxi 'Strength and honour are her clothing; and she shall rejoice in time to come. She openeth her mouth with wisdom; and in her tongue is the law of kindness. She looketh well to the ways of her household; and eateth not the bread of idleness. Her children arise up, and call her blessed; her husband also, and he praiseth her' – but often her talk is more like that of a General rallying her troops than a complaisant wife.

There are 2,751 'paragraphs' to the book; this is how Beeton opens the whole work: 'As with the Commander of an Army, or the leader of any enterprise, so it is with the mistress of a house. Her spirit will be seen through the whole establishment; and just in proportion as she performs her duties intelligently and thoroughly, so will her domestics follow in her path.' The woman she is writing for is in control (or will be when she has used the book) and is held in esteem. 'She ought always to remember that she is the first and the last, the Alpha and Omega in the government of her establishment; and that it is by her conduct that its whole internal policy is regulated. She is, therefore, a person of far more importance in a community than she thinks she is.'

The scope of the book can be seen by looking at a random part of the 'analytical index', which appears at the front of the book: 'Housemaid, recipe for polish for bright grates/Hunter's pudding/Husband and wife/Hysterics/Ice, fruit creams, to make.'

Wonderful. The paragraphs about the footmen's duties etc. are of course not relevant to today's audience, although anyone who reads nineteenth-century novels could do worse than read these extracts out of interest. But other pieces of advice still sound surprisingly modern. She warns against gossips – 'a gossiping acquaintance, who indulges in the scandal and ridicule of her neighbours, should be avoided as the pestilence' – and in friendships too easily made: 'friendships should not be hastily formed, nor the heart given, at once, to every newcomer.' She encourages hospitality, but warns against too much: 'Hospitality is a most excellent virtue; but care must be taken that the love of company, for its own sake, does not become a prevailing passion; for then the habit is no longer hospitality, but dissipation.'

Later versions of *Household Management* (and many were to come) included a table of precedence, but the first edition did not. Isabella Beeton was not expecting her readers to write to an Archbishop or have a Duke to dinner. While she tells a story involving a prince of Soubise and fifty hams, she finishes it by saying 'as we do not write for princes and nobles alone, but that our British sisters may make the best dishes out of the least expensive ingredients, we will also pass the hams…' and elsewhere points out that 'we do not allude to the large assemblies of the aristocracy, but to the smaller parties of the middle classes'.

It was this which made *Household Management* so enduring, a bestseller and a wedding present must-have for a good hundred years, until Constance Spry began to edge her out. Beeton felt safe. She reminded her readers of the importance of sensible and regular shopping, she told you when food was in season (including tables of seasonable food for easy reference) and she gave a rough cost for each recipe in her book. She told her readers to make time for themselves ('it is right that [the mistress] should give some time to pleasures of literature'), told them how to choose guests ('a due mixture of talkers and listeners, the grave and the gay') and reminded them that 'as a general rule, it may be said...it is better to be under-dressed than over-dressed'. She *understood* her audience ('the half-hour before dinner has always been considered as the great ordeal through which the mistress...will either pass with flying colours, or lose many of her laurels') and showed them how to overcome their fears. She knew things could go wrong – guests turning up unexpectedly ('this is an excellent dish for a hasty addition to dinner...it being so easily and quickly made') – or times could be straitened; many of her recipes have various versions, from 'rich' to 'more economical'.

And nowadays? I doubt many of us will be rushing to decapitate a turtle to make turtle soup, but with its sound principles of freshness, economy, seasonality, much of *Household Management* is as trustworthy as ever it was.

ELIZABETH DAVID
1913–1992

MEDITERRANEAN FOOD (1950)

Elizabeth David was a completely different figure from any of the other writers who changed the way the English thought about, prepared, and above all ate, food. Upper class, opinionated, direct, with a feeling of entitlement that was bred in her, and only partially knocked out of her through her troubles in the War, Elizabeth's love of food came upon her almost by chance; it was certainly not fostered in her during her childhood. The audience for which she wrote, at least initially, was different from her predecessors', too; some of her concerns (such as seasonality) were the same, but she was not so much interested in housewifery as in food.

She was born Elizabeth Gwynne, the second of the four daughters of Rupert and Stella Gwynne. Both the Gwynnes and Stella's family, the Ridleys, were rich, and Elizabeth's early childhood was standard for families of her class at the time. The family lived at Wootton Manor, a Jacobean house in Sussex which Rupert, although not the first son, had been given as a wedding present by his parents. From January 1910 Gwynne was the Conservative MP for Eastbourne, and Wootton and the Gwynnes became a centre of political hospitality.

The children, meanwhile – Priscilla, born in 1910, Elizabeth in 1913, Diana in 1915 and Felicité in 1917 – lived in sequestered splendour in the Wing (designed by Detmar Blow), which their parents added on to the house. In common with other children of the time, the children ate nursery food in the nursery, only joining their parents for lunch on Sunday. Both Elizabeth and her older sister Pris remembered their childhood fare as disgusting, with

Elizabeth later writing: 'We ate a lot of mutton and beef plainly cooked, with plain vegetables…Vegetable marrows were yellow, boiled, and watery. There were green turnip tops, spinach, Jerusalem artichokes, parsnips. I hated them all…Junket was slippery and slimy, jam roly-poly greasy…tapioca the most revolting of all, invented apparently solely to torment children.' There was better food than that to be had, mostly fresh from the gardens or fields; the girls collected mushrooms in the autumn and raspberries in the summer, but in general the food was fuel not feast.

Hanging over the family was the lack of an heir. The house would pass on Rupert's death to his younger brother, Roland, who was waiting out the time living nearby with their sister and mother. Rupert, whose pleasures included not only hard work (he became a junior government minister) but also racing, riding and women, did not help the family by dying in 1924 aged only fifty-one. Roland allowed his sister-in-law and her daughters to stay on at Wootton, unless Stella were to remarry when they would have to leave. Stella, cold, distant, interested in her garden and her own social life, kept up the show at Wootton, but within months of their father's death Priscilla and Elizabeth were sent off to boarding school. Pris did not last, but Elizabeth boarded until she was sixteen when she was sent away again, this time to France to study at the Sorbonne for a year and a half. She also took painting lessons, and from Paris was sent on to Munich to learn German and improve her painting.

Although while in Paris she learned both the language and literature of her host country, she learned something else that was to prove much more important in her future life: the love of good food. Not only in the restaurants where she and her fellow-boarders occasionally treated themselves, but from the Robertot's cook, Leontine. Both in Paris and at the Robertot's Normandy farmhouse Elizabeth began to taste new food and discover the joys of simple French cooking.

When Elizabeth finally returned to England in 1932, she was put through the upper-class torment of 'coming out'. It is interesting that she obeyed her mother in this, as she was already shaping up to be something of a rebel. But come out she did, only to shock her family with her announcement that as she clearly was not going to succeed as an artist (her first ambition), she was going to become an actress. She found a job at the Oxford Repertory Company, working as stage manager with occasional small parts. Stanford Holme was the actor-manager in charge, a philandering married man whose wife put up with his various affairs with his young protégées.

So there Elizabeth was in Oxford, sharing digs with a young Joan Hickson, and at the same time as falling in love with the wrong man and learning her trade, she was learning how to cook for herself for the first time. From her letters to her sisters, she was not learning much; sardines on toast and cigarettes were the sorts of suppers she was most often preparing.

In 1934 Elizabeth finally left Stanford and Oxford, but still hoped to become an actress. The problem was that she really was not that good. She had a series of small parts in the new Regent's Park Open Air Theatre, but was never going to make the grade as an actress. She felt that times were tough, but everything is relative. She shared a rented flat with a school friend, bought a fridge with her birthday money from an uncle, and filled it with ready-made food from Selfridges Food Hall. For years Elizabeth, apparently incapable of living on her allowance and admittedly meagre earnings, relied on handouts from her family and loans from her ever loyal sister Pris and astonishingly forbearing brother-in-law, Richard Longland. However she did begin to realise that she had to make some sort of economy so finally, rather than picking up the telephone to Selfridges, she began to use a cooking book her mother had given her.

The Gentle Art of Cookery by Mrs C.F. Leyel and Miss Olga Hartley (1925) is an extraordinary cookbook of its time. Mrs Leyel, chiefly a herbalist and founder of both the Society of Herbalists and the Culpeper shops, mostly approached food from the traditional French angle, but also had a chapter on 'Dishes from *The Arabian Nights*'. Her writing is in some ways similar to Elizabeth David's; she is not hysterical as to exact quantities or timings, and assumes a knowledge of, or at any rate an ease with, cooking. As Elizabeth David later wrote, 'I wonder if I would ever have learned to cook at all had I been given a routine Mrs Beeton to learn from instead of the romantic Mrs Leyel, with her rather wild and imagination-catching recipes.' When, years later, Elizabeth had to abandon her boat and all her possessions she wrote to her sister asking for her to find copies of the cookbooks she had had to leave behind. There were nine in total, among them Leyel's book and three different titles by Marcel Boulestin.

While Regent's Park did not lead her to fame as an actress, it did lead her into the arms of her next lover, Charles Gibson Cowan. Cowan was Elizabeth's polar opposite and practically designed to shock Stella. Working class, Jewish, nine years older, he was also married with a baby. He'd lived as a beggar for six months, and had written a book about it, and was now earning money as an actor/producer/journalist. Elizabeth was entranced by his charm, his intelligence, his literary interests, and before long he had left his wife and they spent the following three years living together in a string of flats. The relationship was complicated, with infidelities on his side and a world of problems caused by their totally different friends, families and backgrounds, but Elizabeth found it hard to break with him.

It was during this time that she first began to travel abroad. She visited friends in Egypt, went to Germany, to the south of France with another friend, and visited her sister Pris in Malta for long periods. This is where her love of the Mediterranean, and her interest in its food, first surfaced. However each time she came back, there Charles was and yet again she could not bring herself to leave him for good.

Until in 1939, with war ever closer, the two adventurers, united by a love of sailing and a lack of anything resembling a real career, decided to leave England and sail to the isles of Greece. Taking with them books, dried food, and a paying guest, they set out on 8th July; within days of their reaching Marseilles war was declared, the paying guest debunked and headed back for England and Elizabeth and Charles decided to sit it out in Marseilles for the time being. Still living on their boat, the *Evelyn Hope*, and cooking on a coal stove, Elizabeth began to include recipes in her letters home. One, for liver, was later used in her first book, with only a few alterations. In the published version she, perhaps unsurprisingly, drops any mention of Oxo, Bovril and tomato ketchup. She revelled in the French markets she found, and added French cookery books to her English collection.

Elizabeth and Charles could not continue to stay in Marseilles; their war involved secret flights on the *Evelyn Hope*, lending a real sense of adventure and danger to Elizabeth's life. From Marseilles to Antibes, to Corsica, it seems that they were often only one step ahead of the war. They were escorted by a patrol boat into Messina only to find that Italy had just declared war on the Allies, and were immediately taken into police custody as spies. When released they were not allowed back to the boat, but were taken to Venice and from there to Trieste, where they were once again arrested (it had just been bombed by the British). Finally they were put on a train to Yugoslavia and from there took themselves to Athens. Writing to her sister Pris, Elizabeth listed the most serious losses of their adventures: the typewriter, Charles's manuscripts and her own collection of recipes which 'I was thinking of writing…up properly and trying to get it published in America.'

After their life on the Mediterranean, both Charles and Elizabeth found it difficult to adapt to city life. However, Elizabeth was still determined not to return to England. Living in hotels as they did, money was as ever tight and once again Elizabeth asked Priscilla for a loan, and for her trust fund money to be released. Her mother Stella wrote a vitriolic letter to Pris saying 'remember she has no morals re money…& will roll you till your last [farthing]…without any feeling or gratitude'. Stella was also furious with Elizabeth for her refusal to engage with any war work when Athens hospitals were 'shrieking for helpers of all kinds'.

Charles, however, did find a job teaching English and the couple decamped to the small island of Syros. This seems to have been a brief respite, an almost happy time in their lives. But then Greece was attacked, surrendering on 24th April 1941, and once again they had to flee, this time in a neighbour's cart, heading for the coast to find a boat to get them to Crete. The journey took four days and once again only offered a brief period of peace. The Battle of Crete, a prolonged and vicious attack on the island from air and land, meant yet again they had to move on, finding berths on one of the last ships evacuating civilians. As they left the island, heading for Egypt, they finally admitted that their affair was over. Charles did not leave Egypt for another five months, but this time the break was truly made.

It was in Egypt that Elizabeth finally joined the war effort. From Cairo she went to Alexandria, where she spent a year, and found a job in cypher work for the navy. It was long, hard, and very dull work, but Alexandria was a busy city, full of bars and restaurants, and it was more than possible to have fun. Elizabeth probably took fun a little to extremes; behind the cool, even arrogant, exterior was an insecurity which she dealt with through drink and relationships with men who could not make her happy. Charles was not the first, nor would he be the last. She shared a flat with an old friend, and they employed a Greek cook, Kyriakou, about whom she later wrote with immense fondness in *Wine and Food* magazine. She tells of him bringing the morning shop into her bedroom with her coffee, emptying the basket onto her bed: 'There were live fish, prawns and crabs and crayfish, slithering and gangling across my eiderdown at seven o'clock in the morning.' Once again, though, the war caused her to move away from Kyriakou and Alexandria, back to Cairo and a new job as a reference librarian for the Ministry of Information. She rented a flat and hired a cook, this time Suleiman, a Sudanese, whose pilaff she included in *Mediterranean Food*.

Again Elizabeth was embroiled with a man, perhaps the only one who really broke her heart: Peter Laing was an American who had been badly wounded in battle and spent six months in hospital outside Cairo. Once recovered he returned to America, and though they took up again after the war she felt forgotten by him. So much so that in July 1944 she wrote home with the surprising news that she was to be married: 'He…is not at all the man I intended to marry, but he seems to love me very much and is apparently able to provide for me in modest comfort.' The calculating tone is chilling, even down to the so-called comforting aside that 'I like the man very much and get on well with him'. Her family cannot have held out much hope for the marriage.

'The man' in question was Ivor Anthony 'Tony' David, an officer in the Indian Army. If her romance with Charles had not lasted partly because of the difference in their backgrounds, this would not prove a difficulty with Tony. But while their class might be more or less equal, their interests and aims were not to be. Elizabeth married for security, and for a rest from the bizarre nomadic life she had been living. They were married on 30th August 1944 and in 1946 moved to New Delhi for Tony's new posting. Elizabeth, perhaps unsurprisingly, hated it. She was too strong a character to fit in as a second fiddle wife, she did not like the other expats, the social life, though busy, was too formal for someone as spontaneous as she. Determined to make Tony leave the army, she finally left India ahead of him, with an attack of sinusitis as her excuse. In August, after less than a year in India, she came home to England after seven years away. She was lent a large flat in Kensington, and once more without a job went back to her old ways of entertaining.

The England she returned to was, in terms of food if nothing else, a shock. She knew about rationing, but had had no real idea of its impact on how one ate. It was not just the restrictions on food that was the problem, either; England had become used to tinned and dried food over fresh. However traumatic her war years had been, she quickly realised one huge advantage of living abroad had been that 'my food had always had some sort of life, colour, guts, stimulus; there had always been bite, flavour, and inviting smells'. None of this was available in the land of powdered eggs. Elizabeth did her best to find good ingredients, and friends returning from abroad came with treats in their suitcases, but even a woman as determined as she could not conjure something from nothing. And so, if she could not eat or cook as she wanted she turned to the only other alternative. She began to write. The spur that urged her on came in the form of a siege; she visited Ross-on-Wye (with a lover, George Lassalle – Tony was still in India) and they were flooded in. Stuck in a small town with filthy food, George encouraged her to pick up a pen. 'I ... started to work out an agonized craving for the sun and furious revolt against that terrible cheerless, heartless food by writing down descriptions of Mediterranean and Middle Eastern cooking. Even to write words like apricot, olives and butter, rice and lemons, oil and almonds, produced assuagement. Later I came to realise that in the England of 1947 those were dirty words I was putting down.' This was the beginning of her new career, the first work she had done that meant anything to her, and the work that in some ways appeared to ease her troubled soul.

Tony David came back from India, having finally left the army. Elizabeth's mother Stella bought them a house in Chelsea. Elizabeth's kitchen became the centre of the house, which was unusual for a woman of her time and class, when the kitchen was where the cooking was done and a room unvisited by guests.

Soon after they moved into the new house, Elizabeth was introduced to the editor of *Harpers Bazaar*, Anne Scott-James, and was given the chance to write an article. 'Rice Again,' her first published piece, was in the March 1949 edition and saw the beginning of her career. It included the recipe for 'Suleiman's Pilaff' which was also in *Mediterranean Food* and was a favourite of my childhood. Scott-James employed Elizabeth as a cookery columnist for the next six years, giving her free rein to write more than a list of recipes and to develop her own voice. Luckily for Elizabeth, Scott-James had told her to keep hold of her own copyrights (which normally belong to the publishing magazine) so a great deal of her work for *Harpers* was later incorporated into *Mediterranean Food*, which (after being turned down by quite a few publishers) finally came out in 1950.

The book was an immediate success; for the first time Elizabeth was in the position of earning money. As well as *Harpers*, she now wrote for the Wine and Food Society's journal, edited by Andre Simon. More journalism followed and she was soon in high demand. Her next book was eagerly awaited, and followed hot on the heels of her first; *French Country Cooking* came out in 1951.

Meanwhile her sister Felicité had moved into a flat at the top of the house and gradually assumed the place that Pris (now divorced and with two small children) had held at the centre of Elizabeth's trust. Elizabeth wrote in longhand, with Felicité typing it up for her.

Although Elizabeth never lived abroad again, the combination of her own itchy feet, her desire to learn yet more about food, and her incessant shortage of money, led her to a new way of life; for a few months of every year she would let out her house and rent somewhere cheaper in rural France or Italy.

Her third book, *Italian Food*, caused her more of a headache than the previous two. Her memories of Italy in the war were not happy, but her friend Norman Douglas encouraged her to write it, and her perpetual panic about money drove her on. She rented a flat in the Palazzo Doria in the middle of Rome and, with good Italian, set to work. It took almost a year and she did not find it easy. It is hard for us to realise now how entrenched the English view was of Italian food – stodgy pasta, did we really want it? But *Italian Food* was to become one of David's most successful and much loved works. Once again, it was not just a collection of recipes, but was an exploration of the essence of Italian food. It was published in 1954 to unanimous literary acclaim, including (to her great joy) being picked by Evelyn Waugh as one of the two best books of 1954. (His son, and my father, Auberon Waugh also said that he thought Elizabeth David was the woman who had done the most to improve British life in the twentieth century.)

Summer Cooking proved an easier work for David to write, and came out in 1955, only a year after the Italian book. In the same year she became cookery columnist for the *Sunday Times*, which should have brought her pleasure, and did bring her kudos, but which also brought her a life-long enemy in the form of her editor Ernestine Carter. Her journalistic career continued to flourish, including a column in *Vogue* on 'the finest foods in season' – a subject central to her food writing. By now her appeal was much broader than it had been in *Mediterranean Food*. The journalism was reaching a wide audience which then went on to buy her books. The war had caused changes in society, and these changes are always reflected in the kitchens. The upper classes had lost servants, while middle-class young women had grown up in rationing and had lost the tradition of fresh cooking. Cooking classes had grown in popularity after the war, as had women's magazines. By the mid fifties, when David's books were being published almost annually, there was a huge market ripe for instruction.

As time went on, David's work became more and more academic and knowledgeable. *Mediterranean Food* was just that, a look at the food of a particular area. By the time her fourth book, *French Provincial Cooking*, was published in 1960, she was writing about history and tradition as much as food. She began writing pamphlets, and indeed her later books, *Spices, Salts and Aromatics in the English Kitchen* (1970) and *English Bread and Yeast Cookery* (1977) are much more specialised and in them she has moved away to yet another audience. She also, it can be seen, was moving away from her early passion and looking more closely at the food of her own country.

As well as the publication of *French Provincial Cooking*, 1960 saw the year of her divorce from Tony David. It had not been much of a marriage for years – perhaps ever – and its final ending came as no surprise to anyone who knew her. Elizabeth had had a series of long and short term affairs throughout her marriage, she had married for convenience and a brief safe harbour. The man she married was not a bad man or a weak one, and she probably did him an unfairness in marrying him at all. *French Provinicial* was dedicated to 'P.H. with love'. Peter Higgins was her lover for some years, finally leaving her for a younger woman, which drove Elizabeth closer to alcohol and sleeping pills.

These probably contributed to the stroke she had in 1977, aged only forty-nine. Although she recovered well and quickly, it did have one worrying effect on her: her sense of taste, especially for salt, was impaired. From then on she had a few trusted people test her dishes for saltiness. The stroke, and this disability (which to most people would be only minor), did shock Elizabeth and affect her self-confidence.

Elizabeth David's other great venture was, in 1965, to open Elizabeth David Ltd, a kitchenware shop, with three friends. She and Peter Trier set off across France in a battered van looking for wholesalers and brought home pots and pans, tableware and batterie de cuisine. The shop became almost an extension of her social life, with her coterie gathering in it for picnic lunches. Despite her name, and the beauty of much of its content, the shop did not flourish. By 1967 it had become little more than a front for a catalogue service, the precursor to the online shop. Her partners tried to adapt to survive, but Elizabeth was not having it. Her high standards were being called into question, she felt, and finally she flounced out and left the whole enterprise.

There is no doubt that Elizabeth David was a difficult woman. Her friends have her as generous, spontaneous, humourous, but her autocratic sense of being right, her inability to put up with fools (or what she saw as fools), her quarrelsomeness and her own demons often isolated her. The way she became more of a historian in her later years, saying to friends that she didn't want to write recipes any more, that 'the excitement of life now is in tracing the texts' was also in a way inward-looking. She relied increasingly on her sister Felicité, both when she was home and abroad, but despite Elizabeth's increasingly frail health, brought to a head after a bad car crash in 1977, Felicité was the first to die, in 1986. They had shared a house for thirty-four years.

Elizabeth's last years were spent in increasingly frail health, in and out of hospital for falls resulting in broken bones, with tuberculosis. She was still working, though. A collection of her essays came out as *An Omelette and a Glass of Wine* in 1984, but her real aim was to finish her final book, a study of ice and ices in history. She was not to succeed; she was finding it increasingly difficult to work, and seemed to be confused at points. Her friend and colleague Jill Norman had the manuscript, which was published posthumously as *Harvest of the Cold Months*.

She died of a stroke at home on 22nd May 1992.

THE BOOK

Elizabeth David began writing *A Book of Mediterranean Food* in 1947, in a spectacularly gray – and hungry – post-war England. From the very opening words of the introduction, the tone is set. This is not a 'how to' book. It is a book which indulges more than the sense of taste – sight and smell are as important to the writer, and reader, as the prosaic 'take...' of other recipes. Her mission statement is simple: 'I hope to give some idea of the lovely cookery of those regions to people who do not already know them, and to stir the memories of those who have eaten this food on its native shores, and who would like sometimes to bring a flavour of those blessed lands of sun and sea and olive trees into their English kitchens.' In 1950, when the book was published, 'stir[ring] the memories' is all the book could do for her readers, but her descriptions of vegetable stalls, 'heaps of shiny fish', the long lists of ingredients the English reader could not hope to find, the dried fruit, the herbs, the saffron, the garlic, bring a sense of those markets to life.

In her preface to the second edition, published only two years after the first, David says that the world of food had changed so rapidly that there would not be a single ingredient, 'however exotic', which could not be found at least somewhere in England. She is being a little disingenuous – the shops of Soho in London's West End might well have come along quite a way in those two years, but for housewives living in the shires there would have been just as little chance of finding saffron or pine-nuts in 1952 as in 1950. And as for *melokhia*, a kind of mallow from which she makes a soup…anyone seen one recently in their greengrocer?

Unlike the other cooks we have considered, David was not writing for an audience of housewives; she was writing for an elite strata of society which had already had some experience of 'abroad'. As time went by she did broaden her ideas about the audience at which her books were aimed, but this first one was more about memories than education. When she did begin to think in that way, her message was very similar to those of our earlier writers: simplicity, seasonality, freshness.

David's writing is very different from that of the earlier writers discussed here, but there are links. Like Acton, she was a cook; like Beeton, she sometimes had an authoritative, know-it-all voice; like so many of the early cookery writers, she believed in real food. In his 1923 book *Simple French Cooking for English Homes*, Marcel Boulestin taught the English that foreign food did not have to be fancy, and David continued to carry that torch. The cooking of the Mediterranean, she writes, 'is honest cooking, too; none of the sham Grande Cuisine of the International Palace Hotel.' It was the fake fanciness of French cooking that alarmed the likes of Woolley and Glasse, but centuries later another truly English woman showed that real foreign cooking did not need flashy tricks. Her years of cooking stews in the galley of the *Evelyn Hope* had taught her that long slow cooking could have the most amazing results, and indeed many of her recipes in *Mediterranean Food* are for ragouts from various regions of the Mediterranean.

To read *Mediterranean Food*, though, is to read more than a cookery book. It is almost a treatise on food and the way others have thought about it. Interspersed throughout the book are quotations, often more than a page long, from other writers: Théophile Gautier on gazpacho (he hated it and called it 'hell-broth'); extracts from Henry James's *A Little Tour in France*; Gertrude Stein; William Beckford; Smollett; and her dear friend from her time in Antibes, Norman Douglas.. There is so much that the book is almost an anthology of food writing at the same time as a recipe book. Although David's voice is sometimes bossy, her wide reading does not make her sound like the eager show-off schoolgirl that comes across from Mrs Beeton's classical references and asides. Whether she is writing about food herself, or quoting others on the subject, the passion for and overriding interest in food shines through.

With *Mediterranean Food* David gave herself a broad brief. She ranged beyond the perhaps more familiar territories of France, Italy and Spain to Greece and the beginnings of the Middle East. Claudia Roden, who had been exiled from Egypt, paid tribute to David when she said that her book 'slightly eased my nostalgic homesickness' and encouraged her to write her own cookery book, *A Book of Middle Eastern Food* (1968). It cannot be underestimated how extraordinary it should be that a woman of David's age and class could get so under the skin of a region through its food, so very different from the nursery food of her childhood.

The book is divided into chapters. As well as the obvious (meat, fish, etc.) she includes one called 'Substantial Dishes'. Many of these are rice dishes – paella, pilaff, risotto – or pasta. In the twenty-first century pasta is everywhere, even in school canteens, so it is hard to imagine a world where pasta was an exotic foreign dish. David has to tell her reader not just how to make sauces (and she chooses very simple ones, such as tomato) but how to cook the spaghetti itself. Also in that recipe are dishes which she obviously found hard to classify – cassoulet from Toulouse ('perhaps a piece of mutton' – at least she says 'perhaps') and a whole baked liver. There is a short chapter on jams, chutneys and preserves which includes stuffed walnuts in syrup (not one I'd recommend trying unless you have very fine motor skills and endless time).

Perhaps the chapter which most resonates the Elizabeth David we know is the one on cold food and salads. Any article on picnics which appears on a brief day of sun in our dismal summers will mention Elizabeth David. Rereading these recipes I am thrown back to my childhood and see how much my mother was indeed influenced by David. There are cold chicken salads, a *boeuf à la mode* (how we children complained about the jelly, and how I love it now). She introduces the reader to tarama – the proper version of the pink taramasalata which you can now buy in plastic tubs in any supermarket. My grandmother, not usually a very patient person, used to make it, beating the roes and the olive oil to a velvety smoothness.

David also tells her readers about hors d'oeuvres, giving recipes for food which, once again, we can now buy in any good supermarket (olives, marinated aubergines, hummus) but which would in 1950 have been glimpses from another world.

The glory of *Mediterranean Food* – and David's other books – is that even now, when we really don't need to look up tomato sauce for pasta, we return again and again to the writing for a sheer greedy wallow in the joy of food. And in among all the luxuriating in taste and smell and texture, there was a missionary zeal. As she wrote in *Harpers* in 1949: 'Unless young people learn now about the art of cooking, and eating and drinking wine, one of the great pleasures of life will be lost to them, and how can they learn to cook if they don't know how food should look and taste and smell?'

PART TWO

THE RECIPES

SOUPS

*I love soup. Really. My ex-husband used to feel rather cheated by it –
even if it was a first course, but especially if it was presented as a whole
supper – and my grandmother said it was 'common' to eat it at lunch,
but I do love it. Never mind the eating of it, there is almost nothing
as comforting as making it. I particularly enjoy making one which
looks ready made but tastes infinitely better. Tomato soup, for instance,
made with slow roasted tomatoes and thyme and celery and fresh stock
(of course) and a potato to thicken. And the real joy is that when you
whizz it up it looks just like Heinz. I'm not sure if that's Heinz being
clever or me, or what's going on in some post-ironic kitchen way, but
I love it.*

*You should always, always, have good stock in your fridge or freezer.
Having said that, mine is nearly always chicken stock; I make vegetable
as needed, and cheat with beef – not with a stock cube, but with a tin
of jellied consommé.*

*The best chicken stock is obviously made with fresh chicken – and
you can get chicken wings for almost nothing. But even if you're just
using up old roast chicken bones, especially if the chicken is a proper
one not a pasty supermarket fowl, you can make a decent stock. Better
than the salt in golden wrapping that passes for a stock cube, anyway.
One of my daughters once stole a packet of stock cubes thinking they
were sweets (I don't know why I had any in the house, either) but
she soon learned her mistake. Some of the very best cooks I know
mistakenly swear that stock is a waste of time, but I think the pro-stock
case was proven when a friend asked, at the last minute, if she could
bring a guest to supper with her, explaining apologetically that he was*

a vegetarian chef scouting around for a place to open a restaurant in the West Country. I cooked a cucumber and mushroom risotto (from Elizabeth David via my grandmother), but in a forgetful moment forgot the vegetarian and used chicken stock. I confessed to my friend, but she told me not to worry. And the vegetarian chef? He raved about the risotto, saying he'd never had a better and what on earth had I put in it? See, you really can't beat a good chicken stock.

My grandmother told me that you should not make a vegetable soup with a chicken stock (always use vegetable stock) but actually in this case I think she was wrong. Although I did once cook a horrible leek and potato soup with chicken stock, which was the occasion of the advice. She was not alone in this view, though. Elizabeth David took her cue from Marcel Boulestin, who wrote in What Shall We Have To-Day? *'the chief thing to remember is that all of these soups…must be made with plain water. When made with the addition of stock they lose all character and cease to be what they were intended to be. The fresh pleasant taste is lost owing to the addition of meat stock, and the value of the soup from an economical point of view is also lost.' Economically, chicken stock is as cheap, if not cheaper than, chips. In point of view of taste…well experiment and try for yourself. Stronger flavoured vegetables can certainly hold a chicken (not beef) stock taste and in my view add to the soup.*

For the joy of verisimilitude I have kept in all the instructions to 'pound' or to put through a 'tammy', but of course you will use your Magimix or equivalent.

HANNAH WOOLLEY

BARLEY-BROTH

Boil the Barley first in two waters, having first pickt it well, then join it with a knuckle of Veal, and seeth them together; to the Broth add Raisins, sweet herbs, large Mace, and the quantity of a fine Manchet sliced together, then season it with salt.

Barley seems to be making something of a fashionable comeback. I'm not a huge fan of it, but it is filling, warming and cheap. This soup, with the addition of raisins and herbs, has a sweetness which might encourage children to eat soup (I suggest you take the bone out before introducing a modern child to the soup). Note how Woolley tells the reader to season with salt at the end – this should always be the case with any sort of pulse, as salt put in early will toughen them. Another good tip if you're cooking pulses such as Puy lentils and you're unsure how old they are is to put in a halved tomato – the acid in it will break down any toughness.

BISK

I'm not going to give you this recipe. It involves ridiculous numbers of ingredients, from a whole leg of beef, to the 'liquor of the marrow-bones of half a dozen peeping Chickens, and as many peeping Pidgeons'. Then you need pallats, noses and lips (of what animal she does not say), sheeps' tongues, cockscombes, roast mutton, lambstones, sweetbreads, oysters, chestnuts, hard boiled eggs...It goes on and on. The interest lies in its name – which comes from the French 'bisque' – and in her bizarre final paragraph after the long recipe: 'Gentlewomen, I must crave your pardon, since I know I have tired your patience in the description of a Dish, which though it be frequently fed in Noblemens houses, and with all this cost and trouble put together by some rare whimsical French Cook, yet I cannot approve of it, but must call it a Miscellaneous hodgpodg of studied vanity; and I have here inserted it not for your imitation, but admiration.' 'Admiration' is clearly not used here in the modern sense.

I think the point is that she needed to show she knew what was in fashion, even if it were only to mock it. Remembering how much of cookery writing is about reassuring the domestic cook, but also about how to hold up her own in society, including this recipe was a master stroke.

TO MAKE A *FRENCH* POTTAGE, CALLED SKINK

Skink, to us, is a purely Scottish soup, so it is interesting to find it here as a French dish. Cullen skink is made from haddock, potatoes and onion, which is all the odder as 'skink' is a Scots word for shin or knuckle of beef, and from that a soup based on beef. Woolley's skink is beef-based, and also uses oatmeal, which to us is another Scots, rather than French, ingredient. Maybe she was just in a muddle. Either way, with a bit of adaptation (mostly in terms of quantities) this would warm and nourish any Frenchman or Scotsman.

Take a leg of Beef, and chop it into three pieces, then boyl it in a Pot with three Pottles of Spring-water, a few Cloves, Mace, and whole Pepper; after the pot is scumm'd put in a bundle of sweet Marjoram, Rosemary, Thyme, Winter-Savoury, Sage, and Parsley, bound up hard, some salt, and two or three great Onions whole, then about an hour before Dinner put in three Marrow-bones, and thicken it with some strained oatmeal, or Manchet sliced and steeped with some Gravy, strong Broth, or some of the pottage, then a little before you dish up the skink, put into it a little fine powder of Saffron, and give it a walm [boiling up] or two; Dish it on large slices of *French* Bread, and Dish the Marrow-Bones on them in a fine clean large Dish; then have two or three Manchets cut into Toasts, and being finely Toasted; lay on the Knuckle of Beef in the middle of the Dish, the Marrow-Bones round about it, and the Toasts round about the Dish brim: serve it hot.

We don't really want the huge bits of meat and bones lying around; that's a little Fred Flinstone for us, I think. I would pull the meat off the bones, and take the marrow out and spread it on the toast to eat with the soup.

TO MAKE POTTAGE OF A CAPON

Take Beef and Mutton, and cut it into pieces; then boyl a large Earthen pot of Water, take out half the water, put in your Meat, and skim it, and when it boyles season it with Pepper and salt; when it hath boyled about two hours, add four or five Cloves, half an hour before you think it is enough, put in your Herbs, Sorrel, Purslain, Burrage, Lettuce, and Bugloss or green Pease; and in the Winter, parlsey-Roots and white Endive; pour the Broth upon light bread toasted, and stew it a while in the Dish covered. If your water consume in boyling, fill it up with water boyling hot. The less there is of the broth, the better it is, though it be but a porringer-full, for then it would be as stiff as Jelly when it is cold.

95

Spot the obvious error: no mention at all of the capon. But I love this recipe for its essence, which, like the broth, is as 'stiff as Jelly': the longer you reduce your broth, or stock, the more delicious it is. Whether you are going to drink the broth as soup, or use it as a stock in a stew or soup or risotto, the same applies. Simmer it down to as little as you dare.

HANNAH GLASSE

Hannah Glasse cooks in the most enormous quantities. Even my mother with her four children, even my paternal grandmother with her six, even myself at university cooking for what sometimes felt like the whole of the rugby team, could never need the amount of food Glasse recommends. Her crawfish soup needs two hundred and fifty crawfish; her 'good gravy soup' asks for a pound each of veal, beef and mutton as well as 'an old cock beat to pieces' (lovely muscular cooking). After all the vegetables and spice needed (four heads of celery included) there are some more meat ingredients – 'an ox's palate...a few cocks-combs, a few of the little hearts of young savoys'. In another life, I should love nothing more than to cook this soup (I nearly wrote 'rustle up', but there's clearly not a lot of rustling going on here) but I have to admit that I am going to have to pass this by...for now at least.

Reading some of these early recipes, even a committed meat eater might quail at the enormous quantities used. Glasse's 'strong broth for soups or gravy' demands a whole leg of beef and four gallons of water. Even my passion for good stock would not take me that far. Her largest soup, if you will, is called 'portable soup'. The recipe begins 'take two legs of beef, about fifty pounds weight' (which might perturb a flat-dwelling modern cook), and ends with tiny cups of very stiff jellied soup. It is, I suppose, essentially stock reduced into solid jelly, of which a walnut sized lump 'will make a pint of water very rich' and is an early and much more delicious form of the hideous stock cube. It's very First World to make something which involves throwing most of it away rather than letting it actually reach your mouth. I remember making a minestrone for which I had to make a stock based on a lot of parma ham which was then thrown away. I still feel guilty about it, but also still remember it as the best minestrone I've ever had.

Although Glasse did not take the later, Beeton, route, and include housewifery in her book, she does occasionally offer 'rules', and those for soup-making show both her practicality and her enjoyment of food. 'First take great care the pots or saucepans and covers be very clean and free from all grease and sand, and that they be well tinned, for fear of giving the broths and soups any brassy taste…' reminds us of how much harder it was to scrub out pans to purity, while 'cover it close, and set it on embers, so that it may do very softly for some time, and both the meat and broths will be delicious' lets us imagine her mouth watering as she writes. I love the way Glasse doesn't 'simmer', but stews or boils 'very softly'. It implies love in her cooking, which Beeton never manages to convey.

Perhaps Glasse's key advice on soups which we should still take is this: 'you must observe in all broths and soups that one thing does not taste more than another; but that the taste be equal, and it has a fine agreeable relish, according to what you design it for; and you must be sure, that all the greens and herbs you put in be cleaned, washed, and picked' (through for bugs). I cooked a beetroot and cumin soup the other day. It came from my head rather than a recipe book, but as I stirred and added and tasted I heard Hannah's voice in my head, urging me not to overdo the cumin.

A CRAW-FISH SOUP

Take a gallon of water, and set it a-boiling; put in it a bunch of sweet-herbs, three or four blades of mace, an onion stuck with cloves, pepper, and salt; then have about two hundred craw-fish, save about twenty, then pick the rest from the shells, save the tails whole; the body and shells beat in a mortar, with a pint of pease green or dry, first boiled tender in fair water, put your boiling water to it, and strain it boiling hot through a cloth till you have all the goodness out of it: set it over a slow fire or stew-hole, have ready a French roll cut very thin, and let it be very dry, put it to your soup, let it stew till half is wasted, then put a piece of butter as big as an egg into a sauce-pan, let it simmer till it is done making a noise, shake in two teaspoonfuls of flour, stirring it about, and an onion; put in the tails of the fish, give them a shake round, put to them a pint of good gravy, let it boil four or five minutes softly, take out the onion, and put to it a pint of the soup, stir it well together, and pour it all together, and let it simmer very softly a quarter of an hour; fry a French roll very nice and brown, and the twenty crawfish, pour your soup into the dish, and lay the roll in the middle, and the craw-fish round the dish.

Fine cooks boil a brace of carp and tench, and may be a lobster or two, and many more rich things, to make a craw-fish soup; but the above is full as good, and wants no addition.

Fish soup of any kind is high on my list of favourites, although slightly spoiled by the memory of a friend passing out face down into a bowl. He'd over refreshed himself before a twenty-first and the parents giving the pre-dance dinner were not particularly impressed. The young amongst us of course found it very funny, and pointed out how much prettier the orangey pink of the soup was on his face than a green one might have been.

This soup is much more simple than it at first looks and if, like Glasse, you decide to ignore the extra fish, and cut down the quantities, is not even particularly expensive.

It is fair to say that the inexperienced, or unconfident, cook, might have difficulty with instructions such as 'let it simmer till it is done making a noise', but I find that such instructions do add to Glasse's charm.

TO MAKE SCOTCH BARLEY-BROTH

Take a leg of beef, chop it all to pieces, boil in three gallons of water with a piece of carrot and a crust of bread, till it is half boiled away; then strain it off, and put it into the pot again with half a pound of barley, four or five heads of celery washed clean and cut small, a large onion, a bundle of sweet-herbs, a little parsley chopped small, and a few marigolds. Let this boil an hour. Take a cock or large fowl, clean picked and washed, and put into the pot; boil it till the broth is quite good, then season with salt, and send it to table, with the fowl in the middle. This broth is very good without the fowl. Take out the onion and sweet-herbs, before you send it to table.

Some make this broth with a sheep's head instead of a leg of beef, and it is very good; but you must chop the head all to pieces. The thick flank (about six pounds to six quarts of water) makes good broth; then put the barley in with the meat, first skim it well, boil it an hour very softly, then put in the above ingredients, with turnips and carrots clean scraped and pared, and cut in little pieces. Boil all together softly, till the broth is very good; then season with salt, and send it to table with the beef in the middle, turnips and carrots round, and pour the broth all over.

We – and even more so, our children – are horribly spoilt when it comes to food. My children refer to anything reheated as 'second-hand food', even a stew deliberately cooked a day before. Unlike English children of earlier generations, they positively insist on sauces with their meat, thinking that a plain grilled chop and vegetables is somehow a let-down. Furthermore the downside of the modern acceptance of foreign food is that good old fashioned English food is disappearing. Cooks such as Jamie Oliver and Gary Rhodes have raised the profile of some English recipes, but few people would recognise a scotch barley-broth, let alone greet one with the joy it deserves.

And yet we are poorer than we were ten years ago, and more aware of our health. A soup like this, full of meat, vegetables and pearl barley would fill and satisfy the bellies of the largest hungry family. A friend used to mock me for being a 'food fascist', insisting on cooking all my children's food rather than buying ready meals. But food fascism was only part of the story. At the time I had four small children and was hideously broke; she was not. It is, always, cheaper to cook from raw ingredients than to buy packet food. And you can eat beef without living off steak; cheap cuts, cooked long and slow, are every bit as delicious as the finest fillet. Belly of pork cooked to melting deliciousness is every bit as fine as roast leg.

The domestic cookery book writers of the past understood the importance of both taste and thrift. In both the soup recipes I have given Glasse suggests a more extravagant version, but adds that the cheaper one is very good.

A GREEN PEASE SOUP

Take a quart of old green pease, and boil them till they are quite tender as pap, in a quart of water; then drain them through sieve and boil a quart of young pease in that water. In the meantime put the old pease into a sieve, pour half a pound of melted butter over them, and strain them through the sieve with the back of a spoon, till you have got all the pulp. When the young pease are boiled enough, add the pulp and butter to the young pease and liquor; stir them together till they are smooth and season with pepper and salt. You may fry a French roll, and let it swim in the dish. If you like it, boil a bundle of mint in the pease.

The mixture of dried and fresh peas makes for a really good soup. You could go modern and add a spoon of crème fraiche if you want, which will look pretty, but isn't entirely necessary.

TO MAKE AN ONION SOUP

Take half a pound of butter, put it into a stew-pan on the fire, let it all melt, and boil it till it has done making any noise; then have ready ten or a dozen middling onions peeled and cut small, throw them into the butter, and let them fry a quarter of an hour; then shake in a little flour, and stir them round; shake your pan, and let them do a few minutes longer, then pour in a quart or three pints of boiling water, stir them round, take a good piece of upper-crust, the stalest bread you have, about as big as the top of a penny-loaf cut small, and throw it in. Season with salt to your palate. Let it boil ten minutes, stirring it often; then take it off the fire, and have ready the yolks of two eggs beat fine, with half a spoonful of vinegar; mix some of the soup with them, then stir it into your soup and mix it well, and pour it into your dish. This is a delicious dish.

TO MAKE AN ALMOND SOUP

Take a quart of almonds, blanch them, and beat them in a marble mortar, with the yolks of twelve hard eggs, till they are a fine paste; mix them by degrees with two quarts of new milk, a quart of cream, a quarter of a pound of double-refined sugar, beat fine, a penny-worth of orange-flour water, stir all well together; when it is well mixed, set it over a slow fire, and keep it stirring quick all the while, till you find it is thick enough; then pour it into your dish, and send it to table. If you don't be very careful, it will curdle.

Almonds have been used in cooking for centuries, with particular joy being taken in white dishes. This is an elegant and unexpected soup.

ELIZA ACTON

Eliza Acton totally understood the principles of soup cooking; her clear prose and firm approach make it impossible to misunderstand her views. Although usually anti-French, she is gracious enough to accept that in the soup department at least, the French knew what they were doing. 'The art of preparing good, wholesome, palatable soups, without great expense, which is so well understood in France, and in other countries where they form part of the daily food of all classes of the people, has hitherto been very much neglected in England; yet it really presents no difficulties which a little practice, and the most common degree of care, will not readily overcome.' These are the words with which she sets out her stall, and they set the tone of the whole book. Not only does she give soup a clear importance, that first sentence addresses four of her other key messages: cost, health, care in cooking and a sense of making good food available to all classes.

102

She is also, of course, strict about the importance of stock, combining strictures about taste with health concerns, referring often to the German nutritionist Leibeg. She also quotes 'one of the most skilful cooks in Europe', M. Carême, on 'the stock-pot of the French artisan', which 'supplies his principal nourishment; and it is thus managed by his wife, who, without the slightest knowledge of chemistry, conducts the process in a truly scientific manner.' See, nothing is new, not even Heston Blumenthal's 'scientific' cooking.

CHESTNUT SOUP

Strip the outer rind from some fine, sound Spanish chestnuts, throw them into a large pan of warm water and as soon as it becomes too hot for the fingers to remain in it, take it from the fire, lift out the chestnuts, peel them quickly, and throw them into cold water as they are done; wipe, and weight them; take three-quarters of a pound for each quart of soup, cover them with good stock, and stew them gently for upwards of three-quarters of an hour, or until they break when touched with a fork; drain, and pound them smoothly, or bruise them to a mash with a strong spoon, and rub them through a fine sieve reversed; mix with them by slow degrees the proper quantity of stock; add sufficient mace, cayenne, and salt to season the soup, and stir it often until it boils. Three-quarters of a pint of rich cream, or even less, will greatly improve it. The stock in which the chestnuts are boiled can be used for the soup when its sweetness is not objected to; or it may in part be added to it.

Chestnuts, 1 ½ 1b.; stewed from 2/3 to 1 hour. Soup, 2 quarts; seasoning of salt, mace, and cayenne: 1 to 3 minutes. Cream, ¾ pint (when used).

At one point I worked as a breakfast chef in the local hotel. The head chef was a terrifying Scottish ex-army cook (odd, given you wouldn't necessarily imagine the army as providing the best food our proud nation has to offer). He had an inveterate hatred of vegetarians, and was enraged at being told that he had to provide vegetarian options on the menu. Each day, while I was feeling sick over the grilled haddocks (I was pregnant at the time and at the best of times am nauseated by cooked breakfast) he would throw meat stock into the vegetarian dish, shouting 'take that, you veggie bastards!' (The gesture was slightly weakened by the fact that he used dried stock granules that can't have had much meat content.) He took a shine to me and taught me how to make a tomato look like a rose. A skill I've never used since.

In any event, I might take his attitude to sneaking in a bit of veal or chicken stock here and dish this soup up to a vegetarian. The rich creaminess of it is irresistible. Like mushroom soup, though, the colour is not that enticing so I would be tempted to add some chopped parsley even just a sprinkling of fresh thyme leaves.

PARSNEP SOUP

Dissolve, over a gentle fire, four ounces of good butter, in a wide stewpan or saucepan, and slice in directly two pounds of sweet tender parsneps; let them stew very gently until all are quite soft, then pour in gradually sufficient veal stock or good broth to cover them, and boil the whole slowly from twenty minutes to half an hour; work it with a wooden spoon through a fine sieve, add as much stock as will make two quarts in all, season the soup with salt and white pepper or cayenne, give it one boil, skim, and serve it very hot. Send pale fried sippets to table with it.

Butter, 4 ½ oz.; parsneps, 2 lbs.: ¾ hour or more. Stock, 1 quart; 20 to 30 minutes; 1 full quart more of stock; pepper, salt: 1 minute.

OBS. – We can particularly recommend this soup to those who like the peculiar flavour of the vegetable.

'Sippets' are rounds of stale bread fried in butter.

I love Eliza here – how clear could she make it that she herself does not like parsnips? Maybe Ann Kirby, the maid who helped her test all the recipes, had a liking for them and so Eliza decided to include this soup in her book.

I have just come back from staying with my brother, who lives in France. He tells me that parsnips have only recently appeared in the shops there, and so are almost a luxury. He cooked possibly the best parsnip soup I have ever eaten. As well as onions, he softened ginger and garlic and chili, added coriander and cumin and stirred coconut milk into the soup. Parsnips have such a definite flavour that they hold their own against the hot and curry flavours. As Glasse notes in her advice to soup cooks 'you must observe in all broths and soups that one thing does not taste more than another; but that the taste be equal'. Nat certainly abided by that in this soup.

Children are odd about soup. My theory is that for them it is too close to the pap they were first fed, so they feel patronised by it. Some French children of my acquaintance, staunch eaters of everything, baulk at soup unless they are told it is not soup but a purée, at which point they gobble it up.

Acton suggests white pepper with this soup, which I personally loathe. I have an uncle who is obsessed with black pepper, and will call for it as soon as he arrives at any table. 'Pepe nero, subito' became his nickname for a while. There was a terrible period (for him and me) when the papers announced an international black pepper shortage and I stock-

piled peppercorns in a way I never would do in the face of snowstorms or nuclear attack. But white pepper is, to me, an abomination. It became very fashionable for a while and I swear to God I was once taken to a Michelin starred restaurant in St Felix Lauragais where white pepper was introduced into every course, even the pudding. Tom, the chef at the hotel in which I briefly worked, loved it because it didn't 'discover itself' (i.e. show) in white sauce or scrambled eggs. But, vide the rose-shaped tomatoes, I think he cared more about show than taste anyway.

JERUSALEM ARTICHOKE, OR PALESTINE SOUP

Wash and pare quickly some freshly-dug artichokes, and to preserve their colour, throw them into spring water as they are done, but do not let them remain in it after all are ready. Boil three pounds of them in water for ten minutes; lift them out, and slice them into three pints of boiling stock; when they have stewed gently in this from fifteen to twenty minutes, press them with the soup, through a fine sieve, and put the whole into a clean saucepan with a pint and a half more of stock; add sufficient salt and cayenne to season it, skim it well, and after it has simmered for two or three minutes, stir it to a pint of rich boiling cream. Serve it immediately.

Artichokes, 3lbs., boiled in water: 10 minutes. Veal stock, 3 pints, 15 to 20 minutes. Additional stock, 1 ½ pint: little cayenne and salt; 2 to 3 minutes. Boiling cream, 1 pint.

OBS: The palest veal stock, as for white soup, should be used for this; but for a family dinner, or where economy is a consideration, excellent mutton-broth, made the day before and perfectly cleared from fat, will answer very well as a substitute; milk too may in part take the place of cream when this last is scarce: the proportion of artichokes should then be increased a little.

Vegetable-marrow, when young, makes a superior soup even to this, which is an excellent one. It should be well pared, trimmed, and sliced tender, pressed through a fine sieve, and mixed with more stock and some cream. In France the marrow is stewed, first in butter, with a large mild onion or two also sliced; and afterwards in a quart or more of water, which is poured gradually to it; it is next passed through a tammy, seasoned with pepper and salt, and mixed with a pint or two of milk and a little cream.

This is another example of why Eliza is so good; she offers cheaper alternatives in a way that might, with luck, help the less confident cook learn to adapt other recipes.

A RICHER WHITE SOUP

Pound very fine indeed six ounces of sweet almonds, then add to them six ounces of the breasts of roasted chickens or partridges, and three ounces of the whitest bread which has been soaked in a little veal-broth, and squeezed very dry in a cloth. Beat these altogether to an extremely smooth paste; then pour to them boiling and by degrees, two quarts of rich veal stock; strain the soup through a fine hair-sieve, set it again over the fire, add to it a pint of thick cream, and serve it, as soon as it is at the point of boiling. When cream is very scarce, or not easily to be procured, this soup may be thickened sufficiently without it, by increasing the quantity of almonds to eight or ten ounces, and pouring to them, after they have been reduced to the finest paste, a pint of boiling stock, which must be again wrung from them through a coarse cloth and with very strong pressure; the proportion of meat and bread also should then be nearly doubled. The stock should be well seasoned with mace and cayenne before it is added to the other ingredients.

Almonds, 6 oz.; breasts of chickens or partridges, 6 oz.; soaked bread, 3 oz.; veal stock, 2 quarts; cream, 1 pint.

<u>OBS</u>. 1. – Some persons pound the yolks of four or five hard-boiled eggs with the almonds, meat and bread for this white soup; French cooks beat smoothly with them an ounce or two of whole rice, previously boiled from fifteen to twenty minutes.

<u>OBS</u>. 2. – A good plain white soup may be made simply by adding to a couple of quarts of pale veal stock or strong well-flavoured veal broth, a thickening of arrow-root, and from half to three-quarters of a pint of cream. Four ounces of macaroni boiled tender and well-drained may be dropped into it a minute or two before it is dished, but the thickening may then be diminished a little.

RABBIT SOUP À LA REINE

Wash and soak through three young rabbits, put them whole into the soup-pot, and pour on them seven pints of cold water, or of clear veal broth; when they have stewed gently about three-quarters of an hour lift them out, and take off the flesh of the backs, with a little from the legs should there not be half a pound of the former; strip off the skin, mince the meat very small, and pound it to the smoothest paste; cover it from the air, and set it by. Put back into the soup the bodies of the rabbits, with two mild onions of moderate size, a head of celery, three carrots, a faggot of savoury herbs, two blades of mace, a half-teaspoonful of pepper-corns, and an ounce of salt. Stew the whole softly three hours; strain it off, let it stand to settle, pour it gently from the sediment, put from four to five pints into a clean stewpan, and mix it very gradually while hot with the pounded rabbit-flesh; this must be done with care, for if the liquid be not added in very small portions at first, the meat will gather into lumps and will not easily be worked smooth afterwards. Add as much pounded mace and cayenne as will season the soup pleasantly, and pass it through coarse but very clean sieve; wipe out the stewpan, put back the soup into it, and stir in when it boils, a pint and a quarter of good cream* mixed with a tablespoonful of the best arrow-root; salt, if needed, should be thrown in previously.

Young rabbits, 3; water, or clear veal broth, 7 pints; ¾ of an hour. Remains of rabbits; onions, 2; celery, 1 head; carrots, 3; savoury herbs; mace, 2 blades; white pepper-corns, a half-teaspoonful, 1 oz.; 3 hours. Soup, 4 to 5 pints; pounded rabbit-flesh, 9 oz.; salt, mace, and cayenne, if needed; cream; 1 ¼ pint; arrow-root, 1 tablespoonful (or 1 ½ oz).

Acton also gives a recipe for brown rabbit soup, in which the joints are first floured and fried before being cooked in water and turned into soup. Mushroom 'catsup' and a dash of vinegar are added with the thickening of rice-flour. My children would obviously prefer the creamy version, and celery and any form of game are an excellent pairing of tastes, but the brown soup is warm and slightly stronger. Either way, I can't sing the praises of rabbit meat enough. It's cheap, delicious, and healthy.

'À la reine' is a culinary term which bears no resemblance to what is going on in this soup. It comes from classical French cooking, and implies the presence of chicken, often with calves' sweetbreads, mushrooms and/ or truffles with a supreme sauce. Perhaps she thought the addition of cream gave it the right to being à la reine.

---

*   We give this receipt exactly as we had it first compounded, but less cream and rather more arrow-root might be used for it, and would adapt it better to the economist.

GOOD VEGETABLE MULLAGATAWNAY

Dissolve in a large stewpan or thick iron saucepan, four ounces of butter, and when it is on the point of browning, throw in four large mild onions sliced, three pounds weight of young vegetable marrow cut in large dice and cleared from the skin and seeds, four large or six moderate-sized cucumbers, pared, split, and emptied likewise of their seeds, and from three to six large acid apples according to the taste; shake the pan often, and stew these over a gentle fire until they are tolerably tender; then strew lightly over the mix well amongst them, three heaped tablespoonsful of mild currie-powder, with nearly a third as much of salt, and let the vegetables stew from twenty to thirty minutes longer; then pour to them gradually sufficient boiling water (broth or stock if preferred) to just cover them, and when they are reduced almost to a pulp press the whole through a hair-sieve with a wooden spoon, and heat it in a clean stewpan, with as much additional liquid as will make two quarts with that which was first added. Give any flavouring that may be needed, whether of salt, cayenne, or acid, and serve the soup extremely hot. Should any butter appear on the surface, let it be carefully skimmed off, or stir in a small dessertspoonful of arrow-root (smoothly mixed with a little cold broth or water) to absorb it. Rice may be served with this soup at pleasure, but as it is of the consistence of winter pease soup, it scarcely requires any addition. The currie-powder may be altogether omitted for variety, and the whole converted into a plain vegetable *potage*; or it may be rendered one of high savour, by browning all of the vegetables lightly, and adding to them rich brown stock. Tomatas, when in season, may be substituted for the apples, after being divided and freed from their seeds.

Butter, 4 oz.; vegetable marrow, pared and scooped, 2lbs.; large mild onions, 4; large cucumbers, 4; or middling-sized, 6; apples, or large tomatas, 3 to 6; 30 to 40 minutes. Mild currie-powder, 3 heaped tablespoonsful; salt, 1 small tablespoonful: 20 to 32 minutes. Water, broth, or good stock, 2 quarts.

The tomato did not come to England until the 1590s. At first it was grown only for its beauty (and perhaps smell), and was believed to be poisonous. By the mid eighteenth century it was used in cooking, but as a committed tomato-phile I have noticed how few of these early recipes do in fact include tomatoes.

This recipe also includes an early mention of curry powder. An ancestor developed and made a modest fortune from a curry powder still available in the East (my daughters brought me some back from Cambodia) and still proudly bearing the name 'Waugh's curry powder'. It is mild and fragrant, and perhaps closer to the curry powders first brought back from India by merchants in the East India Company than some modern preparations.

OX-TAIL SOUP

An inexpensive and very nutritious soup may be made of ox-tails, but it will be insipid in flavour without the addition of a little ham, knuckle of bacon, or a pound or two of other meat. Wash and soak three tails, pour on them a gallon of cold water, let them be brought gradually to boil, throw in an ounce and a half of salt, and clear off the scum carefully as soon as it forms upon the surface; when it ceases to rise, add four moderate-sized carrots, from two to four onions, according to the taste, a large faggot of savoury herbs, a head of celery, a couple of turnips, six or eight cloves, and a half-teaspoonful of pepper-corns. Stew these gently from three hours to three and a half, if the tails be very large; lift them out, strain the liquor, and skim off all the fat; divide the tails into joints, and put them into a couple of quarts or rather more of the stock; stir in, when these begin to boil, a thickening of arrow-root or of rice flour, mixed with as much cayenne and salt as may be required to flavour the soup well, and serve it very hot. If stewed down until the flesh falls away from the bones, the ox-tails will make stock which will be quite a firm jelly when cold; and this, strained, thickened, and well flavoured with spices, catsup, or a little wine, would to many tastes, be a superior soup to the above. A richer one still may be made by pouring good beef broth instead of water to the meat in the first instance.

Ox-tails, 3; water, 1 gallon; salt, 1 ½ oz.; carrots, 4; onions, 2 to 4; turnips, 2; celery, 1 head; cloves, 8; pepper-corns, ½ teaspoonful; faggot of savoury herbs; 3 hours to 3 ½. For a richer soup, 5 to 6 hours. (Ham or gammon of bacon at pleasure, with other flavourings.)

OBS. – To increase the savour of this soup when the meat is not served in it, the onions, turnips, and carrots may be gently fried until of a fine light brown, before they are added to it.

CHEAP FISH SOUPS

An infinite variety of excellent soups may be made of fish, which may be stewed down for them in precisely the same manner as meat, and with the same addition of vegetables and herbs. When the skin is coarse or rank is should be carefully stripped off before the fish is used; and any oily particles which may float on the surface should be entirely removed from it.

In France, Jersey, Cornwall and many other localities, the conger eel, divested of its skin, is sliced up into thick cutlets and made into

112

soup, which we are assured by English families who have it often served at their tables, is extremely good. A half-grown fish is best for the purpose. After the soup has been strained and allowed to settle, it must be heated afresh, and rice and minced parsley may be added to it, or it may be thickened with rice-flour only, or served clear. Curried fish-soups, too, are much to be recommended.

When broth or stock has been made as above with conger eel, common eels, whitings, haddocks, codlings, fresh water fish, or any common kind, which may be at hand, flakes of cold salmon, cod fish, John Dories, or scallops of cold soles, plaice,* &c., may be heated and served in it; and the remains of crabs or lobsters mingled with them. The large oysters sold at so cheap a rate upon the coast, and which are not much esteemed for eating raw, serve admirably for imparting flavour to soup, and the softer portions of them may be served in it after a few minutes of gentle simmering. Anchovy or any other store fish-sauce may be added with good effect to many of these pottages if used with moderation. Prawns and shrimps likewise would generally be considered an improvement to them.

For more savoury preparations, fry the fish and vegetables, lay them into the soup-pot, and add boiling, instead of cold water, to them.

This recipe is perhaps more for the confident cook, or it may be as it is because Acton was realising quite how much space she had devoted to soup. Indeed, her 'observation' at the end of her soup chapter is an apology for it 'so far exceed[ing] the limits within which it ought to have been confined' and promising a later appendix for yet more soups.

Acton uses oysters in this recipe, and indeed the early cooks often used oysters as a thickener or taste fillip. I've not included many recipes which use oysters, as they are no longer the cheap ingredient they once

---

*   Cold vegetables, cut up small, may be added with these at pleasure.

were. They were once the staple of servants and apprentices, rather than the luxury they have now become.

ISABELLA BEETON

A third of Eliza Acton's soup recipes were swiped by Mrs Beeton and included in her Book of Household Management. *But as with all her recipes, Mrs Beeton's soups come from a variety of contributors.*

There is no point in my including obvious soups which are still in circulation, so although Mrs Beeton does of course include recipes for regular vegetable and meat soups, I have chosen soups that we might be less likely to cook. I was very tempted to include Mrs Beeton's recipe for 'Hessian Soup', which begins with the ingredient 'Half an ox's head', but was deterred for various reasons. The first was mere pusillanimity – did I dare ask the butcher for an ox's head? Would my name be mud in West Somerset? My next worry was what would I do with the other half of the head? I could amuse myself by leaving it on one of my daughters' pillows, but decided that would possibly be cruel and undo all my hard work against family vegetarianism. Finally I overcame that fear, and met with the answer that yes of course the butcher could get me an ox head with a little warning. The butcher did not even turn a hair at the question.

However the real reason I have not included hessian soup is that I have to accept, perhaps sadly, that not many people nowadays are really prepared to clean an ox head and rub it all over with salt and then have it bobbing around in a saucepan for six or seven hours. It is a shame, as with the vegetables and split peas, it seems like a nutritious, filling and cheap dish. Mrs Beeton also recommends making a ragout with the best bits of the boiled head to put into a thicker version of the soup and a glass of port. Seems perfect for Boxing Day blues.

The other soup which I felt would not go down well with the modern reader is that for Turtle Soup. This is one of the few recipes where Mrs Beeton does give credit to the creator, in this case M. Ude, and most of the ingredients would be impossible to find, or very expensive, nowadays. Not only would turtles now be very hard to find, even in a good butcher/fishmonger, but the recipe begins with these instructions: 'To make this soup with less difficulty, cut off the head of the turtle the preceding day. In the morning open the turtle by leaning heavily with a knife on the shell of the animal's back, whilst you cut this off all round.' And so it goes on, for two pages. I suggested to my daughter that we experimented 'for my book' with her tortoise, but the idea was not well received. She looked almost as horrified as had my butcher, thirteen years earlier, when he asked how he could help me. I plonked my one year old down on his chopping board. 'Don't you think my baby's delicious?' I asked. 'Could you chop off her leg so I can eat her?' Some jokes need thinking through.

Even in Mrs Beeton's day she refers to the difficulty and expense of buying the turtles, and the fact that this is 'the most expensive soup brought to table.' She also gives a top tip about tinned turtles: 'When live turtle is dear, many cooks use the tinned turtle, which is killed when caught, and preserved by being put in hermetically-sealed canisters, and so sent over to England.'

Although I've done the touristy thing of swimming with turtles in the Indian Ocean (an incredibly happy and worthwhile experience) I do mourn the probability that I shall never eat one. Apparently every bit of them is delicious (M. Ude's/Mrs Beeton's recipe for the soup also includes quenelle of turtle) and not one bit needs to be wasted. In fact it was a long time before scientists could accurately classify them, as every time a ship loaded them up to bring them home the sailors could not resist eating them.

COCOA-NUT SOUP

INGREDIENTS. – 6 oz. of grated cocoa-nut, 6 oz. of rice flour, ½ a teaspoonful of mace; seasoning to taste of cayenne and salt; ¼ of a pint of boiling cream, 3 quarts of medium stock No. 105.

Mode. –Take the dark rind from the cocoa-nut, and grate it down small on a clean grater; weigh it, and allow, for each quart of stock, 2 oz. of the cocoa-nut. Simmer it gently for 1 hour in the stock, which should then be strained closely from it, and thickened for table.

Time. – 2 ¼ hours. Average cost per quart, 1s. 3d.

Seasonable in Autumn.

Sufficient for 10 persons.

THE COCOA-NUT. – This is the fruit of one of the palms, than which it is questionable if there is any other species of tree marking, in itself, so abundantly the goodness of Providence, in making provision for the wants of man. It grows wild in the Indian seas, and in the eastern parts of Asia; and thence it has been introduced into every part of the tropical regions. To the natives of those climates, its bark supplies the material for erecting their dwellings; its leaves, the means of roofing them; and the leaf-stalks, a kind of gauze for covering their windows, or protecting the baby in the cradle. It is also made into lanterns, masks to screen the face from the heat of the sun, baskets, wicker-work, and even a kind of paper for writing on. Combs, brooms, torches, ropes, matting and sailcloth are made of its fibres. With these, too, beds are made and cushions stuffed. Oars are supplied by the leaves; drinking-cups, spoons, and other domestic utensils by the shells of the nuts; milk by its juice, of which, also, a kind of honey and sugar are prepared. When fermented, it furnishes the means of intoxication; and when the fibres are burned, their ashes supply an alkali for making soap. The buds of the tree bear a striking resemblance to cabbage when boiled; but when they are cropped, the tree dies. In a fresh state, the kernel is eaten raw, and its juice is a most agreeable and refreshing beverage. When the nut is imported to this country, its fruit is, in general, comparatively dry, and is considered indigestible. The tree is one of the least productive of the palm tribe.

This is typical of Mrs Beeton. She's cooking for an army, and she is actually quite vague. Look, she doesn't tell you when to put in your cream or how to thicken the soup. An experienced cook would of course know, but the flustered housewife (who is also juggling lots of other dishes for her service à la Francaise) is going to be in a complete panic at the moment she reaches the airy 'thicken for table'.

She also can't resist the little dissertation on the cocoa-nut. Her childlike pleasure in knowledge is shown in the comment about the 'goodness of Providence' which almost undermines her scientific hauteur, but makes her all the more likeable.

The medium stock to which Mrs Beeton refers is made with four pounds of shin of beef, along with chicken carcasses and vegetables. I have made the soup with the good homemade chicken stock which I am never without.

MULLAGATAWNY SOUP

INGREDIENTS. – 2 tablespoonfuls of curry powder, 6 onions, 1 clove of garlic, 1 oz. of powdered almonds, a little lemon-pickle, or mango-juice, to taste; 1 fowl or rabbit, 4 slices of lean bacon; 2 quarts of medium stock, or, if wanted, very good, best stock.

Mode. – Slice and fry the onions of a nice colour; line the stewpan with the bacon; cut up the rabbit or fowl into small joints, and slightly brown them; put in the fried onions, the garlic, and stock, and simmer gently till the meat is tender; skim very carefully, and when the meat is done, rub the curry powder to a smooth batter; add it to the soup with the almonds, which must be first pounded with a little of the stock. Put in seasoning and lemon-pickle or mango-juice to taste, and served boiled rice with it.

Time. – 2 hours. Average cost, 1s. 6d. per quart, with stock.

Seasonable in winter.

Sufficient for 8 persons.

Note. – This soup can also be made with breast of veal, or calf's head. Vegetable Mullagatawny is made with veal stock, by boiling and pulping chopped vegetable marrow, cucumbers, onions, and tomatoes, and seasoning with curry powder and cayenne. Nice pieces of meat, good curry powder, and strong stock, are necessary to make this soup good.

Of course as Mrs Beeton was writing at a time when half the world was coloured pink, the influence of India in England went beyond the paisley pattern and into the food. Anyone who has read Vanity Fair *will remember the scene where Becky Sharpe foolishly eats chillies in her attempt to court fat and foolish Jos Sedley. However although there are many recipes using the word 'curry' in Mrs Beeton's book, none of them go much beyond an addition of curry powder and/or cayenne. Mulligatawny (as it is now more often spelled) is a translation of 'pepper water', and is not a soup that I've seen for years. I had an old-fashioned godfather with an old-fashioned cook and they used to produce Mulligatawny. It came in individual little jugs and you poured it into your bowl. Two other delicious things from those days – rather than horseradish sauce he had freshly-grated horseradish served with beef, and a pudding for children which went on being amazing when you were grown up. Bread fried in butter and drizzled with golden syrup and cream. Heaven.*

SOUP À LA REINE

I.

INGREDIENTS. – 1 large fowl, 1 oz. of sweet almonds, the crumb of 1 ½ French roll, ½ pint of cream, salt to taste, 1 small lump of sugar, 2 quarts of good white veal stock.

Mode. – Boil the fowl gently in the stock till quite tender, which will be in about an hour, or rather more; take out the fowl, pull the meat from the bones, and put it into a mortar with the almonds, and pound very fine. When beaten enough, put the meat back in the stock, with the crumb of the rolls, and let it simmer for an hour; rub it through a tammy, add the sugar, ½ pint of cream that has boiled, and, if you prefer, cut the crust of the roll into small round pieces, and pour the soup over it, when you serve.

Time. – Two hours, or rather more. Average cost, 2s. 7d. per quart.

Seasonable all the year.

Sufficient for 8 persons.

Note. – All white soups should be warmed in a vessel placed in another of boiling water. (See BAIN MARIE.)

II.
(*Economical*)

INGREDIENTS. – Any remains of roast chickens, ½ teacupful of rice, salt and pepper to taste, 1 quart of stock.

Mode. – Take all the white meat and pound it with the rice, which has been slightly cooked, but not much. When it is all well

119

pounded, dilute with the stock, and pass through a sieve. This soup should neither be too clear nor too thick.

Time. – 1 hour. Average cost. – 4d. per quart.

Seasonable all the year.

Sufficient for 4 persons.

Note. – If stock is not at hand, put the chicken-bones in water, with an onion, carrot, a few sweet herbs, a blade of mace, pepper and salt, and stew for 3 hours.

This is classic Mrs Beeton, in that she has given a recipe with a variation which will cost less to produce. She's always keen on using left-overs anyway and wants to prove herself useful to the thrifty housewife. The first version, including pounded almonds, reaches right back into the past when almonds were often used to sweeten or thicken sauces. The second, though on the vague side ('neither too clear nor too thick') is still a perfectly filling supper.

ELIZABETH DAVID

With Elizabeth David we are in a different world from any we have seen so far. David's Mediterranean world – a world we can access fairly easily now – is entirely new. Colour and taste are more important to her than precise quantities and timings. For greed-related reading, rather than straightforward instruction, it is always David we turn to first.

It is not only her powers of description that make her such a joy to read; her erudition (worn much more lightly than Mrs Beeton's) makes her work full of interest and surprises. Theophile Gautier's description of gazpacho, for instance, where he writes that 'at home, a dog of any breeding would refuse to sully its nose with such a compromising mixture…[in Andalucía] the prettiest women do not shrink from swallowing bowlfuls of this hell-broth of an evening' is just one such example.

SOUPE AU PISTOU

The origin of *Pistou* is Genoese, but it has become naturalised in Nice and the surrounding country.

Into 3 pints of boiling water put 1 lb. of French beans cut in inch lengths, 4 medium-sized potatoes, chopped finely, and 3 chopped, peeled tomatoes. Season with salt and pepper and let them boil fairly quickly. When the vegetables are almost cooked, throw in 1/4 lb. of vermicelli and finish cooking gently.

Have ready the following preparation, known as an *aillade*. In a mortar pound 3 cloves of garlic, a handful of sweet basil and a grilled tomato without the skin and pips. When this paste is thoroughly smooth, add 3 tablespoons of the liquid from the *Pistou.* Pour the *Pistou* into a tureen, stir in the *aillade* and some grated Gruyère cheese.

David is, again and again, very stern about tomatoes. She is right. There has been a vast improvement in recent years, but many supermarket tomatoes remain pale and tasteless. It's not worth cooking anything with tomatoes unless you have really sweet, dark, juicy ones. My mother's greenhouse was a thing of beauty. Heavy with the smell of tomato plants, Aladdin would have loved it more than any cave full of jewels. Aubergines and peppers lurked underneath leaves, basil (an entirely different beast from its feeble supermarket cousin) grew tall and strong, and bright blue morning glory trailed up the walls. Picking tomatoes for supper was like Peter Rabbit picking blackberries

– more in the mouth than in the bowl. That greenhouse was very heaven and I think I miss it more than the house itself.

PURÉE LEONTINE

Leontine was the cook of the family David boarded with in Paris, and as such her first real introduction to simple, good French food. For that reason alone (never mind the fresh goodness of this soup) it would be almost rude not to include this recipe.

2 lbs. leeks, 1 cup each of spinach, green peas and shredded lettuce, 1 tablespoon each of chopped parsley, mint, celery, ½ tumbler of olive oil, lemon juice, salt and pepper.

Clean and cut the leeks into chunks. Into a thick marmite put the olive oil and when it is warm put in the leeks, seasoned with salt, pepper and the lemon juice. Simmer slowly for about 20 minutes. Now add the spinach, the peas and the lettuce, stir a minute or two, and add a quart of water. Cook until all the vegetables are soft – about 10 minutes, then press the whole mixture through a sieve. If the purée is too thick add a little milk, and before serving stir in the chopped parsley, mint and celery.

This soup turns out an appetising pale green. Enough for six people.

A MEDITERRANEAN FISH SOUP

A cod's head, a cooked crawfish, 2 pints cockles or mussels, 1 pint prawns, 1 pimento, 1 ½ lb. tomatoes, a lemon, a few celery leaves, a carrot, 2 onions, 6 cloves of garlic, 3 tablespoons rice, coarse salt, ground black pepper, thyme, marjoram, basil, fennel, parsley, a piece of orange peel, ½ pint white wine, 4 pints water, saffron, parsley.

Make a stock with the cod's head, the shells of the crawfish and the prawns, the celery, onions, carrot, a slice each of lemon and orange peel, marjoram, thyme, white wine and water, and a teaspoonful of saffron. Simmer this stock for an hour.

In the meantime chop the tomatoes and put them to cook in a thick pan with the pimento and a clove of garlic, and a very little olive oil, simmering them until reduced to a purée.

Clean the mussels or cockles and open them in a very little water over a quick fire; take them out of their shells and strain the liquid through a muslin.

When the stock has cooked, strain it, return it to the pan, bring it the boil, put in the rice and simmer it for 15 minutes; now add the tomatoes, sieved, the crawfish cut into small pieces, the whole prawns, and stock from the mussels or cockles. Let all this heat together for 5 minutes; by this time the soup should be of a fairly thick and creamy consistency. As the soup bubbles and is ready to serve stir in a handful of fresh parsley, basil, or fennel, the mussels or cockles, a dessertspoon of grated lemon peel and a small clove of garlic crushed in a mortar. Another minute and the soup is ready. The addition of the herbs, the lemon and the garlic at the last moment gives the soup its fresh flavour.

I wanted to include a jellied beetroot soup that seems beautiful and delicious – jellied aspic flavoured with beetroot piled onto a cold poached egg. But when even my brilliant butcher failed to get me a veal knuckle I had to give up.

FISH

I have an admission to make. I barely ever cook fish. My brothers have used my reluctance to do so as way of torturing me by trying to make me admit that I don't actually like fish, but this is not the case. It's true to say that in my wet earlier years I didn't, and never had the same adventurous streak when faced with a milky cooked eye as my brothers. I remember this with shame. However this shame is now comforted by the knowledge that Elizabeth David herself had a problem with fish in her early years – even until adulthood. The difference is that she had no brothers to mock her.

The big summer holiday treat in France was the trip to the sea. My father worked every day, sitting out in the sun with his hat and browning arms, and would just occasionally take a day off. There is a small town on the Mediterranean called Leucate-Plage. It's not at all smart, much more for the French on a day out than a swanky Mediterranean resort. At some point my parents had discovered it, and made it our regular. Papa would get up early, drive the moped to the local post office and ring Madame Jouve, the restaurateur, to ask her what the weather was like on the coast. If he came back with good news we would pile in to the car, bicker for three hours, and arrive furiously hot. Each to his own, there was a plan. Time in the sea, followed by lunch at Madame Jouve, more sea, then pancakes from a van and the journey home. My father was uninterested in sea-bathing, but accepted that this was part of the day.

The big dish was bouillabaisse, with its croutons and rouille and garlic mayonnaise and strange and inexplicable fish swimming in the rich garlicky sauce. And this is where my wetness comes in. Where my parents and brothers would dive in with cries of joy I would order a safer dish, lotte à l'armoricaine – monkfish with a lobster and tomato sauce. I probably only ordered that because I was scared of the scorn with which I would be met were I to order steak. And because the sauce was a very pretty pinky red colour. And I've just checked and my sister was with me on the non-bouillabaisse front.

Years later, when a documentary was made about my father's life, we returned en famille to Leucate. Not only did I eat and love the bouillabaisse, but my one year old restored the family honour by clapping her hands with delight when the dish was produced. And again for the cameras.

Even later when my brother Alexander came to stay with me in France we rang every 'Jouve' in the telephone book trying to track down either the restaurant or the restaurateur in the hope that she would cook us one last meal before she died. Alas, we were too late.

I am not quite sure why cooking fish still makes me so uneasy. Both my brothers are excellent fish cooks, and I have eaten the most amazingly delicious fish dishes made by them. Each time I return home determined to raise my game, but always lose my nerve once more. Rick Stein's Seafood is the best fish cookery book I have come across, including encyclopaedic information on the fish, as well as well illustrated instructions on how to prepare them. Under his guidance I have begun to experiment more with fish and see my brothers are right – it's not hard at all. Any fool can grill or fry a fresh sardine, and any fool can even prepare squid. It's actually really good fun.

Not all the fish available in the nineteenth century still feature in our fishmongers now; I can find 'barbel' in the dictionary 'a cyprinoid fish of the genus barbus', and even that it has a beard or wattle, none of which makes it sound particularly enticing, but I find no modern references to eating it. Even Mrs Beeton, who does include a recipe for

125

it, says 'in England it is esteemed as one of the worst of the fresh-water fish', raising the question as to why she bothered with it at all. She adds that it was 'formerly, if not now, a favourite with the Jews, excellent cookers of fish' and then bizarrely suggests boiling it with a piece of bacon.

The recipes I feature here are therefore for those fish which can easily be found today.

HANNAH WOOLLEY

It is rare for Hannah Woolley to show any sort of fallibility, but I rejoiced at seeing her admission that while she knew that the tongue of a carp is 'an excellent morsel', in 'other Fish you must excuse the weakness of my knowledge'. Even her instruction on how to carve a fish are so strongly worded as to show possible hesitation: 'In Fish that have but one long bone running down the back (as the Sole), the middle is to be carved without dispute; there is none so unacquainted with fare, to contradict it.'

MULLETS FRIED

Part of my terror of cooking fish was my early failure with Red Mullet – no one told me (I whined) that they have to be scaled. Disaster. But despite that they remain one of my favourite fish, and as you can see not in fact difficult to cook at all. You can buy a little fish scaler, or ask the fishmonger to scale them for you.

Scale, draw, and scotch them, after washing wipe them dry, and flowre them, fry them in Clarified Butter; being fried, put to them some Claret-wine, sliced Ginger, grated Nutmeg, and Anchovee, Salt, and sweet Butter beaten up thick, but first rub the dish with a Clove of Garlick: Chuse the least Mullets to fry.

TO BOYL A MULLET

Having scalled your Mullet, you must save their Livers and Roes, then put them in water boyling hot, put to them a Glass of Claret, a bundle of sweet Herbs, with a little Salt and Vinegar, two or three whole Onions, and a Limon sliced; then take some whole Nutmegs and quarter them, and some large Mace, and some Butter drawn with Claret, wherein dissolve two or three Anchovies; Dish up your Fish, and pour on your Sauce, being first seasoned with Salt: Garnish your Dishes with fryed Oysters and Bayleaves; and thus you may season your Liquor for boyling most other Fish.

TO MAKE A HERRING-PYE

Put great store of sliced Onions, with Currans and Raisins of the Sun, both above and under the Herrings, and store of Butter; put them into your Pye, and bake them.

Vague as to quantites and timing, but perfectly simple, cheap and understandable. Onions and raisins are a delicious mix, both in terms of taste and texture.

TO BROYL SCOLLOPS

First boyl the Scollops, then take them out of the shells, and wash them, then slice them, and season them with Nutmeg, Ginger, and Cinamon, and put them into the bottom of your shells again with a little Butter, White-wine, Vinegar, and grated bread, let them be broiled on both sides; if they are sharp, they must have Sugar added to them, for the Fish is luscious, and sweet naturally; therefore you may broyl them with Oyster-Liquor and Gravy, with dissolved Anchovies, minced Onions, and Thyme, with the juice of Limon in it.

TO BOYL A SALMON

Take as much water as will cover it, then take Rosemary, Thyme, and Winter-Savoury, and Salt; boyl all these very well, and then put in some Wine-Vinegar, and when your Salmon is boyled, let him remain in the same water always, untill you have occasion to eat of it.

TO BOYL FLOUNDERS, OR JACKS, THE BEST WAY

Take a pint of White-Wine, the Tops of Young Thyme and Rosemary, a little whole Mace, a little whole Pepper, seasoned with Verjuice, Salt, and a piece of sweet Butter, and so serve it; you may do Fish in the same Liquor three or four times.

TO STEW A TROUT

Take a large Trout fair trim'd, and wash it, put it into a deep pewter Dish; then take half a pint of sweet Wine, with a lump of Butter; and a little whole Mace, Parsley, Savoury and Thyme; mince them all small, and put them into the belly of the Trout, and so let it stew a quarter of an hour; then mince the Yolk of an hard Egg, and strew it on the Trout, lay the Herbs about it, scrape on Sugar, and serve it up.

TO STEW A DISH OF BREAMS

Take your Breams, and dress them, and dry them well, and salt them; then make a Charcoal Fire, and lay them on the Grid-Iron over the Fire being very hot; let them be indifferent brown on both sides, then put a Glass of Claret into a Pewter Dish, and set it over the Fire to boyl, put into it two or three Anchovies, as many Onions, and about half a pint of Gravy, a pint of Oysters, with a little Thyme minced small; when it hath boyled a while, put to it a little melted Butter and a Nutmeg. Then Dish your Bream, and pour all this upon it, and then sett it again on the Fire, putting some Yolks of Eggs over it.

HANNAH GLASSE

On the strength of the length of Glasse's fish chapter, my brothers would probably accuse her of not liking fish either, but in fact most of the fish recipes are included under the Lenten chapter. It is believed that fried fish – that great staple of English takeaway food – came to England in

129

*the seventeenth century via Jewish immigrants from Portugal and Spain.
Glasse gives us fish fried in 'beef-dripping, or hog's lard', but adds 'Some
love fish in batter; then you must beat an egg fine, and dip your fish in just
as you are going to put it in the pan; or as good a batter as any, is a little
ale and flour beat up, just as you are ready for it, and dip the fish, to fry it.'*

*Other suggestions, which I don't think would work, are to use rich
beef-gravy and melted butter as a sauce for lobster, but she does add 'but
the gravy, I think, takes away the sweetness of the butter and lobster,
and the fine flavour of the fish.' All of her fish suggestions outside the
Lent chapter include beef gravy, which seems bizarre to us nowadays.*

TO STEW A BRACE OF CARP

Scrape them very clean, then gut them, wash them and the roes in
a pint of good stale beer, to preserve all the blood, and boil the carp
with a little salt in the water.

In the mean times strain the beer, and put it into a saucepan,
with a pint of red wine, two or three blades of mace, some whole
pepper, black and white, an onion stuck with cloves, half a nutmeg
bruised, a bundle of sweet-herbs, a piece of lemon-peel as big as a
sixpence, an anchovy, a little piece of horse-radish. Let these boil
together softly for a quarter of an hour, covered close; then strain it,
and add to it half the hard roe beat to pieces, two or three spoonfuls
of catchup, a quarter of a pound of fresh butter, and a spoonful of
mushroom pickle, let it boil, and keep stirring it till the sauce is
thick and enough. If it wants any salt, you must put some in: then
take the rest of the roe, and beat it up with the yolk of an egg, some
nutmeg, and a little lemon-peel cut small, fry them in fresh butter
in little cakes, and some pieces of bread cut three-corner-ways and
fried brown. When the carp are enough take them up, pour your

sauce over them, lay the cakes round the dish, with horse-radish scraped fine, and fried parsley. The rest lay on the carp, and then the bread stick about them, and lay round them, then sliced lemon notched, and laid round the dish, and two or three pieces on the carp. Send them to table hot.

The boiling of carp at all times is the best way, they eat fatter and finer. The stewing of them is no addition to the sauce, and only hardens the fish and spoils it. If you would have your sauce white, put in good fish-broth instead of beer, and white wine in the room of red wine. Make your broth with any sort of fresh fish you have, and season it as you do gravy.

Glasse appears to be contradicting herself here, but although the recipe is called stewed carp, in fact it is only the sauce that is stewed, not the fish.

We think of carp as something Frenchmen and Eastern Europeans eat on feast days, and it is pretty much overlooked by English cooks. Thanks to the rise of immigrants from Eastern Europe, though, you should be able to buy carp fairly easily now, even in good supermarkets. It is, however, quite an acquired taste – strong and a little muddy.

My brothers keep telling me that I should not be so fearful of cooking fish, and that there are only a few ways to do it and you can't go wrong. Hannah Glasse sends exactly the same message, and makes me ashamed of my pusillanimity.

TO BROIL SHRIMP, COD, SALMON, WHITING, OR HADDOCK

Flour it, and have a quick clear fire, set your gridiron high, broil it of a fine brown, lay it in your dish, and for sauce have good melted butter. Take a lobster, bruise the body in the butter, cut the meat small, put all together into the melted butter, make it hot and pour it into your dish, or into basins. Garnish with horse-radish and lemon.

Who could find that difficult? And who could not find it delicious?

The word broil is more used by Americans than we English speakers these days, and causes confusion. The R in the word removes the water – broiling is exposing the food to high heat, either under a grill (which of course Glasse would not have had) or on a hot gridiron.

TO DRESS LITTLE FISH

As to all sorts of little fish, such as smelts, roach &c, they should be fried dry and of a fine brown, and nothing but plain butter. Garnish with lemon.

And to boiled salmon the same, only garnish with lemon and horse-radish.

And with all boiled fish, you should put a good deal of salt and horse-radish in the water, except mackerel, with which put salt and mint, parsley and fennel, which you must chop to put into the butter, and some love scalded gooseberries with them. And be sure to boil your fish well; but take great care they don't break.

See? A few simple rules take away the fear.

When my mother went away on foreign travels, leaving my father at home, I'd come down to Somerset for the weekend to keep him company and cook. One day he felt like fish, so he asked me buy some for dinner. 'What do you want?' His forehead creased, and he stared in puzzlement at the fistful of notes he was in the process of handing over to me. 'What's it called? That fearfully expensive one that begins with b?' 'Turbot?' I suggested and his brow cleared. 'Yes. Turbot.' We might not have been very good at the alphabet but we understood one another. Turbot is a luxurious and expensive fish, but it is utterly delicious if you (or someone close to you) feels like affording it.

TO BAKE A TURBUT

Take a dish the size of your turbot, rub butter all over it thick, throw a little salt, a little beaten pepper, and half a large nutmeg, some parsley minced fine and thrown all over, pour in a pint of white wine, cut off the head and tail, lay the turbot in the dish, pour another pint of white wine all over, grate the other half of the nutmeg over it, and a little pepper, some salt and chopped parsley. Lay a piece of butter here and there all over, and throw a little flour all over, and then a good many crumbs of bread. Bake it, and be sure that it is of a fine brown; then lay it in your dish, stir the sauce in your dish all together, pour it into a sauce-pan, shake in a little flour, let it boil, then stir in a piece of butter and two spoonfuls of catchup, let it boil and pour it into basins. Garnish your dish with lemon; and you may add what you fancy to the sauce, as shrimps, anchovies, mushrooms &c. If a small turbot, half the wine will do. It eats finely thus. Lay it in a dish, skim off all the fat, and pour the rest over it. Let it stand till cold, and it is good with vinegar, and a fine dish to set out a cold table.

I'd go for the hot version, as cold fish is all a bit English summer wedding to me.

'Catchup', later ketchup, was (and is) a table sauce that had, by the eighteenth century, become a staple in English kitchens. Originally fishy, various versions developed – mushroom, walnut, mango to name a few, but the tomato version we all know (and may or may not love) did not appear until some time later. You can still buy mushroom ketchup, which is useful in beefing up dishes like cottage pie, or adding to gravy.

To make up for the profligacy of turbot, I now offer you Glasse's much more economical herring and cabbage. Again, it feels faintly Eastern European to me, but there is nothing wrong with that, and this would make a good supper dish.

TO DRESS HERRING AND CABBAGE

Boil your cabbage tender, then put it into a sauce-pan, and chop it with a spoon; put in a good piece of butter, let it stew, stirring lest it should burn. Take some red herrings and split them open, and toast them before the fire, till they are hot through. Lay the cabbage in a dish, and lay the herring on it, and send it to table hot.

Or pick your herring from the bones, and throw all over your cabbage. Have ready a hot iron, and just hold it over the herring to make it hot, and send it away quick.

You have to love the idea of ironing your herring, but obviously we don't have to do that now – your grill will do just as well.

The secret of cabbage, by the way, is butter. Simple as that. For centuries English children have hated cabbage because of the watery, over-cooked, tastelessness with which they are presented. This is a boast, but I can honestly say I have never failed to convert visiting children to cabbage. Shredded and cooked in butter for long enough for it to soften, but not to lose its crunch or colour, no one on earth could not love it. Smoky streaked bacon fried first, and maybe cumin seeds, add to the general deliciousness, but butter is enough.

TO STEW PRAWNS, SHRIMPS OR CRAWFISH

Pick out the tails, lay them by, about two quarts, take the bodies, give them a bruise, and put them into a pint of white wine, with a blade of mace. Let them stew a quarter of an hour, stir them together, and strain them; then wash out the sauce-pan, put to it the strained liquor and tails: grate a small nutmeg in, add a little salt, and a quarter of a pound of butter rolled in flour: shake it all together, cut a pretty thick toast into six pieces, lay it close together in the bottom of your dish, and pour your fish and sauce over it. Send it to table hot. If it be crawfish, or prawns, garnish your dish with some of the biggest claws laid thick round. Water will do in the room of wine, only add a spoonful of vinegar.

ELIZA ACTON

Staying true to her promise to 'supply…thoroughly explicit and minute instructions' so that her recipes can be 'at once understood, and easily followed, by those who have no previous knowledge of the subject', Eliza Acton is the perfect writer for a fish-fearer such as myself. Before the recipes begin, she tells the reader how to spot a fresh fish or crustacean. 'The vivacity of their leaps will show when prawns and shrimps are fresh from the sea' invokes the idea of a wonderful zumba competition in the fishmonger. Nowadays we are likely to ask our fishmongers to clean or de-scale fish, but if you were to choose to do so yourself, Eliza again provides incredibly clear instructions as to how to set about the job. She warns sternly about how the cook will be 'disgraced' if the fish is not cleaned properly, but also gives tips on how to rescue 'tainted' fish (strong vinegar or chloride of soda). However between the first and second editions of the book she seems to have rethought the whole idea of saving slightly off fish 'we are very doubtful whether they can by any process be converted into unquestionably wholesome food.' I'm more than happy to scrape the odd bit of mould from bread or cheddar, but don't think I should go as far as disguising bad fish with vinegar.

Especially useful for the fainthearted amongst us is her overview of which fish can be treated in which manner. Reading her would give confidence to any cook, however inexperienced. Alongside this careful instruction is her usual concern for nutrition, according to Baron Liebeg's ideas. To this end she is particularly keen on boiling fish, urging that they be dropped straight into boiling water to seal in the goodness in the fish. Interestingly, for those who believe that Elizabeth David introduced olive oil to English cooking (forgetting the arrival of the Romans to the country centuries before) Eliza Acton recommends 'fresh, pure olive oil' as 'the best ingredient' for frying fish.

SMALL JOHN DORIES BAKED
(AUTHOR'S RECEIPT. GOOD)

We have found these fish when they were too small to be worth cooking in the usual way, excellent when quite simply baked in the following manner, the flesh being remarkably sweet and tender, much more so than it becomes by frying or broiling. After they have been cleaned, dry them in a cloth, season the insides slightly with fine salt, dredge a little flour on the fish, and stick a few very

136

small bits of butter on them, but only just sufficient to prevent their becoming dry in the oven; lay them singly on a flat dish, and bake them very gently from fourteen to sixteen minutes. Serve them with the same sauce as baked soles.

When extremely fresh, as it usually is in the markets of the coast, fish thus simply dressed *au four* is preferable to that more elaborately prepared by adding various condiments to it after it is placed in a deep dish, and covering it with a thick layer of bread-crumbs, moistened with clarified butter.

The appearance of the John Dories is improved by taking off the heads, and cutting away not only the fins but the filaments of the back.

And that is the whole point of good fish cooking, isn't it...take them fresh, cook them simply and don't necessarily feel you have to muck about with sauces. She does mention using the same sauce as that for baked soles, but this is one of the rare moments when Eliza would have her readers in a quandary. The baked sole recipe only mentions butter and breadcrumbs.

TO BOIL A BRILL

A fresh and full-sized brill always ranks high in the list of fish, as it is of good appearance, and the flesh is sweet and delicate. It requires less cooking than the turbot, even when it is of equal size; but otherwise may be dressed and served in a similar manner. It has not the same rich glutinous skin as that fish, nor are the fins esteemed.

They must be cut off when the brill is cleaned; and it may be put into nearly boiling water, unless it be very large. Simmer it gently, and drain it well upon the fish-plate when it is lifted out; dish it on a napkin, and send lobster, anchovy, crab, or shrimp sauce to table with it. Lobster-coral, rubbed through a sieve, is commonly sprinkled over it for a formal dinner. The most usual garnish for boiled flat fish is curled parsley placed round it in light tufts; how far it is *appropriate*, individual taste must decide.

Brill, moderate-sized, about 20 minutes; large, 30 minutes.

OBS. – The precise time which a fish will require to be boiled cannot be given: it must be watched, and not allowed to remain in the water after it begins to crack.

The italicised 'appropriate' is perfectly barmy, and implies a slight disapproval of the habit of using parsley as a garnish. It is touches like these that make Eliza seem so alive so many years after her death.

SALMON À LA GENEVESE

A fashionable mode of serving salmon at the present day is to divide the larger portion of the body into three equal parts; to boil them in water, or in a marinade; and to serve them dished in a line, but not close together, and covered with a rich genevese sauce. It appears to us that the skin should be stripped from any fish over which the sauce is poured, but in this case it is not customary.

Eliza waxes lyrical about salmon in her introductory notes, saying that it is 'excellent in almost every mode in which it can be cooked or used'. People still seem to think it's a treat, although maybe we've all been to too many weddings where overcooked poached salmon was offered to be able to look at it with true excitement. In this recipe, though, she has moved away from her trademark plain cooking and offered up a rich sauce. As she's so keen on salmon, I offer another of her recipes for the fish.

SALMON À LA ST MARCEL

Separate some cold boiled salmon into flakes, and free them entirely from the skin; break the bones, and boil them in a pint of water for half an hour. Strain off the liquor, put it into a clean saucepan and stir into it by degrees when it begins to boil quickly, two ounces of butter mixed with a large teaspoonful of flour, and when the whole has boiled for two or three minutes add a teaspoonful of essence of anchovies, one of good mushroom catsup, half as much lemon-juice or chilli vinegar, a half saltspoonful of pounded mace, some cayenne, and a very little salt. Shell from half to a whole pint of shrimps, add them to the salmon, and heat the fish very slowly in the sauce by the side of the fire, but do not allow it to boil. When it is very hot, dish and send it quickly to table. French cooks when they re-dress fish or meat of any kind, prepare the flesh with great nicety, and then put it into a stewpan, and pour the sauce upon it, which is, we think, better than the more usual English mode of laying it into the boiling sauce.

SOLES STEWED IN CREAM

Prepare some very fresh middling sized soles with exceeding nicety, put them into boiling water slightly salted and simmer them for two minutes only; lift them out, and let them drain; lay them into a wide stewpan with as much sweet rich cream as will nearly cover them; add a good seasoning of pounded mace, cayenne, and salt;

stew the fish softly from six to ten minutes, or until the flesh parts readily from the bones; dish them, stir the juice of half a lemon to the sauce, pour it over the soles, and send them immediately to table. Some lemon–rind may be boiled in the cream, if approved; and a small teaspoonful of arrow-root, very smoothly mixed with a little milk, may be stirred to the sauce (should it require thickening) before the lemon-juice is added. Turbot and brill may also be dressed by this receipt, time proportioned to their size being of course allowed for them.

Soles, 3 or 4: boiled in water 2 minutes. Cream, ½ to whole pint; salt, mace, cayenne: fish stewed, 6 to 10 minutes. Juice of half a lemon.

OBS. – In Cornwall the fish is laid at once into thick clotted cream, and stewed entirely in it; but this method gives to the sauce, which ought to be extremely delicate, a coarse fishy flavour which the previous boil in water prevents.

At Penzance, grey mullet, after being scaled, are divided in the middle, just covered with cold water, and softly boiled, with the addition of branches of parsley, pepper and salt, until the flesh of the back parts easily from the bone; clotted cream, minced parsley, and lemon-juice are then added to the sauce, and the mullets are dished with the heads and tails laid even to the thick parts of the back, where the fish were cut asunder. Hake, too, is there divided at every joint (having been previously been scaled), dipped into egg, then thickly covered with fine bread-crumbs mixed with plenty of minced parsley, and fried a fine brown; or, the back-bone being previously taken out, the fish is sliced into cutlets, and then fried.

Eliza's 'obs' bring such a freshness to her writing. They are more than just informative, they give the feeling that she has been experimenting and tasting as she cooks. She does not pull her punches, either; of course you don't have to agree with her, but her advice is almost stern and she certainly draws her reader along with her. Personally the very idea of cooking fish in clotted cream turns my stomach, so I'm going to go with Eliza's experimenting and not try that one.

ISABELLA BEETON

ANCHOVY BUTTER OR PASTE

INGREDIENTS – 2 dozen anchovies, ½ lb. of fresh butter.

Mode. – Wash the anchovies thoroughly, bone and dry them, and pound them in a mortar to a paste. Mix the butter gradually with them, and rub the whole through sieve. Put it by in small pots for use, and carefully exclude the air with a bladder, as it soon changes the colour of anchovies, besides spoiling them.

Average cost for this quantity, 2s.

I used to loathe anchovies. Partly because one summer I was very sun-stricken and kept passing out. My mother sat by my bed and fed me anchovies every time I came around. At one point I heard my little brother's voice float up through the floor, 'Is she going to die?' Tortured by this thought, and the sun, and the mouthful of anchovies, I fainted again before I heard the answer. For years afterwards the very smell of anchovies made me shudder at the thought of my incipient death. However I love them now, especially when they're slightly de-anchovified. If you melt them in olive oil, they make a delicious base for a sauce, including, oddly, for lamb. Some love them melted into scrambled eggs. My father loved 'Gentleman's Relish', or Patum Peperium, an anchovy spread which we all fought to be the one to give him for Christmas. (When we were little it was that or fruit gums.

Once I let my imagination run wild and gave him fruit polos. My siblings still mock me.) Invented in 1828, Mrs Beeton would almost certainly have known it, and although the recipe is to this day guarded closely by its manufacturers this recipe, and the next one which just adds mace, cayenne and nutmeg, would have been her closest shot at the spread.

Old-fashioned English gentlemen (there is something very English, and very male about anchovy paste) might well have it as a savoury at the end of the meal; I was brought up in too Francophile a house to want anything savoury after a pudding. Otherwise it is an intrinsic part of tea by the fire on a cold winter's day after a walk.

CURRIED COD

INGREDIENTS. – 2 slices of large cod, or the remains of any cold fish: 3 oz. of butter, 1 onion sliced, a teacupful of white stock, thickening of butter and flour, 1 tablespoonful of curry-powder, ¼ pint of cream, salt and cayenne to taste.

Mode. – Flake the fish, and fry it of a nice brown colour with the butter and onions; put this in a stewpan, add the stock and thickening, and simmer for 10 minutes. Stir the curry-powder into the cream; put it, with the seasoning, to the other ingredients; give one boil, and serve.

Time. – ¾ hour. Average cost, with fresh fish, 3s.

Seasonable from November to March.

Sufficient for 4 persons.

Cod is an easy fish to cook, and was the first one I engaged with. This is a really easy, perfectly good, child-friendly sort of a dish. Mrs Beeton includes quite a lot of 'curried' recipes, but never goes much further than using ready-made curry powder and cayenne. I like to think the curry powder she used was the one invented by my distant ancestor.

JOHN DORY

INGREDIENTS. – ¼ lb. salt to each gallon of water.

Mode. – This fish, which is esteemed by most people a great delicacy, is dressed in the same way as a turbot, which it resembles in firmness, but not in richness. Cleanse it thoroughly and cut off the fins; lay it in a fish kettle, cover with cold water, add salt in the above proportion. Bring it gradually to a boil, and simmer gently for ¼ hour, or rather longer, should the fish be very large. Serve on a hot napkin, and garnish with cut lemon and parsley. Lobster, anchovy, or shrimp sauce, and plain melted butter, should be sent to table with it.

Time. – After the water boils, ¼ to ½ hour, according to size.
Average cost, 3s. to 5s.
Seasonable all the year, but best from September to January.
Note. – Small John Dories are very good, baked.

Although Beeton's book came out six years after Acton's second edition, she does seem to have picked up Acton's theories about nutrition, bringing the fish slowly to the boil rather than putting it in boiling water. But this recipe for poaching fish – whether you do it this way or Acton's – is probably the simplest way of dealing with our finny friends. The goodness lies in the freshness of the fish and of course the sauce, if you want one. If the fish is good enough lemon and parsley will do.

EEL PIE

INGREDIENTS. – 1 lb. of eels, a little chopped parsley, 1 shalot; grated nutmeg; pepper and salt to taste; the juice of ½ a lemon, small quantity of forcemeat, ¼ pint of béchamel, puff paste.

Mode. – Skin and wash the eels, cut them into pieces 2 inches long, and line the bottom of the pie-dish with forcemeat. Put in the eels, and sprinkle them with the parsley, shallots, nutmeg, seasoning, and lemon juice, and cover with puff-paste. Bake for 1 hour, or rather more; make the béchamel hot, and pour it into the pie.

Time. – Rather more than 1 hour.

Seasonable from August to March.

'Forcemeat' is what Mrs Beeton calls stuffing, and you'll find it in the 'Sauces' chapter. And of course, we all buy frozen puff-pastry now and there's nothing wrong with that.

Now look, we're all poorer than we were, and we're only going to get poorer. This really is the time to stop our First World Squeamishness about food and embrace what is around, and cheap. I accept it might be hard to find eel in a fancy London fishmonger, but as someone who suffered for years through being unable to buy ingredients in the countryside (the first River Cafe Cook Book *was particularly tormenting for a greedy woman in Somerset in 1995) I'm happy to turn the tables on the townies occasionally. You can always get eels in those places people pay to go fishing. If you're really lucky they'll have a smokery too and you can buy smoked eel which, served with chopped hard boiled eggs, lemon wedges and parsley, was a particular favourite of our priest.*

Having given that lecture on manning up and eating eel, I find this entry in Mrs Beeton that might put you off again: 'TENACITY OF

LIFE IN THE EEL. – There is no fish so tenacious of life as this. After it is skinned and cut in pieces, the parts will continue to move for a considerable time, and no fish will live so long out of water.'

Despite that I'm going to give you another of her eel recipes:

EELS EN MATELOTE

INGREDIENTS. – 5 or 6 young onions, a few mushrooms, when obtainable; salt, pepper, and nutmeg to taste; 1 laurel-leaf, ½ pint of port wine, ½ pint of medium stock; butter and flour to thicken; 2 lbs. of eels.

Mode. – Rub the stewpan with butter, dredge in a little flour, add the onions cut very small, slightly brown them, and put in all the other ingredients. Wash, and cut up the eels into pieces 3 inches long; put them in the stewpan, and simmer for ½ hour. Make round the dish, a border of croutons, or pieces of toasted bread; arrange the eels in a pyramid in the centre, and pour over the sauce. Serve very hot.

Time. – ¾ hour. Average cost, 1s. 9d. for this quantity.

Seasonable from August to March. *Sufficient* for 5 or 6 persons.

KEGEREE

INGREDIENTS. – Any cold fish, 1 teacupful of boiled rice, 1 oz. of butter, 1 teaspoonful of mustard, 2 soft-boiled eggs, salt and cayenne to taste.

Mode. – Pick the fish carefully from the bones, mix with the other ingredients, and serve very hot. The quantities may be varied according to the amount of fish used.

Time. – ¼ hour after the rice is boiled.

Average cost, 5d., exclusive of the fish.

Kedgeree is part of the Anglo-Indian tradition. Some Scots claim that the dish originated there, went to India and came back as part of Anglo-Indian cuisine. Seems an unlikely story to me. Rice? Very Scottish. Cayenne? Ditto.

I love kedgeree. When I was young it used to be served at two in the morning for breakfast after, or towards the end of, a dance. Those were the days. It was in fact served at breakfast in the Victorian days, and is obviously is a good way of using up cold fish, although we always make it from scratch. Haddock is now the traditional fish to use in kedgeree; I usually use a mixture of smoked and plain. I'm afraid, loving cream as much as Hannah Glasse, I also put in cream as well as curry powder and parsley. We hard-boil the eggs rather than soft boil them. But even this simple recipe of Mrs Beeton's makes a perfectly good supper dish.

SKATE WITH CAPER SAUCE (À LA FRANÇAISE)

INGREDIENTS. – 2 or 3 slices of skate, ½ pint of vinegar, 2 oz. of salt, ½ teaspoonful of pepper, 1 sliced onion, a small bunch of parsley, 2 bay-leaves, 2 or 3 sprigs of thyme, sufficient water to cover the fish.

Mode. – Put in a fish-kettle all the above ingredients, and simmer the skate in them till tender. When it is done, skin it neatly, and pour over it some of the liquor in which it has been boiling. Drain it, put it on a hot dish, pour over it caper sauce, and send some of the latter to table in a tureen.

Time. – ½ hour. Average cost, 4d. per lb.

Seasonable from August to April.

Note. – Skate may also be served with onion sauce, or parsley and butter.

Skate are utterly delicious, elegant and curiously beautiful on the plate. They now sadden me as I was given them by my aunt after visiting my very ill uncle in hospital. She had spent the day in hospital with him, and brought me back and poached us skate wings served just with beurre noir. Typical that even in a crisis she was serving delicious food.

FISH SCALLOP

I

INGREDIENTS. – Remains of cold fish of any sort, ½ pint of cream, ½ tablespoonful of anchovy sauce, ½ teaspoonful of made mustard, ditto of walnut ketchup, pepper and salt to taste. (The above quantities are for ½ lb. fish when picked); bread crumbs.

Mode. – Put all the ingredients into a stewpan, carefully picking the fish from the bones; set it on the fire, let it remain till nearly hot, occasionally stir the contents, but do not allow it to boil. When done, put the fish into a deep dish or scallop shell, with a good quantity of bread crumbs; place small pieces of butter on the top, set in a Dutch oven before the fire to brown, or use a salamander.

Time. – ¼ hour. Average cost, exclusive of the cold fish, 10d.

II

INGREDIENTS. – Any cold fish, 1 egg, milk, 1 large blade of pounded mace, 1 tablespoonful of flour, 1 teaspoonful of anchovy sauce, pepper and salt to taste, bread crumbs, butter.

Mode. – Pick the fish carefully from the bones, and moisten with milk and the egg; add the other ingredients, and place in a deep dish or scallop shells; cover with bread crumbs, butter the top, and brown before the fire; when quite hot, serve.

    Time. – 20 minutes. Average cost, exclusive of the cold fish, 4d.

Isn't that a gloriously 1970s first course? It's the kind of food I think I was brought up to despise, but secretly rather like.

    Mrs Beeton has given us two versions, one of which is more expensive and takes longer to cook. She also gives us a very useful tip – make sure you use up leftover fish.

ELIZABETH DAVID

I was delighted to learn that the young Elizabeth David shared my wetness about fish. However once she began to travel she overcame her fear of cooking them, and distaste at eating them. She knew that to be a good cook you couldn't just write off a whole area of cookery. One of the first fish that pusillanimous fish eaters can contemplate is coquilles St Jacques, or scallops. The confusing thing about this first recipe is that it is given a French name, but contains sherry, with which the French have little truck. Nevertheless it is simple and delicious, and includes the red part. I often wonder what happens to all the red bits of scallops which are not served.

COQUILLES ST JACQUES À LA CRÈME
(SUFFICIENT FOR 2 PEOPLE)

4 scallops, ¼ lb. Mushrooms, 1 teaspoon tomato purée, 2 egg yolks, 2 tablespoons sherry, 1 large cup cream, 2 oz. butter, salt, pepper, lemon juice, parsley.

Cut each cleaned scallop in two. Reserve the red part of the fish and put the remainder in a small pan with the butter, salt and pepper. Cook gently for 5 minutes

At the same time sauté the mushrooms in butter in another pan. Add the sherry, the tomato purée and the cooked mushrooms to the scallops, then stir in the cream and egg yolks, taking care not to let the mixture boil. Put in the red pieces of the scallops, which will be cooked in 2 minutes, the finely chopped garlic, the parsley and a little lemon juice.

Serve with triangles of fried bread.

MOULES MARINIÈRE

3 quarts mussels, 1 small onion, 1 clove of garlic, 1 small glass white wine, a small piece celery, parsley.

Prepare the sauce first; make a little white *roux* in the pan with butter, flour, chopped onion, celery, etc., and the white wine, add the water, and put the mussels in when the liquid has the consistency of a thin soup. The mussels can then be served directly they are opened, a great advantage, as they then do not lose their freshness and savour, which they are apt to do if they are reheated. On no account must the sauce be over-thickened, or you will simply have mussels in a white sauce.

Always serve plenty of French bread with moules mariniere.

My manners hoist me on my own petard where moules are concerned. Our priest asked me to lunch once and gave me mussels. Although I wasn't really crazy about moules I made all the right noises, aware of the hard work involved in de-bearding and preparing them. For ever after, convinced I loved them, the priest would ring me up and say with glee, 'I have some mussels in, come to lunch, I know you love them.' My little brother didn't like them as a child as he was convinced they would bite him inside his throat on the way down; we both love them now.

RAGOUT OF SHELL FISH

12 cooked *scampi* or Dublin Bay prawns, 2 quarts mussels, 6 scallops, ¼ lb. mushrooms, ½ pint white wine, 1 tablespoon concentrated tomato purée, 1 tablespoon flour, 1 onion, 4 cloves of garlic, seasoning, herbs, 1 dessertspoon sugar, 1 oz. butter, parsley.

First of all split the *scampi* tails in half, retaining 6 halves in their shells for the garnish. From the remaining shells remove the flesh and cut it into fairly large pieces.

In a fairly deep pan sauté a sliced onion in butter, when golden add the tomato purée, the chopped garlic, salt, pepper and the sugar and herbs. Simmer 5 minutes. Stir in the flour. When thick pour over the heated wine, and cook this sauce for 15 to 20 minutes. Add the flesh of the *scampi*, the sliced mushrooms, the scallops cut into two rounds each, and the mussels, which should have been very carefully cleaned. Turn up the flame and cook until the mussels have opened. At the last minute add the reserved *scampi* in their shells. Turn into a tureen or deep dish, squeeze over a little lemon, sprinkle with parsley, and serve very hot, in soup plates.

The black shells of the mussels and the pink of the prawns make a very decorative dish. The tails of large crawfish (*langouste*) can be used instead of the Dublin Bay prawns or *scampi*, but of course fewer will be needed, and they can be cut into four or six pieces each.

Enough for 4 to 6 people as a first course.

My mother was careful to teach us that the look of the food on the plate is as important as the taste. I am sure that was partly why she so loved Elizabeth David, who often refers to the visual aspect of food, and writes eloquent and beautiful descriptions of the markets and food of the Mediterranean.

FISH PLAKI

This is a typical Greek way of cooking fish and appears over and over again in different forms.

Wash a large fish, such as bream, chicken turbot, or John Dory. Sprinkle with pepper and salt and lemon juice, and put in a baking dish. Fry some onions, garlic and plenty of parsley in olive oil; when the onions are soft add some peeled tomatoes. Fry gently for a few minutes, add a little water, simmer for a few minutes longer, cover the fish with this mixture, add a glass of white wine, some more sliced tomatoes and thinly sliced lemon. Put in a moderate oven and cook about 45 minutes or longer if the fish is large.

A 'chicken turbot' is merely a very small one – two to three pounds.

TRUITE SAUCE AUX NOIX

Put ½ lb. of peeled walnuts through a mincing machine, then pound them in the mortar with a little salt, adding gradually a cup of water and a little vinegar, stirring all the time as for a mayonnaise.

Serve the sauce with a cold trout which has been simply poached in a *court-bouillon*.

We don't use walnuts enough. My mother went on holiday in Turkey once and came back with a recipe book which seemed to involve a lot of walnuts with meat. Delicious.

MEAT

The early cookbooks make a distinction called 'Made Dishes'. These are basically anything 'made up' rather than simply roasted or boiled meats. They might include fricassées, ragouts and stews, as well as a variety of dishes with 'forcemeat' – stuffing of one kind or another. It's interesting that despite the distrust of French cooking among the early domestic cookery writers, a lot of the vocabulary derives from the French. They may refuse to write 'lardoons' (lardons) for bacon, but 'ragout' (a well-seasoned stew) and 'fricassée' (meat, usually white, browned and then cooked in a sauce made from its own stock) are both French. Perhaps it's not so surprising; whatever Hannah Woolley and her descendants thought of French food, in 1066 the Normans did bring their cookery, their customs and their culinary vocabulary with them. We rear cows but eat beef (boeuf) rear pigs and eat pork (porc), rear sheep and eat (or ate) mutton (mouton). Some English words that did survive to the eighteenth century were later shifted over to more Frenchified words, for instance 'collops' (meaning a thin slice of meat) is apparently from Middle English, but don't tell me it isn't related to 'escalopes', a word of French derivation which superseded it. I might take up talking about collops as a new culinary affectation.

There are wonderfully interesting dishes in the early books – ox-palates stewed with artichoke bottoms, cockscombs and sweetbreads for instance – but I am aware most of us who aren't Fergus Henderson might not be willing to go that far. I've not included recipes for lambs' testicles or stuffed udders, but I am including recipes for tongue. There is no reason on earth why we should be fastidious about these, nor why the only tongue available in most English kitchens is that bright pink pressed abomination. I've cooked tiny little lambs' tongues in a sherry

153

sauce and it is food for the gods. Cheap, at that. One of my favourite recipes inherited from my mother is poached ox tongue served with a mushroom and mustard sauce. (Remember to skin the tongue after poaching.) I shan't give you the recipe, delightful though it sounds, 'to dress pigs petty-toes' (Glasse) as I don't think I'll convince most of you to eat pigs' feet stuffed with their liver, lights and heart (served with dainty croutons round the toes), but think how cheap such a dish would be, how nutritious and how full of taste, and maybe you might waver.

In these early books there is also a range of ideas which are simple in their deliciousness but which might not have occurred to the novice cook. Truffles and morels, for instance, simmered in a little water and then added into soups or sauces, giving an extra richness and depth to the taste. Such ideas also imply that these ingredients were readily available – all the early cookery book writers I discuss were keen to point out that their recipes were economical. I know that truffles can still be found in England – my distinguished cousin not only had a secret still in his cellar, but would return from the hills with his pockets stuffed with truffles. He took the secret of their whereabouts to his grave, and none of his descendants or collaterals has ever found them. Perhaps it is time to train a pig; the dog certainly isn't cutting it. Meanwhile you can cheat with mushroom ketchup, or make your own with a mixture of fresh and dried mushrooms.

I reproduce here Hannah Glasse's basic 'Rules to be observed in all made-dishes.' Most of these rules still apply.

First, that the stew-pans, or sauce-pans, and covers, be very clean, free from sand, and well tinned; and that all the white sauces have a little tartness, and be very smooth and of a fine thickness, and all the time any white sauce is over the fire keep stirring it one way.

154

And as to brown sauce, take great care no fat swims at the top, but that it be all smooth alike, and about as thick as good cream, and not to taste of one thing more than another. As to pepper and salt, season to your palate, but do not put too much of either, for that will take away the fine flavour of everything. As to most made dishes, you may put in what you think proper to enlarge it, or make it good; as mushrooms pickled, dried, fresh, or powdered; truffles, morels, cocks-combs stewed, ox palates cut in little bits, artichoke-bottoms, either pickled, fresh, boiled, or dried ones softened in warm water, each cut in four pieces, asparagus-tops, the yolks of hard eggs, force-meat balls, &c. The best things to give sauce tartness, are mushroom-pickle, white walnut-pickle, elder vinegar, or lemon-juice.

The unsure cook should take heart from this; add what you think makes something taste good. It is often as simple as that. And don't overuse one flavour. There is nothing wrong with trial and error in the kitchen, indeed how else are we to come to new amalgamations of taste and texture? One of my favourite people, if for ever unknown, is whoever first looked at an artichoke and wondered if it would be worth fighting through the thistle to find something worth tasting.

HANNAH WOOLLEY

Be warned: Hannah Woolley's use of sugar is frankly terrifying, not so much on health grounds (although I suppose that too) but on taste grounds. We would certainly not use it in the ways she did. For the purposes of verisimilitude, I have left the ubiquitous sugar in the recipes, but would leave it out of anything you cook.

155

BEEF HASHED

In the making of a Hash of Beef, take some of the Buttock and mince it very small with some Beef-suet, or lard, and some sweet herbs, some beaten Cloves and Mace, Pepper, Nutmeg, and a whole Onion or two; stew altogether in a Pipkin, with some blanched Chesnuts, strong broth, and a little Claret; let it stew softly for the space of three hours, that it may be very tender, then blow off the fat, dish it, and serve it on sippets, you may garnish it with Barberries, Grapes, or Gooseberries.

We would probably use potatoes rather than the sippets (rounds of fried or toasted bread) that are used so often in cookery of this time. Remember that the potato did not arrive in Europe until the second half of the sixteenth century, and that it took some time for the mistrustful natives of England to take to the tuber. This is the sort of dish which was the basis of simple English cooking – meat stretched out with suet, given some of the sweet spices which were so loved then, and dished up with bread. It sounds a bit like the great granny of cottage pie.

OLIVES OF BEEF STEWED AND ROASTED

My first experience of beef olives was of something grey and chewy and totally disgusting that I was only offered in the school canteen. I then met them at the table of my vegetarian mother-in-law. She had been told by her handsome sailor fiancé that she was to learn to cook meat before they met at the altar, and so she did, and became a very good English cook. Her beef olives were something entirely different from those at school and wholly delicious. I did not realise how very old a dish they were, although should probably have guessed – the whole 'forcemeat' style of cooking is very entrenched in England.

156

Take a Buttock of Beef, and cut some of it into thin slices as broad as your hand, then hack them with the back of a knife, Lard them with small Lard, and season them with Pepper, Salt, and Nutmeg; then make a farsing with some sweet herbs, Thyme, Onions, the Yolks of hard Eggs, Beef-suet, or Lard, all minced, some Salt, Barberries, Grapes, or Gooseberries; season it with the former Spices lightly, and work it up together; then lay it on the slices, and roul them up round with some Caul of Veal, Beef, or Mutton, bake them in a Dish in the Oven, or Roast them; then put them in a Pipkin with some butter and Saffron, or none; blow off the Fat from the Gravy, and put it to them, with some Artichoaks, Potato, or Skirrets blanched, being first boyled, a little Claret-wine, and serve them on Sippets, with some slic'd Orange, Limon, Barberries, Grapes, or Gooseberries.

Skirrets are a cousin to parsley, but their roots, which are similar to sweet potatoes, are eaten.

TO STEW VENISON

If you have much Venison, and do make many cold baked Meats, you may stew a Dish in haste thus: When it is sliced out of your Pye, Pot, or Pasty, put it in your stewing-Dish, and set it on a heap of coals, with a little Claret Wine, a sprig or two of Rosemary, half a dozen Cloves, a little grated bread, Sugar, and Vinegar, so let it stew together a while, then grate on Nutmeg, and Dish it up.

One important area of cooking that old cooking books often visit, but new ones seldom do, is using up leftovers. Although my daughters like to complain about 'second-hand food', they're not paying the bills, and

157

good use of leftover meat is an art form in itself. On the other hand I have heard of something disgusting called 'Sunday Lunch Soup', which is to be seriously avoided: apparently people just whizz up all the leftovers – meat, gravy, vegetables, potatoes, Yorkshire puddings – and call it a soup. Save us.

TO MAKE A PIG-PYE

Flea [skin] your Pigg, and cut it into pieces, and season it with Pepper, Salt, Nutmeg, and large Mace, lay into your Coffin good store of Raisins of the Sun, and Currans, and fill it up with sweet Butter, so close it, and serve it hot.

I love the way a pastry case was known as a 'coffin'. You could make this without the pastry, as a pork stew.

TO BROYL A LEG OF PORK

Cut your Pork into slices very thin having first taken off the skinny part of the Fillet, then hack it with the back of your Knife, then mince some Thyme and Sage exceeding small, and mingle it with Pepper and Salt, and therewith season your Collops, then lay them on the Grid-Iron; when they are enough, make sauce for them with Butter, Vinegar, Mustard, and Sugar, and so serve them.

It is noticeable how many more herbs were used in the seventeenth century than most households would use now – winter-savoury, for example, is not in most gardens. But there are some combinations that have been recognised as delicious for centuries; pork and sage is one such.

TO MAKE A FRICASSÉE OF VEAL

Cut your Veal in thin slices, beat it well with a Rowling-pin; season it with Nutmegs, Limon, and Thyme, fry it slightly in the Pan, then beat two Eggs, and one spoonful of Verjuice; put it into the Pan, stir it together, fry it, and Dish it.

TO FRY NEATS-TONGUES

Neats' tongues are calves' tongues, and often appear in recipes with cows' udders. Once boiled, skinned and sliced you can easily forget their provenance, although it is true to say that for the squeamish they do look very ready to chat when you first see them. I love them.

First, boyl them, and after blanch them, and then cut them into thin slices; season them with Nutmeg, Sugar, Cinamon, put to them the Yolks of raw Eggs, and a Limon cut into little square pieces, then Fry them in spoonfuls with sweet butter; make your sauce with White-wine, Sugar, and Butter, heat it hot, and pour it on your Tongues, scrape Sugar on it, and serve it.

TO CARBONADO HENS

Let your sauce be a little White-Wine and Gravy, half a dozen of the Yolks of hard Eggs minced, boyled up with an Onion, add to it a grated Nutmeg; thicken it up with the Yolk of an egg or two, with a Ladle-full of drawn butter; Dish up your hens, and pour over your sauce, strew on Yolks of Eggs minced, and garnish it with Limon.

159

To carbonado is to cut the meat crossways, season it and fry it.

CAPON OR CHICKEN IN WHITE-BROTH

First boil the capon in water and salt, then take three pints of strong Broth, and a quart of White wine, and stew it in a Pipkin, with a quarter of a pound of Dates, half a pound of fine Sugar, four or five blades of large Mace, the Marrow of three Marrow-bones, an handful of white Endive; stew them very leisurely; having so done, strain the yolks of ten Eggs with some of the Broth. Before you dish up the Capon or Chickens, put the Eggs into the Broth, and keep it stirring that it may not curdle, and let it be but a little while upon the fire; the Fowls being dished up, put on the Broth, and garnish the dish with Dates, large Mace, Endive, preserved barberries. You may make a Lere of Almond-Paste, and Grape-Verjuice.

You don't really come by capons – castrated roosters – much nowadays, but there's nothing wrong with a chicken. When we were children my mother used to buy something called 'boiling fowl' from a farmer in the next village. I don't know if you find them any more, either. They were basically older, bigger, and tougher (which is why they needed to be boiled) but full of flavour. And they made an incredible stock.

This dish goes back almost to medieval cookery, with its sweetness, its fruit and its acidic touch of verjuice. But these tastes do seem to be making a comeback – barberries, sweet/sour berries are used in Middle Eastern cooking and chefs like Ottolenghi have brought them back to our consciousness.

A 'Lere' is a binding, used to thicken a sauce (lier, to bind, from the French, like so many other culinary words) but if you've thickened the broth with the egg yolks that is fine. Verjuice is an ingredient brought to England by the Romans, a vinegar-like liquid made from sour pressed grapes or crab apples. It's beginning to make a reappearance in foodie quarters (you can buy it online) but to be honest I think you can go too far with the pursuit of verisimilitude.

TO BOYL A CAPON WITH SAGE AND PARSLEY

First, boyl it in water and salt, then boyl some Parsley, Sage, two or three eggs hard, and chop them; then have a few thin slices of fine Manchet, and stew all together, but break not the slices of bread; stew with some of the broath wherein the Capon boyls, some large Mace, Butter, a little white-wine, or Vinegar, with a few Barberries, or Grapes; dish up the Chickens on the sauce, and serve them with sweet Butter and Limon cut like Dice, the peel being cut like small Lard and boyl a little peel with the chickens.

Whether this was due to bad editing, or just being in a rush, the recipe sounds almost as though Woolley is talking to you, rather than writing it. It also reminds us always to read these recipes through before we begin – the peel to be boiled with the chicken is vital to its taste and the instruction would nowadays have been put firmly at the top of the recipe.

FLORENTINES ON PASTE, OR WITHOUT PASTE

A confusingly named dish for the modern cook; to us a 'florentine' is either an almondy biscuit, or something involving spinach. Ignore that – this is simple and delicious, on or off the pastry.

Take a Leg of Mutton or Veal, shave it into thin slices, and mingle with some sweet Herbs, as sweet Marjoram, Time, Savory, Parsley

161

and Rosemary; being minced very small, a Clove of Garlick, some beaten Nutmeg, Pepper, a minced Onion, some grated manchet, and three or four yolks of raw Eggs, mix all together with a little Salt, some thick slices of interlarded Bacon, lay the Meat round the Dish, on a sheet of Paste, or in the Dish without Paste, being baked, stick Bayleaves round the Dish.

HASHES SEVERAL WAYS

First, of raw Beef, mince it very small with Beef-suet or Lard, some sweet-Herbs, Pepper, Salt, some Cloves and Mace, Chestnuts or Almonds blanch'd, put in whole, some Nutmeg, and a whole Onion or two, and stew it in a Pipkin with some strong broth two hours, put a little Claret to it, and serve it on Sippets, blowing off the fat, and garnish it with Lemon or Barberries.

OTHERWAYS

Cut your Beef, fat and lean, into Gobbets, as big as a Pullets Egg, and put them into a pot or Pipkin with some Carrots cut into pieces as big as a Walnut, some whole Onions, some Parsnips, large Mace, a faggot of sweet herbs, Salt, Pepper, Cloves, with as much water and wine as will cover them, let them thus stew three hours.

HARES ROASTED WITHOUT AND WITH THE SKIN

Take an Hare and flay him, then lard him with small lard, stick him with Cloves, and make a Pudding in his belly, with grated Bread, grated Nutmeg, Cinamon beaten, Salt, Currans, Eggs, Cream and Sugar; having made it stiff, fill the belly of the Hare and so roast it. If you will have your Pudding green, colour it with Spinage; if yellow, with Saffron. Let the Sauce be made of beaten Cinamon, Nutmeg, Ginger, Pepper, Prunes, Currans, a little grated Bread, Sugar and Cloves, all boiled up as thick as Water gruel.

If you roast an Hare with the Skin on, draw out the Bowels, and make a farsing, or stuffing of all manner of sweet herbs minced very small, then roul them in some Butter, and make a ball thereof, put it into the belly, and prick it up close, baste it with butter, and being almost roasted, flay off the Skin, and stick on some Cloves on the Body, bread it with fine grated manchet, Flower and Cinamon, froth it up, and dish it on Sawce, made of grated Bread, Claret-wine, Wine-Vinegar, Cinamon, Ginger, and Sugar, being boiled up to an indifferency.

You can buy hare on the internet – including whole 'with fur', which would please Mrs Woolley. If you live near a shoot you may be able to buy one from the shoot itself or the local butcher. I almost hate to eat them because I love to see them running in the wild – it's about the only animal I'm sentimental about. But they are rich and delicious, so I don't give in to my softness and eat one whenever I meet it on a menu. The only one I've ever cooked myself was given me by my uncle and I wasted it hideously and mucked it up. I'm still cross with myself.

You're unlikely to roast one with the fur on and skin it halfway through the cooking, but I include the recipe just in case…

TO FRY RABBETS WITH SWEET SAUCE

Cut your Rabbet in pieces, wash it, and dry it well in a Cloath, take some fresh Butter, and fry the Rabbet in it; when your Rabbet is little more than half Fryed, take some slices shred very small, a quarter of a pint of Cream, the Yolks of a couple of Eggs, some grated Nutmeg and salt; when the Rabbet is enough, put them into the Pan, and stir them all together; take a little Vinegar, fresh Butter and Sugar, melt it together, and to serve it with Sippets, the Dish Garnished with Flowers, etc.

This, without the ubiquitous sugar, is delicious. Rabbit is a dry meat which can easily take the cream. And as it is a very bony animal, it's a good idea to take it off the bone before serving it. I can't push rabbit enough – apart from anything else, it is so cheap.

Pigeons can also be bought very cheaply, at any rate from country butchers. One of my favourite dishes from the south-west of France is pigeon cooked either with those softly stewed, dark green peas, or (richer but totally heavenly) with ceps. I remember taking my father to a restaurant on a hilltop where they served the birds upside down on toast (or sippets as Hannah Woolley would have them) spread with the mashed livers. My father, knife and fork to the ready at ninety degrees to the table, looked at the pigeons with a scowl. 'Some bugger's stolen my breasts!' he cried.

TO BOYL PIGEONS WITH RICE

Boyl your Pigeons in Mutton-broth, putting sweet-Herbs in their bellies; then take a little Rice, and boyl it in Cream with a little whole Mace, season it with Sugar, lay it thick on their breasts, wringing also the juice of a Limon upon them, and so serve them.

TO STEW COLLOPS OF BEEF

Take of the buttock of Beef thin slices, cross the grain of the Meat; then hack them, and fry them in sweet butter; and being fryed fine and brown, put them in a Pipkin with some strong broth, a little Claret-Wine, and some Nutmeg; steam it very tender, and half an hour before you Dish it, put to it some good Gravy, Elder-Vinegar, and a Clove or two; when you serve it, put some juice of Orange, and three or four slices on it, stew down the Gravy somewhat thick, and put unto it when you Dish it, some beaten butter.

TO MAKE A FRICACIE OF CHICKENS

Scald three or four Chickens, and flea [flay – strip] off the skin and Feathers together, put them in a little water; take half a pint of White-wine, and two or three whole Onions, some large Mace and Nutmeg tyed up in a Cloath, a bundle of sweet-herbs, and a little Salt; and put them all in a Pipkin close covered; let them simmer a quarter of an hour, then take six Yolks of Eggs, half a pound of sweet Butter, four Anchovies dissolved in a little Broath; shred the Anchovies dissolved into the Eggs and Butter, and Capers, and so stir it all together over a Chafing-dish of Coals, till it begin to thicken, then take the Chicken out of the Broath, and put leek upon them; Serve them with Sippets, and Limon sliced.

TO STEW BEEF IN GOBBETS,
THE FRENCH FASHION

Take a Flank of Beef, or any part but the Leg, cut it into slices, or Gobbets as big a Pullets-Eggs, with some Gobbets of Fat, and boyl it in a Pot or Pipkin with some fair Spring-water, scum it clean, and after it hath boyled an hour, put to it Carrots, Parsnips, Turnips, great Onions, some Salt, Cloves, Mace, and whole Pepper; cover it close, and stew it, till be very tender; and half an hour before it is ready put into it some pick'd Thyme, Parsley, Winter-savoury, Sweet Marjoram, Sorrel, and Spinage (being a little bruised with the back of a Ladle) with some Claret-Wine: Then Dish it on fine Sippets, and serve it to the Table hot; Garnish it with Grapes, Barberries, or Gooseberries: Or else use Spices, the bottoms of boyled Artichoakes put into beaten butter, and grated nutmeg, garnished with Barberries.

TO BAKE A BREAST OF VEAL

First, par-boyl it, and take out the long bones, and so lay it in a Dish in Vinegar two or three hours; then take it out, and season it with Pepper and Salt, and so lay it into a thin fine Paste, with good store of fine sweet Herbs, finely chopt, and good store of Butter, or Marrow; then bake it, then put in some juice of Oranges, and Sugar, and serve it hot.

TO BOYL WOODCOCKS, OR SNITES

Boyl them either in strong Broth, or in water and Salt, and being boyled, take out the Guts, and chop them small with the Liver, put to it some Crumbs of grated White-bread, a little Cock-broth, and some large Mace; stew them together with some Gravy, then dissolve the Yolks of two Eggs in some Wine-Vinegar, and a little grated Nutmeg, and when you are ready to Dish it, put in the Eggs, and stir it among the Sauce with a little Butter; Dish them on Sippets, and run the Sauce over them with some beaten Butter and Capers, a Limon minced small, Barberries, or whole pickled Grapes.

'Snites' are probably a misprint for snipe.

TO STEW A BREAST, OR LOYN OF MUTTON

Joynt either your Loyn or Breast of Mutton well, draw it, and stuff it with sweet Herbs, and Parsley minced; then put it in a deep stewing dish with the right side downward, put to it so much White-wine and strong Broath as will stew it, set it on the Coals, put to it two or three Onions, a bundle of sweet Herbs, and a little large Mace; when it is almost stewed, take a handful of Spinage, Parsley and Endive, and put into it, or else some Gooseberries and Grapes; in the Winter time, Samphire and Capers; add these at any time: Dish up your Mutton, and put by the Liquor you do not use, and thicken the other with Yolks of Eggs and sweet butter, put on the sauce and the Herbs over the Meat; Garnish your Dish with Limon and Barberries.

HANNAH GLASSE

Hannah Glasse's meat recipes straddle the old way of cooking and the new. We see meat cooked with sauces we know and still use, such as bread sauce or mushroom sauce. However we also realise that Glasse's was a culture in which every piece of animal was used up. This is no longer the case in England, although peasant cookery in Europe still uses all sorts of body parts we have forgotten. Glasse stuffs udders

167

and uses cockscombs. She advises bruising the brains and adding them to gravy; she stews ox palates and serves pigs' 'pettytoes'. Her writing shows the assumption that many housewives will be slaughtering their own animals, particularly pigs and fowl; her recipe for roasting a goose includes instruction in the best way of plucking it.

In Thomas Hardy's Jude the Obscure (1895) Jude and his wife Arabella have to kill their own pig when the butcher does not appear: Jude is the 'tender-hearted fool' and it is his wife who has the knowledge of how to stick the pig. She urges that it should not be pierced too deep, but must take eight or more minutes to bleed to death; she would rather the pig were singed, but he insists on scalding the skin. Arabella mocks Jude for his ignorance in the ways of butchery, saying that the pig is always starved for a day or two before death to 'save trouble with the innards', and is furious when Jude upsets the pail of blood caught to make blood pudding. These were the dying ways of country life which Hardy was recording, ways which lasted longer in rural France but even there are now the ways of the grandparents, not the young.

Most of Hannah Glasse's recipes are aimed at the regular household, although she does include a chapter called 'Read this CHAPTER, and you will find how expensive a French cook's sauce is.' It includes a 'cullis for all sorts of ragoo' and involves three pounds of veal and half a pound of ham which are stewed together and then thrown away. As she writes 'Now compute the expence, and see if this dish cannot be dressed full as well without this expence.' She could have used the meat in something else, I feel. I remember a haddock soup I made which instructed me to throw away all the haddock; I used it in fish cakes and very good they were too.

Glasse's voice is brisk, but also full of advice. She will point out dishes that are good for large numbers ('Chickens with tongues. A good dish for a great deal of company') and will give variations on recipes according to the season (not for her the twenty-four hour supermarket *with mushrooms packed in plastic) or according to what her reader may find in her cupboard (see 'Chickens boiled with bacon and celery).*

TO DRESS SCOTCH COLLOPS

Take veal, cut it thin, beat it well with the back of a knife or rolling pin, and grate some nutmeg over them; dip them in the yolk of an egg, and fry them in a little butter till they are of a fine brown; then pour the butter from them, and have ready half a pint of gravy, a little piece of butter rolled in flour, a few mushrooms, a glass of white wine, the yolk of an egg, and a little cream mixed together. If it wants a little salt, put it in. Stir it altogether, and when it is of a fine thickness dish it up. It does very well without the cream, if you have none; and very well without gravy, only put in just as much warm water, and either red or white wine.

This recipe is as modern as any Jamie and co. might come up with, although some purists might look at askance at cooking with so much butter. They can go and stand in the corner, to be honest. The other touch, which is very Hannah Glasse, is the alternatives of cooking without either the gravy or the cream. We've all looked in a cupboard and found some ingredient missing – it takes a relaxed cook to know how to adapt, and Glasse encourages her readers to do so without fear.

Those of us who live in the country still have trouble buying veal from butchers. Even the excellent Dulverton butcher, who gamely sold rib of beef on the bone under the counter to preferred customers throughout the foot and mouth crisis in the 90s, won't sell veal. When he did, his shop window was sprayed with red paint by vegetarian anti-hunt activists. For some, veal escalopes are a reminder of bad Italian restaurants in the seventies, where a flabby piece of white meat in soft breadcrumbs passed for Veal Milanese. But I love the gentle taste of veal, and now the calves are no longer stored in dark pens we can all eat it with clear consciences.

TO RAGOO A LEG OF MUTTON

Take all the skin and fat off, cut it very thin the right way of the grain, then butter your stew-pan, and shake some flour into it; slice half a lemon and half an onion, cut them very small, a little bundle of sweet herbs, and a blade of mace. Put all together with your meat into the pan, stir it a minute or two, and then put in six spoonfuls of gravy, and have ready an anchovy minced small; mix it with some butter and flour, stir it altogether for six minutes, and then dish it up.

Leg of lamb is not cheap, but this way it might well go further and does not need a lot of cooking. It's interesting to see Glasse using anchovies with lamb, an idea that has again become fashionable today, with anchovies being tucked under the skin of joints of lamb while roasting. She also uses a lot of lemon and mace in her cooking, a delicious and simple way of lifting a dish.

TO MAKE A WHITE FRICASEY

You may take two chickens or rabbits, skin them and cut them into little pieces. Lay them into warm water to draw out all the blood, and then lay them in a clean cloth to dry: put them into a stew-pan with milk and water, stew them till they are tender, and then take a clean pan, put in half a pint of cream, and a quarter of a pound of butter; stir it together till the butter is melted, but you must be sure to keep it stirring all the time or it will be greasy, and then with a fork take the chicken or rabbits out of the stew-pan and put into the saucepan to the butter and cream. Have ready a little mace dried and beat fine, a very little nutmeg, a few mushrooms, shake all together for a minute or two and dish it up. If you have no mushrooms a spoonful of the pickle does full as well, and gives it a pretty tartness. This is a very pretty sauce for a breast of veal roasted.

Glasse gives quite a few recipes for fricassées. Some add egg yolks, which thicken the sauce, and white wine. Sometimes she suggests garnishing with lemon.

BEEF À LA MODE

You must take a buttock of beef, cut it into two-pound pieces, lard them with bacon, fry them brown, put them into a pot that will just hold them, put in two quarts of broth or gravy, a few sweet-herbs, an onion, some mace, cloves, nutmeg, pepper and salt; when that is done, cover it close, and stew it till it is tender, skim off all the fat, lay the meat in the dish, and strain the sauce over it. You may serve it up hot or cold.

BEEF À LA MODE,
THE FRENCH WAY

Take a piece of the buttock of beef, and some fat bacon cut into little long bits, then take two tea-spoonfuls of salt, one teaspoonful of beaten pepper, one of beaten mace, and one of nutmeg; mix all together, have your larding-pins ready, first dip the bacon in vinegar, then roll it in your spice, and lard your beef very thick and nice; put the meat into a pot with two or three large onions; a good piece of lemon-peel, a bundle of herbs, and three or four spoonfuls of vinegar; cover it down close, and put a wet cloth round the edge of the cover, that no steam can get out, and set it over a very slow fire: when you think one side is done enough (which it will be when quite tender) take it up and lay it in your dish, take off all the fat from the gravy, and pour the gravy over the meat. If you chuse your beef to be red, you may rub it with saltpetre over night.

Note, You must take great care in doing your beef this way that your fire is very slow; it will at least take six hours doing, if the piece be any thing large. If you would have the sauce very rich boil half an ounce of truffles and morel in half a pint of good gravy, till they are very tender, and add a gill of pickled mushrooms, but fresh ones are best; mix all together with the gravy of the meat, and pour it over your beef. You must mind and beat all your spices very fine; and if you have not enough, mix some more, according to the bigness of your beef.

As with so many of these early recipes, the quantities are enormous and you are unlikely to want to cook a whole buttock of beef. More interesting is the declared anti-French Glasse's use both of French terminology (à la mode) and giving of a French version of the dish. Even the most committed Anglophile cooks had occasionally to nod across the Channel. Later Glasse gives a recipe for 'a leg of mutton a la hautgout' – basically hung for a fortnight, rubbed and stuffed with cloves of garlic and roasted. Lamb and garlic – to us the epitome of French cooking.

TO FRICASEY NEATS TONGUES

Take neats tongues, boil them tender, peel them, cut them into thick slices, and fry them in fresh butter; then pour out the butter, put in as much gravy as you shall want for sauce, a bundle of sweet herbs, an onion, some pepper and salt, and a blade or two of mace; simmer all together half an hour, then take out your tongue, strain the gravy, put it with the tongue in the stew-pan again, beat up the yolks of two eggs with a glass of white wine, a little grated nutmeg, a piece of butter as big as walnut rolled in flour, shake all together for four or five minutes, dish it up, and send it to table.

TO FORCE A TONGUE

Boil it till it is tender; let it stand till it is cold, then cut a hole at the root end of it, take out some of the meat, chop it with as much beef suet, a few pippins, some pepper and salt, a little mace beat; some nutmeg, a few sweet herbs, and the yolks of two eggs; chop it all together, stuff it, cover the end with a veal caul or buttered paper, roast it, baste it with butter, and dish it up. Have for sauce good gravy, a little melted butter, the juice of an orange or lemon, and some grated nutmeg; boil it up, and pour it into the dish.

When I was first cooking ox tongues were very cheap; the mad cow crisis did for that. Nevertheless I wish we ate proper tongue more often. I've seen people eat it without the forewarning of what it was and love it; children, who are perhaps particularly susceptible to silly fears about what something is, will love the consistency and taste of fresh tongue.

173

More difficult now would be the recipes involving cockscombs (unless you slaughter your own birds) and ox palates. It's a shame really. What these recipes really do show, though, is a commitment to avoiding wasting any part of the animal or bird. You do still see plates of pigs' snouts and tails for sale in French markets, but I can't say I've ever seen an udder for sale.

TO STUFF A LEG OR SHOULDER OF MUTTON

Take a little grated bread, some beef-suet, the yolks of hard eggs, three anchovies, a bit of onion, some pepper and salt, a little thyme and winter savoury, twelve oysters, and some nutmeg grated; mix all these together, shred them very fine, work them up with raw eggs like a paste, stuff your mutton under the skin in the thickest place, or where you please, and roast it: for sauce, take some of the oyster liquor, some claret, one anchovy, a little nutmeg, a bit of an onion, and a few oysters; stew all these together, then take out your onion, pour sauce under your mutton, and send it to table. Garnish with horse-radish.

We would not serve horse-radish with lamb, but I suspect that the stronger taste of mutton could stand it. As for the rest of the recipe, it could do for lamb just as well as mutton. If you look at the next recipe, and the adjustment that is made for using it for mutton, rather than lamb, this bears out my thinking that stronger tastes were added to the stronger meat.

TO FRY A LOIN OF LAMB

Cut the loin into thin steaks, put a very little pepper and salt, and a little nutmeg on them, and fry them in fresh butter; when enough, take out the steaks, lay them in a dish before the fire to keep hot, then pour out the butter, shake a little flour over the bottom of the pan, pour in a quarter of a pint of boiling water, and put in a piece of butter; shake all together, give it a boil or two up, pour it over the steaks, and send it to table.

Note, You may do mutton the same way, and add two spoonfuls of walnut-pickle.

TO DRESS VEAL À LA BURGOISE

Does she mean bourgeoise? I don't know. Nowadays that would mean vegetables such as carrots and onions are cooked with the meat, but it could just mean cooked in a middle-class French family way. Either way it is good.

Cut pretty thick slices of veal, lard them with bacon, and season them with pepper, salt, beaten mace, cloves, nutmeg, and chopped parsley, then take the stew-pan and cover the bottom with slices of fat bacon, lay the veal upon them, cover it, and set it over a very slow fire for eight or ten minutes, just to be hot and no more, then brisk up your fire and brown your veal on both sides, then shake some flour over it and brown it, pour in a quart of good broth or gravy, cover it close, and let it stew gently till it is enough; when enough, take out the slices of bacon, and skim all the fat off clean, and beat up the yolks of three eggs with some of the gravy; mix all together, and keep it stirring one way till it is smooth and thick, then take it up, lay your meat in the dish, and pour the sauce over it. Garnish with lemon.

A DISGUISED LEG OF VEAL AND BACON

Lard your veal all over with slips of bacon and a little lemon-peel, and boil it with a piece of bacon: when enough, take it up, cut the bacon into slices, and have ready some dried sage and pepper rubbed fine, rub over the bacon, lay the veal in the dish and the bacon round it, strew it all over with fried parsley, and have green sauce in cups, made thus: take two handfuls of sorrel, pound it in a mortar, and squeeze out the juice, put it into a sauce-pan with some melted butter, a little sugar, and the juice of a lemon. Or you may make it thus: beat two handfuls of sorrel in a mortar, with two pippins quartered, squeeze the juice out, with the juice of a lemon or vinegar, and sweeten it with sugar.

A PILLAW OF VEAL

Pilau/pilaff came into the English language from the Turkish right at the beginning of the seventeenth century; it is perhaps surprising therefore how few pilaff recipes there are in eighteenth century cookbooks. This is a very English version: it is neither an Italian risotto nor an Oriental pilaff (although perhaps the peculiar orange garnish, forerunner of so many a pub garnish, is aiming for some sort of Oriental touch) but is, as with so many early English cookery recipes, buttery and eggy and solid.

Take a neck or breast of veal, half roast it, then cut it into six pieces, season it with pepper, salt, and nutmeg: take a pound of rice, put to it a quart of broth, some mace, and a little salt, do it over a stove or very slow fire till it is thick, but butter the bottom of the dish or pan you do it in: beat up the yolks of six eggs and stir into it, then take a little round deep dish, butter it, lay some of the rice at the bottom, then lay the veal on a round heap, and cover it all over with rice, wash it over with the yolks of eggs, and bake it an hour and a half then open the top and pour in a pint of rich good gravy. Garnish with a Seville orange cut in quarters, and send it to table hot.

BOMBARDED VEAL

You must get a fillet of veal, cut out of it five lean pieces as thick as your hand, round them up a little, then lard them very thick on the round side with little narrow thin pieces of bacon, and lard five sheeps tongues (being first boiled and blanched) lard them here and there with very little bits of lemon-peel, and make a well-seasoned force-meat of veal, bacon, ham, beef-suet, and an anchovy beat well; make another tender force-meat of veal, beef-suet, mushrooms, spinach, parsley, thyme, sweet–marjoram, winter savoury, and green onions. Season with pepper, salt, and mace; beat it well, make a round ball of the other force-meat and stuff in the middle of this, roll it up in a veal caul, and bake it; what is left, tie up like a Bologna sausage, and boil it, but first rub the caul with the yolk of an egg; put the larded veal into a stew-pan with some good gravy, and when it is enough skim off the fat, put in some truffles and morels, and some mushrooms. Your force-meat being baked enough, lay it in the middle, the veal round it, and the tongues fried, and laid between, the boiled cut into slices, and fried, and throw all over. Pour on them the sauce. You may add artichoke-bottoms, sweetbreads, and cocks-combs, if you please. Garnish with lemon.

This one is obviously a bit of an effort, but it is interesting to see how many ingredients they thought necessary for a good 'made' dish.

SCOTCH COLLOPS LARDED

Prepare a fillet of veal, cut into thin slices, cut off the skin and fat, lard them with bacon, fry them brown, then take them out, and lay them in a dish, pour out all the butter, take a quarter of pound of butter and melt it in the pan, then strew in a handful of flour; stir it till it is brown, and pour in three pints of good gravy, a bundle of sweet-herbs, and an onion, which you must take out soon; let it boil a little, then put in the collops, let them stew half a quarter of an hour, put in some force-meat balls fried, the yolks of two eggs, a piece of butter, and a few pickled mushrooms; stir all together, for a minute or two till it is thick; and then dish it up. Garnish with lemons.

VEAL BLANQUETS

Roast a piece of veal, cut off the skin and nervous parts, cut it into little thin bits, put some butter into a stew-pan over the fire with some chopped onions, fry them a little, then add a dust of flour, stir it together, and put in some good broth, or gravy, and a bundle of sweet-herbs: season it with spice, make it of a good taste, and then put in your veal, the yolks of two eggs beat up with cream and grated nutmeg, some chopped parsley, a shalot, some lemon-peel grated, and a little juice of lemon. Keep it stirring one way; when enough, dish it up.

Glasse's pork cooking is often going to be problematic for the modern cook. Many recipes begin 'spit your pig', or 'cut off the head'. Often she refers to the pig as 'he' – 'lay him down to the fire, but take care not to scorch him' – which tenderness might hurt some people's feelings. Glasse is clearly dealing with the whole animal – sometimes with added extras. Her 'pig matelote' recipe begins 'gut and scald your pig, cut off the head and pettytoes, then cut your pig in four quarters'. It later instructs the cook to 'skin and gut' two large eels. With the best will in the world, the everyday English cook is not going to be grappling with beheading a pig. I am going to include a couple of her pig recipes. Just cut down the quantities to suit.

A PIG IN JELLY

Cut it into quarters, and lay it into your stew-pan, put in one calf's foot and the pig's feet, a pint of Rhenish wine, the juice of four lemons, and one quart of water, three or four blades of mace, two or three cloves, some salt, and a very little piece of lemon-peel; stove it, or do it over a slow fire two hours; then take it up, lay the pig into the dish you intended it for, then strain the liquor, and when the jelly is cold, skim off the fat, and leave the settling at the bottom. Warm the jelly again, and pour over the pig; then serve it up cold in the jelly.

TO DRESS A PIG THE FRENCH WAY

Spit your pig, lay it down to the fire, let it roast till it is thoroughly warm, then cut it off the spit, and divide it in twenty pieces. Set them to stew in a half a pint of white wine, and a pint of strong broth, seasoned with grated nutmeg, pepper, two onions cut small, and some stripped thyme. Let it stew an hour, then put to it half a pint of strong gravy, a piece of butter rolled in flour, some anchovies, and a spoonful of vinegar, or mushroom pickle: when it is enough, lay it in your dish, and pour the gravy over it, then garnish with orange and lemon.

TO MAKE A PRETTY DISH OF
A BREAST OF VENISON

Take half a pound of butter, flour your venison, and fry it of a fine brown
on both sides; then take it up and keep it hot covered in the dish: take
some flour, and stir it into the butter till it is quite thick and brown (but
take great care it don't burn) stir in half a pound of lump-sugar beat fine,
and pour in as much red wine as will make it of the thickness of a ragoo;
squeeze in the juice of a lemon, give it a boil up, and pour it over the
venison. Don't garnish the dish, but send it to table.

*When I lived on Exmoor, I was regularly given venison by cousins or
farmers. It is traditional to give the owner of the land on which the kill
happens some of the meat, so occasionally a huge hunk of meat would
be passed on to me. I was poor and had lots of children, so I made sure I
could tenderise the toughest old stag into something not just edible, but
delicious. I remember the pail in the scullery of our rented house with
a shoulder of venison tenderising over almost a week so that we could
make a feast for the christening of one of our daughters. That was not
the sort of venison that could have been used in this recipe. Now you can
buy venison that has been reared for the table at upmarket butchers and
supermarkets, and this recipe for a 'pretty dish' would suit that. In my
secret heart though I prefer the story of a piece of meat delivered on the
back of a truck, marinading for days, stewing or slow roasting for hours,
its whole life and death story taking place within a few miles.*

TO ROAST A TURKEY

*This is a long recipe, but its interest lies in showing how little has
changed in our ways of cooking: 1747, and the reader is being told*

180

to serve bread sauce with turkey. Now we would use milk rather than water for the sauce, but the spices used and the principles are the same. 'England', as Glasse's contemporary, Voltaire, wrote, 'has forty-two religions and only two sauces'.

The best way to roast a turkey is to loosen the skin on the breast of the turkey, and fill it with force-meat made thus: take a quarter of a pound of beef-suet, as many crumbs of bread, a little lemon peel, an anchovy, some nutmeg, pepper, parsley, and a little thyme. Chop and beat them all well together, mix them with the yolk of an egg, and stuff up the breast; when you have no suet, butter will do: or you may make your force-meat thus: spread bread and butter thin, and grate some nutmeg over it: when you have enough roll it up, and stuff the breast of the turkey; then roast it of a fine brown, but be sure to pin some white paper on the breast until it is near enough. You must have good gravy in the dish, and bread sauce made thus: take a good piece of crumb, put it into a pint of water, with a blade or two of mace, two or three cloves, and some whole pepper. Boil it up five or six times, then with a spoon take out the spice you had before put in, and then you must pour off the water (you may boil an onion in it if you please); then beat up the bread with a good piece of butter and a little salt or onion-sauce made thus: take some onions, peel them and cut them into thin slices, and boil them half an hour in milk and water; then drain the water from them and beat them up with a good piece of butter; shake a little flour in, and stir it altogether with a little cream, if you have it (or milk will do); put the sauce into boats, and garnish with lemon.

Another way to make sauce: Take half a pint of oysters, strain the liquor, and put the oysters with the liquor into a sauce-pan, with a blade or two of mace; let them just lump, then pour in a glass of white wine, let it boil once, and thicken it with a piece of

181

butter rolled in flour. Serve this up in a basin by itself, with good gravy in the dish for everybody who don't love oyster-sauce. This makes a pretty side-dish for supper, or a corner-dish of a table for dinner. If you chafe it in the dish, add half a pint of gravy to it, and boil it up together. This sauce is good either with boiled or roasted turkies or fowls; but you may leave the gravy out, adding as much butter as will do for sauce, and garnishing with lemon.

This slightly stream of consciousness way of writing might not be the one to soothe a flustered housewife on Christmas morning: we can see why Mrs Beeton's more ordered way of writing gained public popularity a century later.

TO STEW A TURKEY OR FOWL IN CELERY SAUCE

You must judge according to the largeness of your turkey or fowl, what celery or sauce you want. Take a large fowl, put it into a saucepan or pot, and put to it one quart of good broth or gravy, a bunch of celery washed clean and cut small, with some mace, cloves, pepper, and allspice tied loose in a muslin rag; put in an onion and a sprig of thyme; let these stew softly till they are enough, then add a piece of butter rolled in flour; take up your fowl, and pour the sauce over it. An hour will do a large fowl, or a small turkey; but a very large turkey will take two hours to do softly. If it is overdone or dry it is spoiled; but you may be a judge of that, if you look at it now and then. Mind to take out the onion, thyme, and spice, before you send it to table.

Note, A neck of veal done this way is very good, and will take two hours doing.

TO ROAST A FOWL WITH CHESTNUTS

First take some chestnuts, roast them very carefully so as not to burn them, take off the skin, and peel them, take about a dozen of them cut small, and bruise them in a mortar; parboil the liver of the fowl, bruise it, cut about a quarter of a pound of ham or bacon, and pound it; then mix them all together, with a good deal of parsley chopped small, a little sweet-herbs, some mace, pepper, salt, and nutmeg; mix these together and put into your fowl, and roast it. The best way of doing it is to tie the neck and hang it up by the legs to roast with a string, and baste it with butter. For sauce take the rest of the chestnuts peeled and skinned, put them into some good gravy, with a little white wine, and thicken it with a piece of butter rolled in flour; then take up your fowl, lay it in the dish, and pour in the sauce. Garnish with lemon.

Don't think I'm expecting you to cook this in the eighteenth century way. This is delicious and so easy now that we can buy peeled chestnuts, use a Magimix, and don't have to cook with our heads up a chimney basting a hanging fowl.

CHICKENS ROASTED WITH FORCE-MEAT AND CUCUMBERS

This one is more fiddly, but unusual and excellent. We hardly ever eat cooked cucumbers, though one of my favourite risottos uses cucumber and strips of its skin. They are delicious cooked; the skin loses its toughness and both it and the flesh have an intensified taste which is more interesting than the wet slices of nothingness so often added to an English salad.

183

Take two chickens, dress them very neatly, break the breast-bone, and make force-meat thus: take the flesh of a fowl, and of two pigeons, with some slices of ham or bacon, chop them all well together, take the crumb of a penny loaf soaked in milk and boiled, then set to cool; when it is cool mix it all together, season it with beaten mace, nutmeg, pepper, and a little salt, a very little thyme, some parsley, and a little lemon-peel, with the yolks of two eggs; then fill your fowls, spit them, and tie them at both ends; after you have papered the breast, take four cucumbers, cut them in two, and lay them in salt and water two or three hours before; then dry them, and fill them with some of the force-meat (which you must take care to save) and tie them with a packthread, flour them and fry them of a fine brown; when your chickens are enough, lay them in the dish and untie your cucumbers, but take care the meat do not come out; then lay them round the chickens with the fat side downwards, and the narrow end upwards. You must have some rich fried gravy, and pour into the dish; then garnish with lemon.

Note, One large fowl done this way, with the cucumbers laid round it, looks very pretty, and is a very good dish.

A PRETTY WAY OF STEWING CHICKENS

Take two fine chickens, half boil them, then take them up in a pewter, or silver dish, if you have one; cut up your fowls, and separate all the joint bones one from another, and then take out the breast bones. If there is not liquor enough from the fowls, add a few spoonfuls of water they were boiled in, put in a blade of mace, and a little salt; cover it close with another dish, set it over a stove or chaffing-dish of coals, let it stew till the chickens are enough, and then send them hot to the table in the same dish they were stewed in.

184

Note, This is a very pretty dish for any sick person, or for a lying-in lady. For change it is better than butter, and the sauce is very agreeable and pretty.

N.B. You may do rabbits, partridges, or moor-game this way.

Simple, clean and very good. Glasse's appreciation of dishes that look pretty is one of her charms.

CHICKENS BOILED WITH BACON AND CELERY

Boil two chickens very white in a pot by themselves, and a piece of ham, or good thick bacon; boil two bunches of celery tender, then cut them about two inches long, all the white part, put it into a saucepan with half a pint of cream, a piece of butter rolled in flour, and some pepper and salt; set it on the fire, and shake it often: when it is thick and fine, lay your chickens in the dish and pour your sauce in the middle, that the celery may lie between the fowls, and garnish the dish all round with slices of ham or bacon.

Note, If you have cold ham in the house, that, cut into slices and broiled, does full as well, or better, to lay around the dish.

TO DRESS A DUCK WITH GREEN PEAS

Put a deep stew-pan over the fire, with a piece of fresh butter; singe your duck and flour it, turn it in the pan two or three minutes, then pour out all the fat, but let the duck remain in the pan; put to it half a pint of good gravy, a pint of pease, two lettuces cut small, a small bundle of sweet-herbs, a little pepper and salt, cover them close, and let them stew for half an hour, now and then give the pan a shake; when they are just done, grate in a little nutmeg, and put in a very little beaten mace, and thicken it either with a piece of butter rolled in flour, or the yolk of an egg beat up with two or three spoonfuls of cream; shake it all together for three or four minutes, take out the sweet-herbs, lay the duck in the dish, and pour the sauce over it. You may garnish with boiled mint chopped, or let it alone.

This could come from Elizabeth David. My brother's mouth waters when he sees a duck flying overhead, he loves to eat them so much. They are a large part of the cooking tradition of the south-west of France where we spent our summer holidays, and are often eaten with braised peas. The sauce there would not be thickened with cream, however.

TO DRESS A DUCK WITH CUCUMBERS

Take three or four cucumbers, pare them, take out the seeds, cut them into little pieces, lay them in vinegar for two or three hours before, with two large onions peeled and sliced, then do your duck as above; then take the duck out, and put in the cucumbers and onions, first drain them in a cloth, let them be a little brown, shake a little flour over them; in the mean time let your duck be stewing in the saucepan with half a pint of gravy for a quarter of an hour, then add to it the cucumbers and onions, with pepper and salt to your palate, a good piece of butter rolled in flour, and two or three spoonfuls of red wine; shake all together, and let it stew together for eight or ten minutes, then take up your duck, and pour the sauce over it.

Or you may roast your duck, and make this sauce and pour over it, but then a quarter of a pint of gravy will be enough.

186

PIGEONS BOILED WITH RICE

Take six pigeons, stuff their bellies with parsley, pepper, and salt, rolled in a very little piece of butter; put them into a quart of mutton broth, with a little beaten mace, a bundle of sweet-herbs, and an onion; cover them close, and let them boil a full quarter of an hour; then take out the onion and sweet-herbs, and take a good piece of butter rolled in flour, put it in and give it a shake, season it with salt, if it wants it, then have ready half a pound of rice boiled tender in milk; when it begins to be thick (but take great care it do not burn) take the yolks of two or three eggs, beat up with two or three spoonfuls of cream and a little nutmeg, stir it together till it is quite thick, then take up the pigeons and lay them in a dish; pour the gravy to the rice, stir all together and pour over the pigeons. Garnish with hard egg cut into quarters.

Sometimes all these garnishes of hard boiled eggs and wedges of lemon remind me of nothing so much as pub meals in the seventies; it's odd what remained in our national cooking consciousness.

PIGEONS IN FRICANDOS

After having trussed your pigeons with their legs in their bodies, divide them in two, and lard them with bacon; then lay them in a stew-pan with the larded side downwards, and two whole leeks cut small, two ladlefuls of mutton broth, or veal gravy; cover them close over a very slow fire, and when they are enough make your fire very brisk, to waste away what liquor remains: when they are of a fine brown take them up, and pour out all the fat that is left in the pan; then pour in some veal gravy to loosen what sticks to the

187

pan, and a little pepper; stir it about for two or three minutes and pour it over the pigeons. This is a pretty little side-dish.

TO ROAST PIGEONS WITH A FARCE

Make a farce with livers minced small, as much sweet suet or marrow, grated bread and hard egg, an equal quantity of each; season with beaten mace, nutmeg, a little pepper, salt and a little sweet-herbs; mix all these together with the yolk of an egg, then cut the skin of your pigeon between the legs and the body, and very carefully with your finger raise the skin from the flesh, but take care you do not break it: then force them with this farce between the skin and flesh, then truss the legs close to keep it in; spit them and roast them, dredge them with a little flour, and baste them with a piece of butter; save the gravy which runs from them, and mix it up with a little red wine, a little of the force-meat and some nutmeg. Let it boil, then thicken it with a piece of butter rolled in flour, and the yolk of an egg beat up, and some minced lemon; when enough lay the pigeons in the dish and pour in the sauce. Garnish with lemon.

PIGEONS IN PIMLICO

Take the livers, with some fat and lean of ham or bacon, mushrooms, truffles, parsley, and sweet-herbs; season with beaten mace, pepper, and salt; beat all this together, with two raw eggs, put it into the bellies, roll them in a thin slice of veal, over that a thin slice of bacon, wrap them up in white paper, spit them on a small spit, and roast them. In the meantime make for them a ragoo of truffles and mushrooms chopped small with parsley cut small; put to it half a pint of good veal gravy, thicken with a piece of butter rolled in flour. An hour will do your pigeons; baste them, when enough lay them in your dish, take off the paper, and pour your sauce over them. Garnish with patties, made thus: take veal and cold ham, beef-suet, an equal quantity, some mushrooms, sweet-herbs, and spice, chop them small, set them on the fire, and moisten with milk or cream; then make a little puff-paste, roll it and make little patties, about an inch deep and two inches long; fill them with the above ingredients, cover them close and bake them; lay six of them round a dish. This makes a fine dish for a first course.

A STEWED PHEASANT

Take your pheasant and stew it in veal gravy, take artichoke bottoms parboiled, some chestnuts roasted and blanched: when your pheasant is enough (but it must stew till there is just enough for sauce, then skim it) put in the chestnuts and artichoke bottoms, a little beaten mace, pepper, and salt just enough to season it, and a glass of white wine, and if you don't think it thick enough, thicken it with a little piece of butter rolled in flour: squeeze in a little lemon, pour the sauce over the pheasant, and have some force-meat balls fried and put into the dish.

Note, A good fowl will do full as well, trussed with the head on like a pheasant. You may fry sausages instead of force-meat balls.

Glasse goes on to give recipes for a variety of birds which we rarely eat any longer, such as russ and reiss. Ortolans, the eating of which was finally outlawed in France as late as 2007 and provided the 'last meal' of President Mitterand have a mention here, as do larks and other birds such as plovers, snipe and woodcock, which are still available but are so high-end I'm not including them here.

189

I have included pheasants as anyone who lives in the countryside can get them comparatively cheaply. In France they are rare and very expensive; my brother's French children ooh and ah when they see one cross the road, whereas my children, brought up in rural Somerset, are totally bored by them. One of my daughters, aged three, once said solemnly to a pheasant in a field 'I ate your brother yesterday – and he was delicious.' The same daughter addressed a duck being pulled out of the oven with the words, 'well, you won't be saying quack any more'. I think I can safely say I've brought up my children with no false sentimentality where eating is concerned.

TO MAKE A CURREY THE INDIAN WAY

Take two small chickens, skin them and cut them as for a fricasey, wash them clean, and stew them in about a quart of water, for about five minutes, then strain off the liquor and put the chickens in a clean dish; take three large onions, chop them small, and fry them in about two ounces of butter, then put in the chickens and fry them together till they are brown, take a quarter of an ounce of turmerick, a large spoonful of ginger and beaten pepper together, and a little salt to your palate: strew all these ingredients over the chickens whilst it is frying, then pour in the liquor, and let it stew about half an hour, then put in a quarter of a pint of cream, and the juice of two lemons, and serve it up. The ginger, pepper and turmerick must be beat very fine.

TO BOIL THE RICE

Put two quarts of water to a pint of rice, let it boil till you think it is done enough, then thow in a spoonful of salt, and turn it out

190

into a cullender; then let it stand about five minutes before the fire to dry, and serve it up in a dish by itself. Dish it up and send it to table, the rice in a dish by itself.

So maybe only the presence of ginger and turmeric makes this a curry, but it is nevertheless a fascinating recipe, as it is the first published curry recipe in Britain. Although curry was commercially available in London from 1784, Glasse's book pre-dates that by some years, and it was not until East India officials began to return from India at the beginning of the nineteenth century that curry began to exert any sort of hold over the English. Even then it took some time. One of the funniest scenes in Thackeray's Vanity Fair *is when social climber Becky Sharp, determined to entrap her friend's brother Jos Sedley, claims to love all things Indian, including its food. She tries the curry that Jos's mother has made for him and is mortified by its heat.* Vanity Fair *was published in 1848, but set before and during the Napoleonic wars. By the middle of the nineteenth century writers such as Acton and Beeton claimed curry as a naturalised English dish – and now, in the twenty-first century, chicken tikka masala is apparently Britain's most popular dish, overtaking even fish and chips.*

TO MAKE A PELLOW THE INDIAN WAY

Take three pounds of rice, pick and wash it very clean, put it into a cullender, and let it drain very dry; take three quarters of a pound of butter, and put it into a pan over a very slow fire till it melts, then put in the rice and cover it over very close, that it may keep all the steam in; add to it a little salt, some whole pepper, half a dozen blades of mace, and a few cloves. You must put in a little water to keep it from burning, then stir it up very often, and let it stew till the rice is soft. Boil two fowls, and fine piece of bacon of about two pounds weight as common, cut the bacon in two pieces. Lay it in the dish with the fowls, cover it over with the rice, and garnish it with about half a dozen hard eggs and a dozen of onions fried whole and very brown.

Note, This is the true Indian way of dressing them.

This, what with the bacon and the lack of any spice other than mace and cloves, is not a very convincing Indian dish. However, as we have established, there was no one really in a position to argue with her.

ELIZA ACTON

Acton opens her section on meat with a chapter on the very foundations of meat cookery – 'boiling roasting, &c'. She stresses how important it is to master the very basics 'of what is called plain cookery, which is, in fact, of more importance than any other, because it is in almost universal request in this country for families of moderate fortune'. There we have the nub of her belief, a belief that should be shared by cookery teachers today who instead spend hours in computer suites designing sandwiches or making fancy cakes rather than knuckling down with the principles of pot roasting or soup. As Acton declaims, 'A thorough practical knowledge of the processes described…will form a really good cook far sooner and more completely than any array of mere receipts can do.'

The different basic methods of cooking meat are introduced: Roasting 'which is quite the favourite mode of dressing meat in this country', steaming, stewing etc. She is firm on the subject of stewing, stressing that 'this very wholesome, convenient and economical mode of cookery is by no means so well understood or profited by in England as on the continent, where its advantages are fully appreciated.'

192

A great deal in that section of her book is in fact irrelevant to us, dealing as it does with ways of managing the 'enormous coal-fires constantly kept burning' in most kitchens. There are wonderful line drawings of different kinds of pans and spits, some of which look more like medieval instruments of torture than anything which could produce food. There is a 'conjuror' on which to broil meat, and a 'salamander' used to brown the surface of a dish 'without putting it at the fire'. Shaped like a large spoon on the end of a long handle, it was held in the fire until red hot and then over the meat to brown it – like a primitive grill. 'It is very much used in a superior order of cookery', Acton writes, adding, 'A kitchen shovel is sometimes substituted for it on an emergency.'

Further to help the ignorant housewife, line drawings of the beasts, divided up and numbered, show which cut comes from where on the animal. There is an outline of how to treat each part. 'Of bull-beef we only speak to warn our readers that it is of all meat the coarsest and the most rank in flavour.'

There are a few simple stews at the beginning of her chapter – with cabbage is called German, with leeks Welsh, English includes port and mushroom catsup. 'An intelligent cook', Acton adds, 'will find it easy to vary [this class of dishes] in numberless ways. Mushrooms, celery, carrots...' etc. etc.

A noticeable difference between Acton's recipes and the earlier ones is the repeated reference to butchers. No longer is there any suggestion that the housewife is wrestling with a whole carcass; ox tails 'should be sent from the butcher ready jointed', but there are recipes teaching the cook how to salt meat herself.

The re-dishing up of leftovers was one of Acton's priorities, and again one which could be taught to many a modern housewife in our throw-away age.

AN EXCELLENT HASH OF COLD BEEF

Put a slice of butter into a thick saucepan, and when it boils throw in a dessertspoonful of minced herbs, and an onion (or two or three eschalots) shred small: shake them over the fire until they are lightly browned, then stir in a tablespoonful of flour, a little cayenne, some mace or nutmeg, and half a teaspoonful of salt. When the whole is well coloured, pour to it three-quarters of a pint more of broth or gravy, according to the quantity of meat to be served in it. Let this boil gently for fifteen minutes; then strain it, add half a wineglassful of mushroom or of compound catsup, lay in the meat, and keep it by the side of the fire until it is heated through and is on the point of simmering, but be sure not to let it boil. Serve it up in a very hot dish, and garnish it with fried or toasted sippets of bread.

A COMMON HASH OF COLD BEEF OR MUTTON

Take the meat from the bones, slice it small, trim off the brown edges, and stew down the trimmings with the bones well broken, an onion, a bunch of thyme and parsley, a carrot cut into thick slices, a few pepper-corns, four cloves, some salt, and a pint and a half of water. When this is reduced to little more than three quarters of a pint, strain it, clear it from the fat, thicken it with a large dessertspoonful of rice-flour, or rather less of arrow-root, add salt and pepper if needed, boil the whole for a few minutes, then lay in the meat and heat it well. Boiled potatoes are sometimes sliced hot into a very common hash.

OBS. – The cook should be reminded that if the meat in a hash or mince be allowed to boil, it will immediately become hard, and can then only be rendered eatable by *very long stewing*, which is by no means desirable for meat which is already sufficiently cooked.

BRESLAW OF BEEF (GOOD)

Trim the brown edges from half a pound of undressed roast beef, shred it small, and mix it with four ounces of fine breadcrumbs, a teaspoonful of minced parsley, and two-thirds as much of thyme, two ounces of butter broken small, half a cupful of gravy or cream, a high seasoning of pepper and cayenne and mace or nutmeg, a small teaspoonful of salt, and three large eggs well whisked. Melt a little butter in a deep dish, pour in the beef, and bake it half an hour; turn it out, and send it to table with brown gravy in a tureen. When cream or gravy is not at hand, an additional egg or two and rather more butter must be used. We think that grated lemon-rind improves the breslaw. A portion of fat from the joint can be added where it is liked. The mixture is sometimes baked in buttered cups.

Beef, ½ lb.; bread-crumbs, 4 oz.; butter, 2 oz.; gravy or cream, ½ cupful; parsley, 1 teaspoonful; thyme, two-thirds of teaspoonful; eggs, 3 or, if small, 4; salt, 1 teaspoonful; pepper and nutmeg, ½ teaspoonful each: bake ½ hour.

There is quite a variety of hashes in Modern Cookery, some topped with breadcrumbs, others with mashed potato – a cottage pie by any other name.

Ox cheeks seem to be back in fashion, in restaurants at least. Think of a cow and you can't but imagine the soft tenderness of its cheek. Delicious.

OX-CHEEK STUFFED AND BAKED
(GOOD, AND NOT EXPENSIVE)

Cleanse, with the greatest nicety, a fresh ox-cheek by washing, scraping it lightly with a knife, and soaking out the blood; then put it into plenty of warm water, and boil it gently for about an hour. Throw in a large teaspoonful of salt, and carefully remove all the scum as it rises to the surface. Let it cool after it is lifted out, and then take away the bones, remembering always to work the knife close to them, and to avoid piercing the skin. When the cheek has become cold, put into it a good roll of forcemeat then skewer or bind up the cheek securely, and send it to a moderate oven for an hour or an hour and a half. It should be baked until it is exceedingly tender quite through. Drain it well from fat, dish it, withdraw the skewers, or unbind it gently, and either sauce it with a little good brown gravy, or send it to table with melted butter in a tureen, a cut lemon, and cayenne, or with any sauce which may be considered more appropriate.

Acton waxes lyrical on the joys of veal and the uses to which all part of the animal can be put. The udder was apparently used by the French instead of butter; boiled and then pounded it was used in forcemeats (stuffings). And as for the head – she has ten different recipes for that tasty morsel, including one called 'the Warder's way' which carries this 'obs': 'The skin, with the ear, may be left on the head for this receipt, and the latter slit into narrow strips from the tip to within an inch and a half of the base; which will give it a feathery and ornamental appearance, the head may then be glazed or not at pleasure.' I don't think we'll be trying that one. She also recommends stewed calf's feet as cheap and good, pointing out as so often the nutritional as well as the economic value of the cut.

Many of her veal recipes come with the oyster sauce which was so popular in her day.

196

BOILED BREAST OF VEAL

Let both the veal and the sweet-bread be washed with exceeding nicety, cover them with cold water, clear off the scum as it rises, throw in a *little* salt, add a bunch of parsley, a large blade of mace, and twenty white pepper-corns; simmer the meat from an hour to an hour and a quarter, and serve it covered with rich onion sauce. Send it to table very hot. The sweet-bread may be taken up when half done, and curried, or made into cutlets, or stewed in brown gravy. When onions are objected to, substitute white sauce and a cheek of bacon for them, or parsley and butter, if preferred to it.

1 to 1 ¼ hour.

Don't make the mistake I did the first time I attempted sweetbreads. You can't just throw them in merrily as Acton suggests. Before cooking they have to be soaked and skinned, which is not an easy job. It is however well worth the effort once you know what you're doing.

STEWED SHOLDER OF VEAL (ENGLISH RECEIPT)

Bone a shoulder of veal, and strew the inside thickly with savoury herbs minced small: season it well with salt, cayenne, and pounded mace; and place on these a layer of ham cut in thick slices and freed from rind and rust. Roll up the veal, and bind it tightly with a fillet; roast it for an hour and a half, then simmer it gently in good brown gravy for five hours; add forcemeat-balls before it is dished; skim the fat from the gravy, and serve it with the meat. This receipt, for which we are indebted to a correspondent on whom we can depend, and which we have not therefore considered it necessary to test ourselves, is for a joint which weighs ten pounds before it is boned.

As ever, Acton cooks in huge quantities. But this is a fine, simple recipe and if Acton can trust her correspondent so can we.

The next recipe marries veal with mushrooms, a pairing with which we are all familiar. But the basting with béchamel, which gives the meat a thick creamy crust, is interesting.

NECK OF VEAL À LA CRÈME (OR AU BÉCHAMEL)

Take the best end of a neck of white and well-fed veal, detach the flesh from the ends of the bones, cut them sufficiently short to give the joint a good square form, fold and skewer the skin over them, wrap a buttered paper round the meat, lay it at a moderate distance from a clear fire, and move the paper and continue the basting with a pint, or more, of *béchamel* or of rich white sauce, until the veal is sufficiently roasted, and well encrusted with it. Serve some *béchamel* under it in the dish, and send it very hot to table. For variety, give the *béchamel* in making it a high flavour of mushrooms, and add some small buttons stewed very white and tender, to the portion reserved for saucing the joint.

2 to 2 ¼ hours.

KNUCKLE OF VEAL EN RAGOUT

Cut in small thick slices the flesh of a knuckle of veal, season it with a little fine salt and white pepper, flour it lightly, and fry it in butter to a pale brown, lay it into a very clean stewpan or saucepan, and just cover it with boiling water; skim it clean, and add to it a faggot of thyme and parsley, the white part of a head of celery, a small quantity of cayenne, and a blade or two of mace. Stew it very softly from an hour and three-quarters to two hours and a half. Thicken and enrich the gravy if needful with rice-flour and mushroom catsup or Harvey's sauce, or with a large teaspoonful of flour, mixed with a slice of butter, a little good store-sauce and a glass of sherry or Madeira. Fried forcemeat-balls may be added at pleasure. With an additional quantity of water, or of broth (made with the bones of the joint), a pint and a half of young green peas stewed with the veal for an hour will give an agreeable variety of this dish.

KNUCKLE OF VEAL WITH RICE

Pour over a small knuckle of veal rather more than sufficient water to cover it; bring it slowly to a boil; take off all the scum with great care, throw in a teaspoonful of salt, and when the joint has simmered for about half an hour, throw in from eight to twelve ounces of well washed rice, and stew the veal gently for an hour and a half longer, or until both the meat and rice are perfectly tender. A seasoning of cayenne and mace in fine powder with more salt should it be required, must be added twenty or thirty minutes before they are served. For a superior stew good veal broth may be substituted for the water.

Veal, 6 lbs.; water, 3 to 4 pints; salt, 1 teaspoonful; 30 to 40 minutes. Rice, 8 to 12 oz.: 1 ½ hour.

OBS. – A quart or even more of full grown green peas added to the veal as soon as the scum has been cleared off will make a most excellent stew. It should be well seasoned with white pepper, and the mace should be omitted. Two or three cucumbers, pared and freed from the seeds, may be sliced into it when it boils, or four or five young lettuces shred small may be added instead. Green onions also, when they are liked, may be used to give it flavour.

199

She is always a little hesitant about using onions, which makes me suspect her assistant as being anti-onion.

Every early recipe involving rice suggests boiling it for far longer than we would nowadays. Whether this is a matter of difference in fashion, or whether it arrived in England treated in some different way, I really don't know. In any event I would advise leaving it until much later to add the rice.

SPRING-STEW OF VEAL

Cut two pounds of veal, free from fat, into small half-inch thick cutlets; flour them well, and fry them in butter with two small cucumbers sliced, sprinkled with pepper, and floured, one moderate sized lettuce, and twenty-four green gooseberries cut open lengthwise and seeded. When the whole is nicely browned, lift it into a thick saucepan, and pour gradually into the pan half a pint, or rather more, of boiling water, broth, or gravy. Add as much salt and pepper as it requires. Give it a minute's simmer, and pour it over the meat, shaking it well round the pan as this is done. Let the veal stew gently from three-quarters of an hour to an hour. A bunch of green onions cut small may be added to the other vegetables if liked; and the veal will eat better, if slightly seasoned with salt and pepper before it is floured; a portion of fat can be left on it if preferred.

Veal 2 lbs.; cucumbers, 2; lettuce, 1; green gooseberries, 24; water or broth, ½ pint or more: ¾ to 1 hour.

SWEET-BREADS SIMPLY DRESSED (ENTRÉE)

In whatever way sweet-breads are dressed, they should first be well soaked in lukewarm water, the thrown into boiling water to *blanch*

200

them, as it is called, and to render them firm. If lifted out after they have boiled from five to ten minutes according to their size, and laid immediately into fresh spring water to cool, their colour will be the better preserved. They may then be generally stewed for three-quarters of an hour in veal gravy, which with the usual additions of cream, lemon, and egg-yolks, may be converted into a fricassée sauce for them when they are done; or they may lifted from it, *glazed*, and served with good Spanish gravy; or, the glazing being omitted, they may be sauced with the sharp *Maître d'Hôtel* sauce. They may also be floured, and roasted in a Dutch oven, being often basted with butter, and frequently turned. A full sized sweet-bread, after having been blanched, will require quite three-quarters of an hour to dress it.

Blanched 5 to 10 minutes. Stewed ¾ hour or more.

BLANQUETTE OF VEAL OR LAMB, WITH MUSHROOMS (ENTRÉE)

Slice very thin the white part of some cold veal, divide and trim it into scallops not larger than a shilling, and lay it into a clean saucepan or stewpan. Wipe with a bit of new flannel and a few grains of salt, from a quarter to half a pint of mushroom-buttons, and slice them into a little butter which just begins to simmer; stew them in it from twelve to fifteen minutes, without allowing them to take the slightest colour; then lift them out and lay them on the veal. Pour boiling to them a pint of *sauce tournée*; let the *blanquette* remain near, but not close to the fire for awhile; bring it nearer, heat it slowly, and when it is on the point of boiling mix a spoonful or two of the sauce from it with the well beaten yolks of four fresh eggs; stir them to the remainder; add the strained juice of half a small lemon; shake the saucepan above the fire until the sauce is just set, and serve the *blanquette* instantly.

201

IRISH STEW

Take two pounds of small thick mutton cutlets with or without fat, according to the taste of the persons to whom the stew is to be served; take also four pounds of good potatoes, weighed after they are pared; slice them thick, and put a portion of them in a flat layer into a large thick saucepan or stewpan; season the mutton well with pepper, and place some of it on the potatoes; cover it with another layer, and proceed in the same manner with all, reserving plenty of the vegetable for the top; pour in three-quarters of a pint of cold water, and add, when the stew begins to boil, an ounce of salt; let it simmer gently for two hours, and serve it very hot. When the addition of onion is liked, strew some minced over the potatoes.

Mutton cutlets, 2 lbs.; potatoes, 4 lbs.; pepper, ½ oz.; salt, 1 oz.; water ¾ pint: 2 hours.

OBS. – For a real Irish stew the potatoes should be boiled to a mash: an additional quarter of an hour may be necessary for the full quantity here, but for half to it two hours are quite sufficient.

Her other recipe for Irish stew suggests that the top layer of the stew should be of potatoes, and that they should be browned before sent to table, and this is the way we always had it. It is the only dish I remember my father ever cooking, taking inordinate pride in his achievement.

Although Acton has given two recipes for the dish, she does seem quite unimpressed by it, saying 'it is, of course, suited only to a quite plain family dinner'.

MUTTON KIDNEYS À LA FRANÇAISE (ENTRÉE)

Skin six or eight fine fresh mutton kidneys, and without opening them, remove the fat; slice them rather thin, strew over them a large dessertspoonful of minced herbs, of which two-thirds should be parsley and the remainder thyme, with a tolerable seasoning of pepper or cayenne, and some fine salt. Melt two ounces of butter in a frying-pan, put in the kidneys and brown them quickly on both sides; when nearly done, stir amongst them a dessertspoonful of flour and shake them well in the pan; pour in the third of a pint of gravy (or of hot water in default of this), the juice of half a lemon, and as much of Harvey's sauce, or of mushroom catsup, as will flavour the whole pleasantly; bring these to the point of boiling, and pour them into a dish garnished with fried sippets, or lift out the kidneys first, give the sauce a boil and pour it on them. In France, a couple of glasses of champagne, or, for variety, of claret, are frequently added to this dish; one of port wine can be substituted for either of these. A dessertspoonful of minced eschalots may be strewed over the kidneys with the herbs; or two dozens of very small ones previously stewed until tender in fresh butter over a gentle fire, may be added after they are dished. This is a very excellent and approved receipt.

Fried 6 minutes.

Like the Irish stew, I think of kidneys as a very male sort of food. I suspect this is partly because this was one thing my husband used to make; I love kidneys but do find the pungent smell of piss as they cook quite off-putting. Once it's cooked out, no taste remains and they are delicious if not overcooked into bullets.

It is interesting to see how little attention Acton pays to pork. She tells her readers how to roast various cuts of pig, but only after warning them of how 'proverbially, and we believe even dangerously unwholesome [it is] when ill fed, or in any degree diseased'. She tells us how to cure ham and bacon, and how to make sausage meat and sausages, but there are barely no 'made dishes' involving pork in her work.

FRICASEED FOWLS OR CHICKENS (ENTRÉE)

To make a fricassée of good appearance without great expense, prepare, with exceeding nicety, a couple of plump chickens, strip off the skin, and carve them very neatly. Reserve the wings, breasts, merrythoughts, and thighs; and stew down the inferior joints with a couple of blades of mace, a small bunch of savoury herbs, a few white pepper-corns, a pint and a half of water, and a small half-teaspoonful of salt. When something more than a third part reduced, strain the gravy, let it cool, and skim off every particle of fat. Arrange the joints which are to be fricasseed in one layer if it can be done conveniently, and pour to them as much of the gravy as will nearly cover them; add the very thin rind of half a fine fresh lemon, and simmer the fowls gently from half to three-quarters of an hour; throw in sufficient salt, pounded mace, and cayenne, to give the sauce a good flavour, thicken it with a large teaspoonful of arrow-root, and stir to it the third of a pint of rich boiling cream; then lift the stewpan from the fire, and shake it briskly round while the beaten yolks of three fresh eggs, mixed with a spoonful or two of cream, are added; continue to shake the pan gently above the fire till the sauce is just set, but it must not be allowed to boil, or it will curdle in an instant.

½ to ¾ hour.

This is a very superior fricassée to the dished up leftovers of roast chicken in sauce that I used to give my children on a Sunday night. Perhaps loveliest of all is the old word, 'merrythought', which is the breastbone.

By 1845 the English had a better understanding of what a curry should be than Hannah Glasse had managed, and Eliza Acton must, somewhere, have had a genuine Indian curry, as she compares it to an English one, where 'turmeric and cayenne pepper prevail…often far too powerfully'. She is already complaining of the over 'red or yellow hue' of the English curry; how I wish she could see a generic High Street chicken tikka masala. She does include tastes we recognise in a curry, recommending stewing grated coconut for an hour or so in the sauce, and offers up a recipe for curry powder (see below). Chili itself does not yet seem to have arrived in England. Acton continues wary of her old nemesis, onions, and adds garlic to her list of ingredients only to be used economically.

There is also mention of curry-paste, 'which has attracted some attention of late, and the curries made with it are very good, and quickly and easily prepared.' And there we have the beginnings of convenience food.

MR ARNOTT'S CURRIE-POWDER

Turmeric, eight ounces.
Coriander seed, four ounces.
Cummin seed, two ounces.
Fenugreek seed, two ounces.
Cayenne, half an ounce. (More or less of this last to the taste)

Let the seeds be of the finest quality. Dry them well, pound, and sift them separately through a lawn-sieve, then weigh, and mix them in the above proportions. This is an exceedingly agreeable

205

and aromatic powder, when all the ingredients are perfectly fresh and good, but the preparing is rather a troublesome process. Mr Arnott recommends that when it is considered so, a 'high-caste' chemist should be applied to for it.

In a footnote to the recipe, Acton can't resist fiddling with the proportions – the sign of a true cook. 'We think', she writes, 'it would be an improvement to diminish by two ounces the proportion of turmeric, and to increase that of the coriander seed; but we have not tried it.'

A BENGAL CURRIE

Slice and fry three large onions in two ounces of butter, and lift them out of the pan when done. Put into a stewpan three other large onions and a small clove of garlic which have been pounded together, and smoothly mixed with a dessertspoonful of the best pale turmeric, a teaspoonful of powdered ginger, one of salt, and one of cayenne pepper; add to these the butter in which the onions were fried, and half a cupful of good gravy; let them stew for about ten minutes, taking care that they shall not burn. Next, stir to them the fried onions and half a pint more of gravy; add a pound and a half of mutton, or of any other meat, free from bone and fat, and simmer it gently for an hour, or more should it not then be perfectly tender.

Fried onions, 3 large; butter, 2 oz.; onions pounded, 3 large; garlic, 1 clove; turmeric, 1 dessertspoonful; powdered ginger, salt, cayenne, each 1 teaspoonful; gravy, ½ cupful: 10 minutes. Gravy, ½ pint; meat, 1 ½ lb.: 1 hour or more.

A DRY CURRIE

Skin and cut down a fowl into small joints, or a couple of pounds of mutton, free from fat and bone, into very small thick cutlets; rub them with as much currie-powder, mixed with a teaspoonful of flour and one of salt, as can be made to adhere to them: this will be from two to three tablespoons. Dissolve a good slice of butter in a deep, well-tinned stewpan or saucepan, and shake it over a brisk fire for four or five minutes, or until it begins to take colour; then put in the meat, and brown it well and equally, without allowing a morsel to be scorched. The pan should be shaken vigorously every minute or two, and the meat turned in it frequently. When this is done, lift it out and throw in the stewpan two or three large onions finely minced, and four or five eschalots when these last are liked; add a morsel of butter if needful, and fry them until they begin to soften; then add a quarter of a pint of gravy, broth, or boiling water, and a large acid apple, or two moderate-sized ones, of a good boiling kind, with the hearts of two or three lettuces, or of one hard cabbage, shred quite small (tomatas or cucumbers freed from their seeds can be substituted for these when in season). Stew the whole slowly until it resembles a thick pulp, and add to it any additional liquid that may be required, should it become too dry; put in the meat, and simmer the whole very softly until this is done, which will be in from three-quarters of an hour to an hour.

Prawns, shrimps, or the flesh of boiled lobsters may be slowly heated through, and served in this currie sauce with good effect.

CURRIED EGGS

Boil six or eight fresh eggs quite hard, as for salad, and put them aside until they are cold. Mix well together from two to three ounces of good butter, and from three to four dessertspoonsful of currie-powder; shake them in a stewpan or thick saucepan, over a clear but moderate fire for some minutes, then throw in a couple of mild onions finely minced, and fry them gently until they are tolerably soft: pour to them, by degrees, from half to three-quarters of a pint of broth or gravy, and stew them slowly until they are reduced to pulp; mix smoothly a small cup of thick cream with two teaspoonsful of wheaten or of rice-flour, stir them to the currie, and simmer the whole until the raw taste of the thickening is gone. Cut the eggs into half-inch slices, heat them quite through in the sauce without boiling them, and serve them as hot as possible.

ISABELLA BEETON

Like Eliza Acton, Beeton opens her section on meat with introductory remarks about the basic forms of cooking, and different types of oven and kitchen equipment. She also gives detailed notes on the different breeds of animal reared for the table.

As previously discussed, Beeton's recipes were taken from a variety of sources, including those we have already looked at in this book. She gives many recipes for reusing cold meats, and is very aware of economy in her recipes, often giving variations to suit the pockets of her readers.

The recipes in Household Management *have moved forward in one way at least – there are no recipes for udder, or any of the more extreme parts of the body. There are still recipes for such things as bullock's heart, but there is a sense that this is dying out in popularity: 'this is an excellent family dish, is very savoury, and, though not seen at many good tables, may be recommended for its cheapness and economy.'*

We will begin with one of the great English dishes; a dish which is still unknown to the greediest Frenchman, to whom a 'Boule de Suif' is not a dumpling but a prostitute in a short story by Maupassant.

BEEF-STEAK AND KIDNEY PUDDING

INGREDIENTS. – 2 lb. of rump-steak, 2 kidneys, seasoning to taste of salt and black pepper, suet crust made with milk in the proportion of 6 oz. of suet to each 1 lb. of flour.

Mode. – Procure some tender rump steak (that which has been hung a little time), and divide it into pieces about an inch square, and cut each kidney into 8 pieces. Line the dish with crust made with suet and flour in the above proportion, leaving a small piece of crust to overlap the edge. Then cover the bottom with a portion of the steak and a few pieces of kidney, season with salt and pepper (add some flour to thicken the gravy, but it is not necessary), and then add another layer of steak, kidney, and seasoning. Proceed in this manner till the dish is full, when pour in sufficient water to come within 2 inches of the top of the basin. Moisten the edges of the crust, cover the pudding over, press the two crusts together, that the gravy may not escape, and turn up the overhanging paste. Wring out a cloth in hot water, flour it, and tie up the pudding; put it into boiling water, and let it boil for at least 4 hours. If the water diminishes, always replenish with some, hot in a jug, as the pudding should be kept covered all the time and not allowed to stop boiling. When the cloth is removed, cut out a round piece in the top of the crust, to prevent the pudding bursting, and send it to table in the basin, either in an ornamental dish, or with a napkin pinned round it. Serve quickly.

Time. – For a pudding with 2 lbs. of steak and 2 kidneys allow 4 hours.

Average cost, 2s. 8d.

Sufficient for six persons.

Seasonable all the year, but more suitable in winter.

Note. – Beef-steak pudding may be very much enriched by adding a few oysters or mushrooms.

Immediately following this entirely English dish, contributed, Beeton says 'by a Sussex lady, in which county the inhabitants are noted for their savoury puddings' is 'Beef-steaks with fried potatoes, or Biftek aux pommes-de-terre (à la mode Française)'. Steak and chips. Many of her cold beef recipes also involve potatoes – variations on cottage pies. It seems the potato was finally finding a home in the English kitchen.

BEEF CAKE

INGREDIENTS. – The remains of cold roast beef; to each pound of cold meat allow ¼ lb. of bacon or ham; seasoning to taste of pepper and salt, 1 small bunch of minced savoury herbs, 1 or 2 eggs.

Mode. – Mince the beef very finely (if underdone it will be better), add to it the bacon, which must also be chopped very small, and mix well together. Season, stir in the herbs, and bind with an egg, or 2 should 1 not be sufficient. Make it into small square cakes, about ½ inch thick, fry them in hot dripping, and serve in a dish with good gravy poured round them.

Time. – 10 minutes. Average cost, exclusive of the cold meat, 6d.

Seasonable at any time.

BUBBLE-AND-SQUEAK (COLD MEAT COOKERY)

INGREDIENTS. – A few thin slices of cold boiled beef; butter, cabbage, 1 sliced onion, pepper and salt to taste.

Mode. – Fry the slices of beef gently in a little butter, taking care not to dry them up. Lay them on a flat dish, and cover with fried greens. The greens may be prepared from cabbage sprouts or green savoys. They should be boiled till tender, well drained, minced, and placed, till quite hot, in a frying-pan with butter, a sliced onion, and seasoning of pepper and salt. When the onion is done, it is ready to serve.

Time. – Altogether, ½ hour.

Average cost, exclusive of the cold beef, 3d.

Seasonable at any time.

This is not bubble and squeak as my mother made it – that was cabbage and mashed potato fried together – but is still a very good Sunday or Monday night supper.

FRICANDEAU OF BEEF

INGREDIENTS. – About 3 lbs. of the inside fillet of the sirloin (a piece of the rump may be substituted for this), pepper and salt to taste, 3 cloves, 3 blades of mace, 6 whole allspice, 1 pint of stock, or water, 1 glass of sherry, 1 bunch of savoury herbs, 2 shallots, bacon.

Mode. – Cut some bacon into thin strips, and sprinkle over them a seasoning of pepper and salt, mixed with cloves, mace and allspice, well pounded. Lard the beef with these, put it into a saucepan with the stock or water, sherry, herbs, shalots, 2 cloves, and more pepper and salt. Stew the meat gently till tender, when take it out, cover it closely, skim all the fat from the gravy, and strain it. Set it on the fire, and boil, till it becomes a glaze. Glaze the larded side of the beef with this, and serve on sorrel sauce, which is made as follows: Wash and pick some sorrel, and put it into a stewpan with only the water than hangs about it. Keep stirring, to prevent its burning, and when done, lay it in a sieve to drain. Chop it, and stew it with a small piece of butter and 4 or 5 tablespoonfuls of good gravy, for an hour, and rub it through a tammy. If too acid, add a little sugar; and a little cabbage-lettuce boiled with the sorrel will be found an improvement.

Time. – 2 hours to gently stew the meat.
Average cost, for this quantity, 4s.
Sufficient for 6 persons.
Seasonable at any time.

BRISKET OF BEEF, À LA FLAMANDE

INGREDIENTS. – About 6 or 8 lbs. of the brisket of beef, 4 or 5 slices of bacon, 2 carrots, 1 onion, a bunch of savoury herbs, salt and pepper to taste, 4 cloves, 4 whole allspice, 2 blades of mace.

Mode. – Choose that portion of the brisket which contains the gristle, trim it, and put it into the stewpan with the slices of bacon, which should be put under and over the meat. Add the vegetables, herbs, spices and seasoning, and cover with a little weak stock or water; close the stewpan as hermetically as possible, and simmer very gently for 4 hours. Strain the liquor, reserve a portion of it for sauce, and the remainder boil quickly over a sharp fire until reduced to a glaze, with which to glaze the meat. Garnish the dish with scooped carrots and turnips, and when liked, a little cabbage; all of which must be cooked separately. Thicken and flavour the liquor that was saved for sauce, pour it round the meat, and serve. The beef may also be garnished with glazed onions, artichoke-bottoms etc.

Time. – 4 hours. Average cost, 7d. per lb.
Sufficient for 6 or 8 persons.
Seasonable at any time.

Brisket is often overlooked as a cut. It is cheap and if cooked slowly for a long time very tender. My grandmother used to brown it in butter, surround it in mushrooms and cook it in a lidded pot for hours.

Isabella Beeton, patriotic and authoritative, adds a wonderful note to this recipe, part of which I reproduce here for comedy value.

FRENCH BEEF. – It has been all but universally admitted, that the beef of France is greatly inferior in quality to that of England, owing to inferiority of pasturage. Mr Curmer, however, one of the latest writers on the culinary art, tells us that this is a vulgar error, and that French beef is far superior to that of England. This is mere vaunting on the part of our neighbours, who seem to want *la gloire* in everything…No, M. Curmer, we are ready to acknowledge the superiority of your cookery, but we have long since made up our minds as to the inferiority of your raw material.

And who, we may now ask, is M. Curmer?

A shift we can see in between Acton's and Beeton's books is from mutton to lamb. Acton has very few lamb recipes; Beeton still has many mutton recipes, but also concerns herself with lamb.

BREAST OF LAMB AND GREEN PEAS

INGREDIENTS. – 1 breast of lamb, a few slices of bacon, ½ pint of stock, 1 lemon, 1 onion, 1 bunch of savoury herbs, green peas.
Mode. – Remove the skin from a breast of lamb, put it into a saucepan of boiling water, and let it simmer for 5 minutes. Take it out and lay it in cold water. Line the bottom of a stewpan with a few thin slices of bacon; lay the lamb on these; peel the lemon, cut it into slices, and put these on the meat to keep it white and make it tender; cover with 1 or 2 more slices of bacon; add the stock, onion, and herbs, and set it on a slow fire to simmer very gently

until tender. Have ready some green peas, put these on a dish, and place the lamb on the top of these. The appearance of this dish may be much improved by glazing the lamb, and spinach may be substituted for the peas when variety is desired.

Time. – 1 ½ hour. Average cost, 10d. per pound.

Sufficient for three persons.

Seasonable, grass lamb, from Easter to Michaelmas.

SHOULDER OF LAMB STUFFED

INGREDIENTS. – Shoulder of lamb, forcemeat, trimmings of veal or beef, 2 onions, ½ head of celery, 1 faggot of savoury herbs, a few slices of fat bacon, 1 quart of stock.

Mode. – Take the blade bone out of a shoulder of lamb, fill up its place with forcemeat, and sew it up with coarse thread. Put it into a stewpan with a few slices of bacon under and over the lamb, and add the remaining ingredients. Stew very gently for rather more than 2 hours. Reduce the gravy, with which glaze the meat, and serve with peas, stewed cucumbers, or sorrel sauce.

Time. – Rather more than 2 hours. Average cost, 10d. to 1s. per lb.

Sufficient for 4 or 5 persons.

Seasonable from Easter to Michaelmas.

LAMB'S SWEETBREADS, LARDED, AND ASPARAGUS (AN ENTRÉE)

INGREDIENTS. – 2 or 3 sweetbreads, ½ pint of veal stock, white pepper and salt to taste, a small bunch of green onions, 1 blade of pounded mace, thickening of butter and flour, 2 eggs, nearly ½ pint of cream, 1 teaspoonful of minced parsley, a very little grated nutmeg.

Mode. – Soak the sweetbreads in lukewarm water, and put them into a saucepan with sufficient boiling water to cover them, and let them simmer for 10 minutes; then take them out and put them into cold water. Now lard them, lay them in a stewpan, add the stock, seasoning, onions, mace, and a thickening of butter and flour, and stew gently for ¼ hour or 20 minutes. Beat up the egg with the cream, to which add the minced parsley and a very little grated nutmeg. Put this to the other ingredients; stir it well till quite hot, but do not let it boil after the cream is added, or it will curdle. Have ready some asparagus-tops, boiled; add these to the sweetbreads, and serve.

Time. – Altogether ½ hour. Average cost, 2s. 6d. to 3s. 6d. each.

Sufficient – 3 sweetbreads for 1 entrée.

Seasonable from Easter to Michaelmas.

BROILED VEAL CUTLETS
A L'ITALIENNE (AN ENTRÉE)

INGREDIENTS. – Neck of veal, salt and pepper to taste, the yolk of 1 egg, bread crumbs, ½ pint of Italian sauce.

Mode. – Cut the veal into cutlets, flatten and trim them nicely; powder over them a little salt and pepper; brush them over with the yolk of an egg, dip them into bread crumbs, then into clarified butter, and, afterwards, in the breadcrumbs again; broil or fry them over a clear fire, that they may acquire a good brown colour. Arrange them in the dish alternately with rashers of broiled ham, and pour the sauce in the middle.

Time. – 10 to 15 minutes, according to the thickness of the cutlets.

Average cost, 10d. per pound
Seasonable from March to October.

For us, meat (except for spring lamb) has no sense of seasonality. I have included none of Mrs Beeton's recipes for pork, as they are mostly either 'how to' cure, smoke or pickle hams, or basic roasting recipes. There is even one for 'Fried Ham and Eggs (a Breakfast Dish)'. You could substitute much cheaper pork for the veal in the following recipes.

VEAL À LA BOURGEOISE
(EXCELLENT)

INGREDIENTS. – 2 to 3 lbs. of the loin or neck of veal, 10 or 12 young carrots, a bunch of green onions, 2 slices of lean bacon, 2 blades of pounded mace, 1 bunch of savoury herbs, pepper and salt to taste, a few new potatoes, 1 pint of green peas.

Mode. – Cut the veal into cutlets, trim them, and put the trimmings into a stewpan with a little butter; lay in the cutlets and fry them a nice brown colour on both sides. Add the bacon, carrots, onions, spice, herbs, and seasoning; pour in about a pint of boiling water, and stew gently for two hours on a very slow fire. When done, skim off the fat, take out the herbs, and flavour the gravy with a little tomato sauce and ketchup. Have ready the peas and potatoes, boiled *separately*; put them with the veal, and serve.

Time. – 2 hours. Average cost, 2s. 9d.

Sufficient for 5 or 6 persons.

Seasonable from June to August with peas; – rather earlier when these are omitted.

SCOTCH COLLOPS, WHITE
(COLD MEAT COOKERY)

INGREDIENTS. – The remains of cold roast veal, ½ teaspoonful of grated nutmeg, 2 blades of pounded mace, cayenne and salt to taste, a little butter, 1 dessertspoonful of flour, ¼ pint of water, 1 teaspoonful of anchovy sauce, 1 tablespoonful of lemon-juice, ¼ teaspoonful of lemon-peel, 1 tablespoonful of mushroom ketchup, 3 tablespoonfuls of cream, 1 tablespoonful of sherry.

Mode. – Cut the veal into thin slices about 3 inches in width; hack them with a knife, and grate on them the nutmeg, mace, cayenne, and salt, and fry them in a little butter. Dish them, and make a gravy in the pan by putting in the remaining ingredients. Give one boil, and pour it over the collops; garnish with lemon and slices of toasted bacon, rolled. Forcemeat balls may be added to this dish. If cream is not at hand, substitute the yolk of an egg beaten up well with a little milk.

Time. – about 5 or 7 minutes

Seasonable from May to October.

This can also be made from scratch, with raw meat, but of course would take longer to cook.

VEAL COLLOPS (AN ENTRÉE)

INGREDIENTS. – About 2 lbs. of the prime part of the leg of veal, a few slices of bacon, forcemeat, cayenne to taste, egg and bread crumbs, gravy.

Mode. – Cut the veal into long thin collops, flatten them, and lay on each a piece of thin bacon of the same size; have ready some forcemeat, which spread over the bacon, spinkle over all a little cayenne, roll them up tightly, and do not let them be more than two inches long. Skewer each one firmly, egg and bread crumb them, and fry them a nice brown in a little butter, turning the occasionally, and shaking the pan about. When done, place them on a dish before the fire, put a small piece of butter in the pan, dredge in a little flour, add ¼ pint of water, 2 tablespoonfuls of lemon-juice, a seasoning of salt, pepper, and pounded mace; let the whole boil up, and pour it over the collops.

Time. – from 10 to 15 minutes. Average cost, 10d. per lb.

Sufficient for 5 or 6 persons.

Seasonable from March to October.

CALF'S LIVER AUX FINES HERBES & SAUCE PIQUANTE

INGREDIENTS. – A calf's liver, flour, a bunch of savoury herbs, including parsley ; when liked, two minced shalots ; 1 teaspoonful of flour, 1 tablespoonful of vinegar, 1 tablespoonful of lemon juice, pepper and salt to taste, ¼ pint water.

Mode. – Procure a calf's liver as white as possible, and cut it into slices of a good and equal shape. Dip them in flour, and fry them of a good colour in a little butter. When they are done, put them on a dish, which keep hot before the fire. Mince the herbs very fine, put them in the frying-pan with a little more butter, add the remaining ingredients, simmer gently until the herbs are done, and pour over the liver.

Time. – According to the thickness of the slices, from 5 to 10 minutes. Average cost, 10d. per lb.

Sufficient for 7 or 8 persons.

Seasonable from March to October.

The whiteness of a calf's liver is obviously a bit of a moot point nowadays, as the whiter the veal the more cruelly it has been treated. A long time ago I was told by the butcher in Dulverton that he did not stock veal since his shop had been attacked for doing so. This is a pro-stag hunting, seriously rural part of England. However veal is now produced more humanely – indeed there is a specialist veal farm just outside Bampton, a few miles from Dulverton, and I don't think it's ever been under any pressure.

MINCED VEAL AND MACARONI (A PRETTY SIDE OR CORNER DISH)

INGREDIENTS. – ¾ lb. of minced cold roast veal, 3 oz. of ham, 1 tablespoonful of gravy, pepper and salt to taste, ¼ teaspoonful of grated nutmeg, ¼ lb. of bread crumbs, ¼ lb. of macaroni, 1 or 2 eggs to bind, a small piece of butter.

Mode. – Cut some nice slices from a cold fillet of veal, trim off the brown outside, and mince the meat finely with the above proportion of ham: should the meat be very dry, add a spoonful of good gravy. Season highly with pepper and salt, add the grated nutmeg and bread crumbs, and mix these ingredients with 1 or 2 eggs well beaten, which should bind the mixture and make it like forcemeat. In the mean time, boil the macaroni in salt and water, and drain it; butter a mould, put some of the macaroni at the bottom and sides of it, in whatever form is liked; mix the remainder with the forcemeat, fill the mould up to the top, put a plate or small dish on it, and steam for ½ hour. Turn it out carefully, and serve with good gravy poured round, but not over, the meat.

Time. – ½ hour. Average cost, exclusive of the cold meat, 10d.
Seasonable from March to October.

Note. – To make a variety, boil some carrots and turnips separately in a little salt and water; when done, cut them into pieces about 1/8 inch in thickness; butter an oval mould, and place these in it, in white and red stripes alternately, at the bottom and sides. Proceed as in the foregoing recipe, and be very careful in turning out the mould.

This is gloriously Victorian, especially in the technicolor version Beeton suggests as an alternative. However the basic premise is yet another good way of using up leftover meat.

MOULDED MINCED VEAL

INGREDIENTS. – ¾ lb. of cold roast veal, a small slice of bacon, 1/3 teaspoonful of minced lemon-peel, ½ onion chopped fine, salt, pepper, and pounded mace to taste, a slice of toast soaked in milk, 1 egg.

Mode. – Mince the meat very fine, after removing from it all skin and outside pieces, and chop the bacon; mix these well together, adding the lemon-peel, onion, seasoning, mace and toast. When all the ingredients are thoroughly incorporated, beat up an egg, with which bind the mixture. Butter a shape, put in the meat, and bake for ¾ hour; turn it out of the mould carefully, and pour round it a good brown gravy. A sheep's head dressed in this manner is an economical and savoury dish.

Time. – ¾ hour. Average cost, exclusive of the meat, 6d.
Seasonable from March to October.

STEWED SWEETBREADS (AN ENTRÉE)

INGREDIENTS. – 3 sweetbreads, 1 pint of white stock, thickening of butter and flour, 6 tablespoonfuls of cream, 1 tablespoonsful of lemon-juice, 1 blade of pounded mace, white pepper and salt to taste.

Mode. – Soak the sweetbreads in warm water for 1 hour, and boil them for 10 minutes; take them out, put them into cold water for a few minutes; lay them in a stewpan with the stock, and simmer them gently for rather more than ½ hour. Dish them; thicken the gravy with a little butter and flour; let it boil up, add the remaining ingredients, allow the sauce to get quite *hot* but *not boil*, and pour it over the sweetbreads.

Time. – to soak 1 hour, to be boiled 10 minutes, stewed rather more than ½ hour.

Average cost, from 1s. to 5s., according to the season.

Sufficient for an entrée.

Season. – in full season from May to August.

Note. – A few mushrooms added to this dish, and stewed with the sweetbreads, will be found an improvement.

Mrs Beeton's white stock is a basic veal and chicken stock, made with onions, carrot, celery, pepper, salt and mace. Regular chicken stock will do.

CHICKEN OR FOWL PIE

INGREDIENTS. – 2 small fowls or 1 large one, white pepper and salt to taste, ½ teaspoonful of grated nutmeg, ½ teaspoonful of pounded mace, forcemeat, a few slices of ham, 3 hard-boiled eggs, ½ pint water, puff crust.

Mode. – Skin and cut up the fowls into joints, and put the neck, leg, and backbones in a stewpan, with a little water, an onion, a bunch of savoury herbs, and a blade of mace; let these stew for about an hour, and, when done, strain off the liquor: this is for gravy. Put a layer of fowl at the bottom of a pie-dish, then a layer of ham, then one of forcemeat and hard-boiled eggs cut in rings: between the layers put a seasoning of pounded mace, nutmeg, pepper, and salt. Proceed in this manner until the dish is full, and pour in about ½ pint of water; border the edge of the dish with puff crust, put on the cover, ornament the top, and glaze it by brushing over it the yolk of an egg. Bake from 1 ¼ to 1 ½ hour, should the pie be very large, and, when done, pour in, at the top, the gravy made from the bones. If to be eaten cold, and wished particularly nice, the joints of the fowls should be boned, and placed in the dish with alternate layers of force-meat; sausage meat may be also be substituted for the forcemeat, and is now very much used. When the chickens are boned, and mixed with sausage-meat, the pie will take about 2 hours to bake. It should be covered with a piece of paper when about half-done, to prevent the paste from being dried up or scorched.

Time. – For a pie with unboned meat, 1 ¼ to 1 ½ hour; with boned meat and sausage or forcemeat, 1 ½ to 2 hours.

Average cost, with 2 fowls, 6s. 6d.

Sufficient for 6 or 7 persons.

Seasonable at any time.

CURRIED FOWL

INGREDIENTS. – 1 fowl, 2 oz. of butter, 3 onions sliced, 1 pint of white veal gravy, 1 tablespoonful of curry-powder, 1 tablespoonful of flour, 1 apple, 4 tablespoonfuls of cream, 1 tablespoonful of lemon-juice.

Mode. – Put the butter into a stewpan, with the onions sliced, the fowl cut into small joints, and the apple peeled, cored, and minced. Fry of a pale brown, add the stock, and stew gently for 20 minutes; rub down the curry-powder and the flour with a little of the gravy, quite smoothly, and stir this to the other ingredients; simmer for rather more than ½ hour, and just before serving, add the above proportion of hot cream and lemon juice. Serve with boiled rice, which may either be heaped lightly on a dish by itself, or put round the curry as a border.

Time. – 50 minutes. Average cost, 3s. 3d.

Sufficient for 3 or 4 persons.

Seasonable in the winter.

Note. – This curry may be made of cold chicken, but undressed meat will be found far superior.

This curry, and others in Beeton's book like it, are pretty much what English curries remained for over a hundred years. The one curry in her book which seems a little more adventurous is based on M. Soyer's recipe (she actually credits him). Soyer was a Frenchman who was the most famous chef of the time, first for royalty, and then at the Reform Club. His recipe for curry, which Beeton calls 'Fowl Pillaw' (an Indian dish) is basically a fowl boiled with rice and with some spices, which include 'cardamum, cloves, allspice, coriander-seed and cinnamon'. It is served with crisped bacon and hard-boiled eggs, which make it less authentic.

I remember people cooking yellow curries, made mostly from curry powder, in my childhood. They used to come with chopped banana, sliced cucumbers, desiccated coconut and mango chutney on little dishes. They were a huge treat and delicious in an impure sort of way, and totally different from what you would find in a high street restaurant, which is different again from what an Indian will cook you at home. Madhur Jaffrey (whose first Indian cookery book was surprisingly published as long ago as 1973), educated the English in how to cook authentic Indian food. She must have taken a few years to reach West Somerset.

RAGOUT OF FOWL

INGREDIENTS. – The remains of cold roast fowls, 3 shalots, 2 blades of mace, a faggot of savoury herbs, 2 or 3 slices of lean ham, 1 pint of stock or water, pepper and salt to taste, 1 onion, 1 desertspoonful of flour, 1 tablespoonful of lemon-juice, ½ teaspoonful of pounded sugar, 1 oz. of butter.

Mode. – Cut the fowls up into neat pieces, the same as for a fricassée; put the trimmings into a stewpan with the shalots, mace, herbs, ham, onion and stock (water may be substituted for this). Boil it slowly for 1 hour, strain the liquor, and put a small piece of butter into a stewpan; when melted, dredge in sufficient flour to dry up the butter, and stir it over the fire. Put in the strained liquor, boil for a few minutes, and strain it again over the pieces of fowl. Squeeze in the lemon-juice, add the sugar and a seasoning of pepper and salt, make it hot, but do not allow it to boil; lay the fowl neatly on the dish, and garnish with croutons.

Time. – altogether 1 ½ hour. Average cost, exclusive of the cold fowl, 9d.

Seasonable at any time.

This is a total family favourite, but without the sugar and served with rice (also cooked in the chicken stock) rather than croutons. Croutons seem to take over from where sippets left off.

Beeton has endless recipes for dished up cold chicken, all variations on braising them in some sort of gravy, covering them in a béchamel or frying them in breadcrumbs. Although not very exciting in a culinary way, they do back up one of her key tenets – economy.

PIGEON PIE (EPSOM GRAND-STAND RECIPE)

INGREDIENTS. – 1 ½ lb of rump-steak, 2 or 3 pigeons, 3 slices of ham, pepper and salt, to taste, 2 oz. of butter, 4 eggs, puff crust.

Mode. – Cut the steak into pieces about 3 inches square, and with it line the bottom of a pie-dish, seasoning it well with pepper and salt. Clean the pigeons, rub them with pepper and salt inside and out, and put into the body of each rather more than ½ oz. of butter; lay them on the steak, and a piece of ham on each pigeon. Add the yolks of 4 eggs, and half fill the dish with stock; place a border of puff paste round the edge of the dish, put on the cover and ornament it in any way that may be preferred. Clean three of the feet, and place them in a hole made in the crust at the top: this shows what kind of a pie it is. Glaze the crust, - that is to say, brush it over with the yolk of an egg, - and bake it in a well-heated oven for about 1 ¼ hour. When liked, a seasoning of pounded mace may be added.

Time. – 1 ¼ hour, or rather less. Average cost, 5s. 3d.

Sufficient for 5 or 6 persons. *Seasonable* at any time.

Although the modern cook might not want to put the feet on display in the way suggested, this is an important recipe for a couple of reasons. Firstly, there are a lot of these pie recipes which involve beginning with meat, then adding another – the main – ingredient. There is another called giblet pie, for instance, which uses stewed giblets with the beef. The other reason this recipe is important is because of its provenance – the Epsom Grand-Stand in which Mrs Beeton spent large parts of her childhood.

Pigeons are delicious birds; we eat a lot of them when we're in France, where they're bred for the table. The ones you buy in England might not be so good – a little tougher, probably. So stewing them, as per the following recipe, is a good way to treat them.

STEWED PIGEONS

INGREDIENTS. – 6 pigeons, a few slices of bacon, 3 oz. of butter, 2 tablespoonfuls of minced parlsey, sufficient stock to cover the pigeons, thickening of butter and flour, 1 tablespoonful of mushroom ketchup, 1 tablespoonsful of port wine.

Mode. – Empty and clean the pigeons thoroughly, mince the livers, add to these the parsley and butter, and put it into the insides of the birds. Truss them with the legs inward, and put them into a stewpan, with a few slices of bacon placed over and under them; add the stock, and stew gently for rather more than ½ hour. Dish the pigeons, strain the gravy, thicken it with butter and flour, add the ketchup and port wine, give one boil, pour over the pigeons, and serve.

Time. – Rather more than ½ hour. Average cost, 6d. to 9d. each.

Sufficient for 4 or 5 persons.

Seasonable from April to September.

For some reason Beeton includes rabbit in the poultry section of her book. Again, they are a meat best eaten in France where they are bred for the table and are young and tender. Beeton tells us that the way to pick a rabbit is by its claws; if they are smooth and sharp the animal is young, if they are blunt and rugged, and the ears are dry and tough, then it is old. *Country butchers often have rabbits in their freezers. These may well be old, so the trick is to soak them overnight in brine, which tenderises them. It is worth getting right as they are a cheap and nutritious, if bony, meat. A real treat when you cook rabbits is the livers, kidney and heart fried in butter and then the pan deglazed with a little sherry. This often develops into an ugly greedy scrum in our family.*

RABBIT À LA MINUTE

INGREDIENTS. – 1 rabbit, ¼ lb. of butter, salt and pepper to taste, 2 blades of pounded mace, 3 dried mushrooms, 2 tablespoonfuls of minced parsley, 2 teaspoonfuls of flour, 2 glasses of sherry, 1 pint of water.

Mode. – Empty, skin, and wash the rabbit thoroughly, and cut it into joints. Put the butter into a stewpan with the pieces of rabbit: add salt, pepper, and pounded mace, and let it cook until three parts done; then put in the remaining ingredients, and boil for about 10 minutes: it will then be ready to serve. Fowls or hare may be dressed in the same manner.

Time. – Altogether, 35 minutes. Average cost, from 1s. to 1s. 6d. each.

Sufficient for 4 or 5 persons.

Seasonable from September to February.

RABBIT PIE

INGREDIENTS. – 1 rabbit, a few slices of ham, salt and white pepper to taste, 2 blades of pounded mace, ½ teaspoonful of grated nutmeg, a few forcemeat balls, 3 hard-boiled eggs, ½ pint of gravy, puff crust.

Mode. – Cut up the rabbit (which should be young), remove the breastbone, and bone the legs. Put the rabbit, slices of ham, forcemeat balls, and hard eggs, by turns, in layers, and season each layer with pepper, salt, pounded mace, and grated nutmeg. Pour in about ½ pint of water, cover with crust, and bake in a well-heated oven for about 1 ½ hour. Should the crust acquire too much colour, place a piece of paper over it to prevent its burning. When done, pour in at the top, by means of the hole in the middle of the crust, a little good gravy, which may be made of the breast- and leg-bones of the rabbit and 2 or 3 shank-bones, flavoured with onion, herbs, and spices.

Time. – 1 ½ hour. Average cost, from 1s. to 1s. 6d. each.

Sufficient for 5 or 6 persons.

Seasonable from September to February.

Note. – The liver of the rabbit may be boiled, minced, and mixed with the forcemeat balls, when the flavour is liked.

RAGOUT OF RABBIT OR HARE

INGREDIENTS. – 1 rabbit, 3 teaspoonfuls of flour, 3 sliced onions, 2 oz. of butter, a few thin slices of bacon, pepper and salt to taste, 2 slices of lemon, 1 bay-leaf, 1 glass of port wine.

Mode. – Slice the onions, and put them into a stewpan with the flour and butter; place the pan near the fire, stir well as the butter melts, till the onions become a rich brown colour, and add, by degrees, a little water or gravy till the mixture is of the consistency of cream. Cut some thin slices of bacon; lay in these with the rabbit, cut into neat joints; add a seasoning of pepper and salt, the lemon and bay-leaf, and let the whole simmer until tender. Pour in the port wine, give one boil, and serve.

Time. – about ½ hour to simmer the rabbit.

Average cost, from 1s. to 1s. 6d. each.

Sufficient for 4 or 5 persons.

Seasonable from September to February.

JUGGED HARE
(VERY GOOD)

INGREDIENTS. – 1 hare, 1 ½ lb. of gravy beef, ½ lb. of butter, 1 onion, 1 lemon, 6 cloves; pepper, cayenne, and salt to taste; ½ pint of port wine.

Mode. – Skin, paunch, and wash the hare, cut it into pieces, dredge them with flour, and fry in boiling butter. Have ready 1 ½ pints of gravy, made from the above proportion of beef, and thickened with a little flour. Put this into a jar; add the pieces of fried hare, an onion stuck with six cloves, a lemon peeled and cut in half, and a good seasoning of pepper, cayenne, and salt; cover the hare down tightly, put it up to the neck into a stewpan of boiling water, and let it stew until the hare is quite tender, taking care to keep the water boiling. When nearly done, pour in the wine, and add a few forcemeat balls: these must be fried or baked in the oven for a few minutes before they are put to the gravy. Serve with red-currant jelly.

Time. – 3 ½ to 4 hours. If the hare is very old, allow 4 ½ hours.

Average cost, 7s.

Sufficient for 7 or 8 persons.

Seasonable from September to the end of February.

It is often assumed that jugged hare (or rabbit) must contain the animal's blood; this is not at all the case. Neither Hannah Glasse nor Isabella Beeton includes blood in her recipes, and neither can be accused of culinary squeamishness. 'Jugging' is the process of cooking – in other words the boiling of the meat in a jar.

ELIZABETH DAVID

PEBRONATA DE BOEUF
(A CORSICAN RAGOUT)

The beef is cut into dice and browned in olive oil. Add white wine, all kinds of herbs and seasoning, and simmer very slowly.

When it is nearly cooked add the following pebronata sauce: a thick tomato purée to which you have added pimentos, onions, garlic, thyme, parsley, pounded juniper berries and red wine.

FILET DE BOEUF A L'AMIRAL

Slice 5 or 6 onions and fry them in dripping; take them out of the pan and add to them 4 or 5 fillets of anchovies chopped, 2 tablespoons of chopped bacon, pepper, thyme, marjoram, parsley and 2 yolks of eggs.

Cut a fillet of beef into slices, but not right through, and between each slice put some of the prepared stuffing. Tie the fillet up and put it in a covered pan with dripping, and bake it slowly in the oven.

This recipe harks back to the sort of thing Woolley was cooking: the use of anchovies, the stuffing which includes a range of herbs…and yet here it is in 1950.

In her chapter 'substantial dishes' David mostly gives recipes for risotti and pasta. The only one I am going to include here is Suliman's Pilaff, mostly because it was one of the great treats of our childhood and the very thought of it still makes me happy. On the other hand it was my sister's one escape card; she was allowed to pick out the raisins, much to her siblings' disgust. It is a brilliant way to use up cold roast lamb.

SULIMAN'S PILAFF
(ONE OF THE MOST COMFORTING
DISHES IMAGINABLE)

Into a thick pan put 3 or 4 tablespoons of good dripping or oil, and when it is warm put in 2 cupfuls of rice and stir for a few minutes until the rice takes on a transparent look. Then pour over about 4 pints of boiling water and cook very fast for about 12 minutes. The time of cooking varies according to the rice, but it should be rather under than overdone.

In the meantime, have ready a savoury preparation of small pieces of cooked mutton, fried onions, raisins, currants, garlic, tomatoes and pine nuts, if you can get them, or roasted almonds, all sautéed in dripping with plenty of seasoning.

Put your strained rice into a thick pan and stir in the meat and onion mixture add a little more dripping if necessary, and stir for a few minutes over a low flame before serving.

Hand with the pilaff a bowl of sour cream or Yoghourt.

RAGOUT DE MOUTON À LA CATALANE

2 lb. leg or loin of mutton, an onion, 2 cloves of garlic, a tablespoon of concentrated tomato purée or ½ lb. of fresh tomatoes, ½ lb. of bacon, herbs, ½ lb. of chick peas, white wine or port.

Cut the meat and the bacon into thick squares; brown them on each side in pork or bacon fat or oil; add the garlic and the tomato purée or the fresh tomatoes, skinned and chopped, and plenty of thyme or marjoram or basil, and 2 bay leaves. Pour over a glass of sweet white wine, or port. Cover the pan and cook very gently for 2 hours, until the meat is tender.

231

Have ready the chick peas, soaked and cooked. When the mutton is about ready put the drained chick peas and the meat mixture together into a fireproof dish, put a layer of breadcrumbs on the top and cook in a gentle oven for an hour until a slight crust has formed on the top, and the chick peas are absolutely soft.

Chickpeas and mutton/lamb are a perfect combination. Of course you can cheat and use tinned ones, but it really is worthwhile to think ahead and soak your own. I made this recently with the leg of a wether, as we call it in Somerset, or hog and the strong taste of the meat worked brilliantly with the sweet wine and tomatoes. We don't usually cook bacon with lamb, but we have already seen earlier cooks combine the two successfully.

VEGETABLES

HANNAH WOOLLEY

Woolley has very few recipes for vegetables, and of those she does have they include so much sugar and rosewater that they are unlikely to appeal to today's tastes. For instance her 'Spinage-Tart' is cooked and drained and cooked again and full of rosewater and sugar and cinnamon. Her last sentence 'it will be of a green colour' does not indicate much interest in the vegetable.

MUSHROOMS STEWED

Take them fresh gathered, and cut off the end of the stalk; and as you peel them, put them in a dish with White-wine; after they have layn half an hour, drain them from the Wine, and put them between two Dishes, and set them on a soft fire without any liquor, and when they have stewed a while, pour away the liquor that proceeded from them, then put to your Mushrooms a sprig of Time, a whole Onion, four or five corns of whole pepper, two or three Cloves, a piece of an Orange, a little Salt, and some sweet butter, with some pure gravy of Mutton; cover them and set them on a very gentle fire, so let them stew softly till they are enough and very tender; when you dish them, blow off the fat from them, and take out the Time, the Spice, and Orange, then wring in the juice of Lemon, and strew some Nutmeg thereon.

233

TO FRY ARTICHOAKS

When they are boyled, and sliced fitting for that purpose, you must have your Yolks of Eggs beaten with a grated Nutmeg or two; when your Pan is hot, you must dip them into the Yolks of Eggs, and charge your Pan; when they are fryed on both sides, pour on drawn butter: And if you will fry *Spanish* Potato's, then the Sauce is, Butter, Vinegar, Sugar, and Rose-water; these for a need may serve for Second-Course Dishes.

Look at that. Hannah Woolley is the first known writer to give a recipe for potatoes, but it appears very grudging, and isn't even given its own heading. 'If you will fry' seems as though you're crazy to consider it, and the italicised 'Spanish' makes it seem grudging too. As so often, she sprays her sugar around. The artichoke recipe though is positively modern.

TO MAKE A SALLET OF GREEN PEASE

Cut up as many green Pease as you think will make a Sallet, when they are newly come up about half a Foot high; then set your Liquor over the Fire, and let it boyl, and then put them in; when they are boyled tender put them out, and drain them very well; then mince them, and put in some good sweet butter, salt it, and stir it well together.

Not what we would call a salad at all.

HANNAH GLASSE

Most of Glasse's recipes for vegetables come in the chapter dedicated to Lent, which in itself makes them seem worthy rather than delicious. However as a lot of the recipes involve a fair amount of cream, the air of fasting is soon dissipated.

It is interesting to see the vegetables that she cooks; some are totally alien to us nowadays. She cooks skirrets, which are a relation of parsley and of which the roots are eaten. She cooks cardoons (chardoons) which are available now, but not everywhere. A plant that looks like celery but tastes more like artichoke, it is tough and hard work to prepare. Like old celery, it needs stringing and long cooking. Glasse suggests boiling them, then frying them in butter, or cooking them in red wine and then grating Cheshire cheese over them and browning them with 'a cheese-iron'.

This recipe, for the underused and underrated sorrel, is good, although I'm not convinced by the orange garnish.

SORREL WITH EGGS

First your sorrel must be quite boiled and well strained, then poach three eggs soft, and three hard, butter your sorrel well, fry some three-corner toasts brown, lay the sorrel in the dish, lay the soft eggs on it, and the hard between; stick the toast in and about it. Garnish with quartered orange.

TO FRY ARTICHOKES

First blanch them in water, then flour them, fry them in fresh butter, lay them in your dish and pour melted butter over them.

Or you may put a little red wine into the butter, and season with nutmeg, pepper and salt.

Some of the recipes are just ideas, as good recipes often are. Scrambled eggs on toast with either broccoli (brockely) or asparagus for example.

BROCKELY IN SALLAD

Brockely is a pretty dish, by way of salad in the middle of a table. Boil it like asparagus…lay it in your dish, beat up with oil and vinegar, and a little salt. Garnish with stertion-buds.

Or boil it, and have plain butter in a cup. Or farce French rolls with it, and buttered eggs together, for change.

Hannah Woolley's unwilling-seeming mention of potatoes seems a thing of the past with Glasse, who offers a few recipes for the still comparatively new vegetable. Some of them are indeed so simple that it suggests how unsure the English must still have been about them – she tells her readers how to boil and fry them, for example, but faintly more adventurous is the following recipe, although it still involves sugaring.

TO MAKE POTATOE CAKES

Take potatoes, boil them, peel them, beat them in a mortar, mix them with yolks of eggs, a little sack, sugar, a little beaten mace, a little nutmeg, a little cream or melted butter, work it up into a paste; then make it into cakes, or just what shapes you please with moulds, fry them brown in fresh butter, lay them in plates or dishes, melt butter with sack and sugar, and pour over them.

TO DRESS SPINACH

Pick and wash your spinach well, put it into a sauce-pan, with a little salt. Cover it close, and let it stew till it is just tender; then throw it into a sieve, drain all the liquor out, and chop it small, as much as the quantity of a French roll, add half a pint of cream to it, season with salt, pepper, and grated nutmeg, put in a quarter of a pound of butter, and set it a stewing over the fire a quarter of an hour, stirring it often. Cut a French roll into long pieces, about as thick as your finger, fry then poach six eggs, lay them round on the spinach, stick the pieces of roll in and about the eggs. Serve it up either for a supper, or a side-dish at a second course.

Glasse also has a wonderful way of cooking spinach and peas 'when you have not room on the fire to do it by itself'. You put the vegetable in a tin box and put the box in whatever liquid is boiling on the fire. The advice is interesting in its reminding us how much harder the very basics of cooking were when you were dealing with an open fire.

TO STEW CUCUMBERS

Pare twelve cucumbers, and slice them as thick as a half crown, lay them in a coarse cloth to drain, and when they are dry, flour them and fry them brown in fresh butter; then take them out with an egg-slice, lay them in a plate before the fire, and have ready one cucumber whole, cut a long piece out of the side, and scoop out all the pulp; have ready fried onions peeled and sliced, and fried brown with the sliced cucumber. Fill the whole cucumber with the fried onion, season with pepper and salt; put on the piece you cut out, and tie it round with a pack-thread. Fry it brown, first flouring it, then take it out of the pan and keep it hot; keep the pan on the fire, and with one hand put in a little flour, while with the other you stir it. When it is thick put in two or three spoonfuls of water, and half a pint of white or red wine, two spoonfuls of catchup, stir it together, put in three blades of mace, four cloves, half a nutmeg, a little pepper and salt, all beat fine together; stir it into the sauce-pan, then throw in your cucumbers, give them a toss or two, then lay the whole cucumbers in the middle, the rest round, pour the sauce all over, untie the cucumbers before you lay it into the dish. Garnish the dish with fried onions, and send it to table hot. This is a pretty side-dish at a first course.

TO RAGOO FRENCH BEANS

Take a quarter of a peck of French beans, string them, do not split them, cut them in three across, lay them in salt and water, then take them out and dry them in a coarse cloth, fry them brown, then pour out all the fat, put in a quarter of a pint of hot water, stir it into the pan by degrees, let it boil, then take a quarter of a pound of fresh butter rolled in a very little flour, two spoonfuls of catchup, one spoonful of mushroom-pickle, and four of white wine, an onion stuck with six cloves, two or three blades of mace beat, half a nutmeg grated, a little pepper and salt; stir it all together for a few minutes, then throw in the beans; shake the pan for a minute or two, take out the onion, and pour them into your dish. This is a pretty side-dish, and you may garnish with what you fancy, either pickled French beans, mushrooms, or samphire, or anything else.

TO RAGOO CELERY

Wash and make a bunch of celery very clean, cut it in pieces, about two inches long, put it into a stew pan with just as much water as will cover it, tie three or four blades of mace, two or three cloves, about twenty corns of whole pepper in a muslin rag loose, put it into the stew-pan, a little onion, a little bundle of sweet-herbs; cover it close, and let it stew softly till tender; then take out the spice, onion and sweet-herbs, put in a half an ounce of truffles and morels, two spoonfuls of catchup, a gill of red wine, a piece of butter as big as an egg rolled in flour, six farthing French rolls, season with salt to your palate, stir it all together, cover it close, and let it stew till the sauce is thick and good. Take care the rolls do not break, shake your pan often, when it is enough, dish it up, and garnish with lemon. The yolks of six hard eggs, or more, put in with the rolls, will make it a fine dish. This for a first course.

If you would have it white, put in white wine instead of red, and some cream for a second course.

Glasse makes the recipe sound a lot more complicated than she need; once again her voice comes through sounding more like a neighbour telling a recipe over a fence than a writer.

PEASE FRANÇOISE

Take a quart of shelled pease, cut a large Spanish onion or two middling ones small, and two cabbage or Silesia lettuces cut small, put them into a sauce-pan, with half a pint of water, season them with a little salt, a little beaten pepper, and a little beaten mace and nutmeg. Cover them close, and let them stew a quarter of an hour, then put in a quarter of a pound of fresh butter rolled in a little flour, a spoonful of catchup, a little piece of burnt butter as big as a nutmeg; cover them close, and let it simmer softly an hour, often shaking the pan. When it is enough, serve it up for a side-dish.

A FARCE MEAGRE CABBAGE

Take a white-heart cabbage, as big as the bottom of a plate, let it boil five minutes in water, then drain it, cut the stalk flat to stand in the dish, then carefully open the leaves, and take out the inside, leaving the outside leaves whole. Chop what you take out very fine, take the flesh of two or three flounders or plaice clean from the bone; chop it with the cabbage and the yolks and whites of four hard eggs, a handful of picked parsley, beat all together in a mortar, with a quarter of a pound of melted butter; mix it up with the yolk of an egg, and a few crumbs of bread, fill the cabbage, and tie it together, put it into a deep stew pan, or sauce-pan, put to it half a pint of water, a quarter of a pound of butter rolled in a little flour, the yolks of four hard eggs, an onion stuck with six cloves, whole pepper and mace tied in a muslin rag, half an ounce of truffles and morels, a spoonful of catchup, a few pickled mushrooms; cover it close, and let it simmer an hour. If you find it is not enough, you must do it longer. When it is done, lay it in your dish, untie it, and pour the sauce over it.

TO MAKE AN ARTICHOKE PYE

Boil twelve artichokes, take off all the leaves and choke, take the bottoms clear from the stalk, make a good puff-paste crust, and lay a quarter of a pound of good fresh butter all over the bottom of your pye; then lay a row of artichokes, strew a little pepper, salt, and beaten mace over them, then another row, and strew the rest of your spice over them, put in a quarter of a pound more of butter in little bits, take half an ounce of truffles and morels, boil them in a quarter of a pint of water, pour the water into the pye, cut the truffles and morels very small, throw all over the pye; then have ready twelve eggs boiled hard, take only the hard yolks, lay them all over the pye, pour in a gill of white wine, cover your pye and bake it. When the crust is done, the pye is enough. Four large blades of mace and twelve peppercorns well beat will do, with tea-spoonful of salt.

ELIZA ACTON

Now, in the mid nineteenth century, the recipes for vegetables come in greater quantity and are more recognisable to the modern eye. Vegetables are boiled and served with butter, with perhaps some parsley added. They are mashed with butter (again) and milk or cream. There are still some hangovers from previous generations' cooking – the spices such as cayenne would not often now be seen, for instance (although cumin seeds are delicious).

However, one way in which Acton's cooking of vegetables does differ from ours (or mine, anyway), is in the lengths of time she boils them. 'Vegetables when not sufficiently cooked are known to be so exceedingly unwholesome and indigestible, that the custom of serving them crisp, which means, in reality, only half-boiled, should be altogether disregarded when health is considered of more importance than fashion', she writes. She suggests boiling cabbage for an hour to an hour and a half and carrots for an hour and a half to two hours, a feat which might even make school and hospital canteens quail. To counteract the overcooking she recommends bicarbonate of soda be added to the water to keep the colour of the vegetables.

The actual vegetables cooked form a bridge between the eighteenth and twentieth centuries too, although often they appear in ways long gone. Brussels sprouts on toast, for instance, or slices of boiled or baked beetroot served with the cheese course; the latter is a delicious idea and works well with goat cheese.

Potatoes have clearly now taken a firm hold in the kitchens of England. 'There is no vegetable commonly cultivated in this country, we venture to assert, which is comparable in value to the potato...It must be very nutritious, or it would not sustain the strength of thousands of people whose almost sole food it constitutes, and who, when they can procure a sufficient supply of it to satisfy fully the demands of hunger, are capable of accomplishing the heaviest daily labour.' It is ironic that Modern Cookery was published in the same year as the potato blight first gripped Ireland, leaving a million dead of starvation. Acton has stern words to say to the English potato cook: 'The wretched manner in which it is dressed in many English houses renders it comparatively valueless.' It is perhaps for that reason that the first vegetable recipe is 'To boil potatoes (As in Ireland)'.

Another point of interest is how often the recipes come from France; the 'made dishes' in Acton's book are resolutely English, but she turns her face across the Channel for vegetable cooking.

POTATO RISSOLES (FRENCH)

Mash and season the potatoes with salt, and white pepper or cayenne, and mix with them plenty of minced parsley, and a small quantity of green onions, or eschalots; add sufficient yolks of eggs

242

to bind the mixture together, roll it into small balls, and fry them in plenty of lard or butter over a moderate fire, or they will be too much browned before they are done through. Ham, or any other kind of meat finely minced, may be substituted for the herbs, or added to them.

TO DRESS DANDELIONS LIKE SPINACH, OR AS A SALAD (VERY WHOLESOME)

This common weed of the fields and highways is an excellent vegetable, the young leaves forming an admirable adjunct to a salad, and much resembling endive when boiled and prepared in the same way, or in any of the modes directed for spinach. The slight bitterness of its flavour is to many persons very agreeable; and it is often served at well-appointed tables. It has also, we believe, the advantage of possessing valuable medicinal qualities. Take the roots before the blossom is at all advance, if they can readily be found in that state; if not, pluck off and use the young leaves only. Wash them as clean as possible, and boil them tender in a large quantity of water salted as for sprouts or spinach. Drain them well, press them dry with a wooden spoon, and serve them quite plain with melted butter in a tureen; or, squeeze, chop, and heat them afresh, with seasoning of salt and pepper, a *morsel* of butter rolled in flour, and a spoonful or two of gravy or cream. A very large portion of the leaves will be required for a dish, as they shrink exceedingly in the cooking. For a salad, take them very young and serve them entire, or break them quite small with the fingers; then wash and drain them. Dress them with oil and vinegar, or with any other sauce which may be preferred with them.

243

Rather than resorting to supermarket bags of mixed leaves, send your children out into the highways and byways searching for dandelion leaves. After all, as Action reassures us, they are 'often served at well-appointed tables'.

STEWED LETTUCES

Strip off the outer leaves, and cut away the stalks; wash the lettuces with exceeding nicety, and throw them into water salted as for all green vegetables. When they are quite tender, which will be in from twenty to thirty minutes, according to their age, lift them out and press the water thoroughly from them; chop them a little, and heat them in a clean saucepan with a seasoning of pepper and salt, and a small slice of butter; then dredge in a little flour and stir them well; add next a small cup of broth or gravy, boil them quickly until they are tolerably dry, then stir in a little pale vinegar or lemon-juice, and serve them as hot as possible, with fried sippets around them.

Many of Acton's vegetable dishes involve stewing with gravy after the long boiling, which perhaps only reinforced the foreigner's view of the English as a nation of meat eaters. Now, when we rather like the vegetable to taste of itself, we are unlikely to take gravy-saturated vegetables to our hearts or palates.

This stewed lettuce dish resembles the French way of cooking peas and lettuce – stewed together long and slow with baby onions. Cooked lettuce is delicious and hardly ever eaten. And the following recipe – where the peas are stewed – is also similar. As for plain boiled peas, Acton is very strict on their account: 'Never, on any account, boil or mix mint with them unless it be expressly ordered, as it is particularly distasteful to many persons. It should be served in small heaps round them, if at all.'

GREEN PEAS À LA FRANÇAISE, OR FRENCH FASHION

Throw a quart of young and freshly-shelled peas into plenty of spring water with a couple of ounces of butter, and with the hand work them together until the butter adheres well to the peas; lift them out, and drain them in a cullender. Put them into a stewpan or thick saucepan without any water, and let them remain over a gentle fire, and be stirred occasionally for twenty minutes from the time of their first beginning to simmer; then pour to them as much boiling water as will just cover them; throw in a small quantity of salt, and keep them boiling quickly for forty minutes: stir well amongst them a small lump of sugar which has been dipped quickly into water, and a thickening of about half an ounce of butter very smoothly mixed with a teaspoonful of flour; shake them over the fire for two minutes, and serve them directly heaped high in a very hot dish: there will be no sauce except that which adheres to the peas if they be properly managed. We have found marrowfats excellent, dressed by this receipt. Fresh and good butter should be used with them always.

Peas, 1 quart; butter, 2 oz.: 20 minutes. Water to cover the peas; little salt: 40 minutes. Sugar small lump; butter, ½ oz.: flour, 1 teaspoonful: 2 minutes.

GREEN PEAS WITH CREAM

Boil a quart of young peas perfectly tender in salt and water, and drain them as dry as possible. Dissolve an ounce and a half of butter in a clean stewpan, stir smoothly to it when it boils a dessertspoonful of flour, and shake these over the fire for three or four minutes, but without allowing them to take the slightest colour; pour gradually to them a cup of rich cream, add a small lump of sugar pounded, let the sauce boil, then put in the peas and toss them gently in it until they are very hot: dish, and serve them quickly.

Peas, 1 quart: 18 to 25 minutes. Butter, 1 ½ oz.; flour, 1 dessertspoonful: 3 to 5 minutes. Sugar, 1 saltspoonful; cream, 1 cupful.

Cucumbers are still making an appearance as more than a watery salad adjunct. Interestingly, some recipes are now coming from further afield than France. Acton suggests cooking maize (corn on the cob) as they do in America. And there is this West Indian recipe for cucumbers.

MANDRANG, OR MANDRAM
(WEST INDIAN RECEIPT)

Chop together very small, two moderate-sized cucumbers, with half the quantity of mild onion; add the juice of a lemon, a saltspoonful or more of salt, a third as much of cayenne, and one or two glasses of Madeira, or of any other dry white wine. This preparation is to be served with any kind of roast meat.

CUCUMBERS À LA POULETTE

The cucumbers for this dish may be pared and sliced very thin; or quartered, freed from the seeds, and cut into half-inch lengths; in either case they should be steeped in a little vinegar and sprinkled with salt for half an hour before they are dressed. Drain, and then press them dry in a soft cloth; flour them well, put a slice of butter into a stewpan or saucepan bright in the inside, and when it begins to boil throw in the cucumbers, and shake them over a gentle fire for ten minutes, but be careful to prevent their taking the slightest colour; pour to them gradually as much strong, but very pale veal stock or gravy as will nearly cover them; when it boils skim off the fat entirely, add salt and white pepper if needed, and when the cucumbers are quite tender, strew in a large teaspoonful of finely-minced parsley, and thicken the sauce with the yolks of two or three eggs. French cooks add the flour when the vegetable has stewed in the butter, instead of dredging it upon them at first, and this is perhaps the better method.

VEGETABLE MARROW

It is customary to gather this when not larger than a turkey's egg, but we should say that the vegetable is not then in its perfection. The flesh is whiter and of better flavour when the gourd is about six inches long; at least we have found it so with the kinds which have fallen under our observation. It may either be boiled in the skin, then pared, halved, and served up on a toast; or quartered, freed from the seed, and left until cold, then dipped into egg and fine crumbs of bread, and fried; or it may be cut into dice, and reheated in a little good white sauce; or strewed tender in butter, and served in well-thickened veal gravy, flavoured with a little lemon-juice. It may likewise be mashed...and in that form will be found excellent. The French make a fanciful dish of the marrows thus: they boil them tender in water, and halve them lengthwise as usual, they then slice a small bit off each to make them stand evenly in the dish, and after having hollowed the insides, so as to leave a mere shell, about half an inch thick, they fill them with a rich mince of white meat, and pour white sauce round them; or they heap fried bread-crumbs over the tops, place the dish in the oven for a few minutes, and serve them without sauce.

Size of turkey's egg, 10 to 15 minutes; moderate-sized, 20 to 30; large, ¾ to 1 hour.

The size of the marrow – six inches – makes it more what we would call a courgette (or zucchino). This style of cookery writing – which is really more a list of ideas than recipes – is pretty much the direction Elizabeth David later took, and is the style most beloved by people at ease in their kitchens. For those who are still insecure, weighing, measuring, double-checking, looking at colour pictures, it is too scary.

I can never look at a stuffed marrow without remembering one (and it was a proper marrow, not a collection of courgettes) which my mother stuffed for a big dinner party of strangers who had been put with us for a neighbour's dance. At some point the dish was balanced – or not – on the edge of the table and ended upside down on the floor, which happened to be covered in rush matting. What to do? Scoop it up and pass it on round the table. I doubt we even managed it within the five second rule either. No one was hurt.

Tomatoes did not come to England until the end of the sixteenth century, and even then were grown for ornamental not culinary purposes. In fact, they were thought to be poisonous, or at the very least seriously unhealthy. The first cookbook including tomatoes was not published (and then in Italy) until 1692; the fruit was more usually used to decorate the table. It took until the middle of the eighteenth century before the English regularly used tomatoes in cooking. For me, a life without tomatoes is barely worth contemplating. Although their acidic content is meant to exacerbate arthritis, I spend six weeks in France eating them, sweet and fresh, until my knuckles swell. That's my choice. Perhaps what I miss most about my childhood home is the greenhouse, with its heady smell of warm tomato leaves and the juicy fruit tumbling at the gentlest touch into my hand. Acton has quite a few tomato recipes, including one for a purée (more or less a passata but with cream added) which she recommends be served with calves' heads or beef palates, or added to gravy for pork. Otherwise she likes them roasted, stewed (in gravy, of course, with cream and arrowroot added) or 'forced' (stuffed).

FORCED TOMATAS (ENGLISH RECEIPT)

Cut the stems quite close, slice off the tops of eight fine tomatas, and scoop out the insides; press the pulp through a sieve and mix with it one ounce of fine crumbs of bread, one of butter broken very small, some pepper or cayenne, and salt. Fill the tomatas with the mixture, and bake them for ten minutes in a moderate oven; serve them with brown gravy in the dish. A few small mushrooms stewed tender in a little butter, then minced and added to the tomata pulp, will very much improve this receipt.

Bake 10 minutes.

FORCED TOMATAS (FRENCH RECEIPT)

Let the tomatas be well shaped and of equal size; divide them nearly in the middle leaving the blossom-side the largest, as this is only to be used; empty them carefully of their seeds and juice, and fill them with the following ingredients, which must previously be stewed tender in butter but without being allowed to brown:

249

minced mushrooms and shalots, with a moderate proportion of parsley, some lean of ham chopped small, a seasoning of cayenne, and little fine salt, if needed; let them cool, then mix with them about a third as much of fine crumbs of bread, and two yolks of eggs; fill the tomatas, cover them with fine crumbs, moisten them with clarified butter, and bake them in a brisk oven until they are well coloured. Serve them as a garnish to stewed rump or sirloin of beef, or to a boned and forced leg of mutton.

Minced lean of ham, 2 oz.; bread-crumbs, 2 oz.; shalots, 4 to 8; parsley, full teaspoonful; cayenne, ¼ saltspoonful; little salt, if needed; butter, 2 oz.; yolks of eggs, 2 to 3;: baked 10 to 20 minutes.

OBS. – The French pound the whole of these ingredients with a bit of garlic, before they fill the tomatas with them, but this is not absolutely necessary, and the garlic, if added at all, should be parboiled first, as its strong flavour, combined with that of the eschalots, would scarcely suit the general taste. When the lean of a dressed ham is at hand, only the herbs and vegetables will need to be stewed in the butter; this should be mixed with them into the forcemeat, which an intelligent cook will vary in many ways.

The English centuries-long distrust of garlic is shown here. You can almost hear Acton hissing 'foreign food' through her teeth. Beeton continued this hatred, saying that 'the smell of this plant is generally considered offensive', although she admits that 'it was in greater repute with our ancestors than it is with ourselves'.

TURNIPS STEWED IN BUTTER (GOOD)

This is an excellent way of dressing the vegetable when it is mild and finely grained; but its flavour otherwise is too strong to be agreeable. After they have been washed, wiped quite dry, and pared, slice the turnips nearly half an inch thick, and divide them into dice. Just dissolve an ounce of butter for each half-pound of the turnips, put them in as flat as they can be, and stew them very gently indeed, from three-quarters of an hour to a full hour. Add a seasoning of salt and white pepper when they are half done. When thus prepared, they may be dished in the centre of fried or nicely broiled mutton cutlets, or served by themselves.

For a small dish: turnips, 1 ½ lb.; butter, 3 oz.; seasoning of white pepper; salt, ½ teaspoonful, or more: ¾ to 1 hour. Large dish: turnips, 2 lb.; butter 4 oz.

TO FRY JERUSALEM ARTICHOKES

Boil them from eight to twelve minutes; lift them out, drain them on a sieve, and let them cool; dip them into beaten eggs, and cover them with fine breadcrumbs. Fry them a light brown, drain, pile them in a hot dish, and serve them quickly.

SALSIFY

We are surprised that a vegetable so excellent as this should be so little cared for in England. Delicately fried in batter – which is a common mode of serving it abroad – it forms a delicious second course dish: it is also good when plain-boiled, drained, and served in gravy, or even with melted butter. Wash the roots, scrape gently off the dark outside skin, and throw them into cold water as they are done, to prevent their turning black; cut them into lengths of three or four inches, and when all are ready put them into plenty of boiling water with a little salt, a

251

small bit of butter, and a couple of spoonsful of white vinegar or the juice of a lemon: they will be done in from three-quarters of an hour to an hour. Try them with a fork, and when perfectly tender, drain, and serve them with white sauce, rich brown gravy, or melted butter.

STEWED ONIONS

Strip the outer skin from four or five fine Portugal onions, and trim the ends, but without cutting into the vegetable; arrange them in a saucepan of sufficient size to contain them all in one layer, just cover them with good beef or veal gravy, and stew them very gently indeed for a couple of hours: they should be tender quite through, but should not be allowed to fall to pieces. When large, but not mild onions are used, they should be first boiled for half an hour in plenty of water, then drained from it, and put into boiling gravy: strong, well-flavoured broth of veal or beef, is sometimes substituted for this, and with the addition of a little catsup, spice, and thickening, answers very well. The savour of this dish is heightened by flouring lightly and frying the onions of a pale brown before they are stewed.

Portugal onions, 4 or 5 (if fried, 15 to 20 minutes); broth or gravy, 1 to 1 ½ pint: nearly or quite 2 hours.

OBS. – When the quantity of gravy is considered too much, the onions may be only half covered, and turned when the under-side is tender, but longer time must then be allowed for stewing them.

STEWED CHESTNUTS

Strip the outer rind from forty or fifty fine sound Spanish chestnuts, throw them into a large saucepan of hot water, and bring it to the point of boiling; when the second skin parts from them easily, lift them out, and throw them into plenty of cold water; peel, and wipe them dry; then put them into a stewpan or bright saucepan, with as much highly-favoured cold beef or veal gravy as will nearly cover them, and stew them very gently from three-quarters of an hour to a full hour: they should be quite tender, but unbroken. Add salt, cayenne, and thickening if required, and serve the chestnuts in their gravy. We have found it an improvement to have them floured and lightly browned in a little good butter before they are stewed, and also to add some thin strips of lemon-rind to the gravy.

Chestnuts, 40 or 50; gravy, ¾ pint, or more: ¾ to 1 hour.

OBS. – A couple of bay leaves and a slice of lean ham will give an improved flavour to the sauce should it not be sufficiently rich: the ham should be laid under the chestnuts, but not served with them. When these are to be browned, or even otherwise, they may be freed readily from the second skin by shaking them with a small bit of butter in a frying-pan over a gentle fire.

ISABELLA BEETON

Sometimes Beeton seems as modern as the latest food fad; her introductory comments on vegetables are in her keen, learned vein, but some of the footnotes to her recipes would please the most eager nutritionist. She tells us the 'constituent properties of the Artichoke' ('starch, 30, albumen 10, uncrystalizable sugar 148', etc), information which I doubt much of her audience needed. Medical information is also included, such as the diuretic and aperient qualities of the asparagus. More useful to the cook, however, is the way she tells her reader when each vegetable is in season. Both economically and ecologically minded readers nowadays should be interested in this; I am amazed how little people know about what vegetable grows at which time of the year. Beeton also offers various tips on how to arrange vegetables (try arranging Brussels sprouts 'on the dish in the form of a pineapple' if you will) and how to keep the vegetables' colour. As well as the use of bicarbonate of soda, thrown into the water before it boils, she suggests putting 'a large piece of cinder into a muslin bag' to boil with artichokes.

One other advantage for cooks is that Beeton puts her vegetable recipes in alphabetical order, unlike the shambolic approach of earlier writers.

Like earlier writers, though, (whose ideas, as we have seen, she often took) she often cooks many vegetables into what must have been a watery pulp (¾ hour for a large cabbage and 1 ¾ to 2 ¼ hours for carrots) and suggests that many vegetable dishes be stewed in rich gravy. Others are served with cream or melted butter.

ASPARAGUS PEAS

INGREDIENTS. – 100 heads of asparagus, 2 oz. of butter, a small bunch of parsley, 2 or 3 green onions, flour, 1 lump of sugar, the yolks of 2 eggs, 4 tablespoonfuls of cream, salt.

Mode. – Carefully scrape the asparagus, cut it into pieces of equal size, avoiding that which is in the least hard or tough, and throw them into cold water. Then boil the asparagus in salt and water until three-parts done; take it out, drain, and place it on a cloth to dry the moisture away from it. Put it into a stewpan with the butter, parsley, and onions, and shake over a brisk fire for 10 minutes. Dredge in a little flour, add the sugar, and moisten with boiling water. When boiled a short time and reduced, take out the parsley and onions, thicken with the yolks of 2 eggs beaten with the cream; add a seasoning of salt, and when the whole thing is on the point of simmering, serve. Make the sauce sufficiently thick to adhere to the vegetable.

Time. – Altogether, ½ hour. Average cost, 1s. 6d. a pint.
Seasonable in May, June, and July.

ASPARAGUS PUDDING
(A DELICIOUS DISH, TO BE SERVED
WITH THE SECOND COURSE)

INGREDIENTS. – ½ pint of asparagus peas, 4 eggs, 2 tablespoonfuls of flour, 1 tablespoon of *very finely* minced ham, 1 oz. of butter, pepper and salt to taste, milk.

Mode. – Cut up the nice green tender parts of asparagus, about the size of peas; put them into a basin with the eggs, which should be well beaten, and the flour, ham, butter, pepper, and salt. Mix all these ingredients well together, and moisten with sufficient milk to make the pudding of the consistency of thick batter; put it into a pint buttered mould, tie it down tightly with a floured cloth, place it in boiling water, and let it boil for 2 hours; turn it out of the mould on to a hot dish, and pour plain melted butter round, but not over, the pudding. Green peas pudding may be made in exactly the same manner, substituting peas for the asparagus.

Time. – 2 hours. Average cost, 1s. 6d. per pint.
Seasonable in May, June, and July.

STEWED RED CABBAGE

INGREDIENTS. – 1 red cabbage, a small slice of ham, ½ oz. of fresh butter, 1 pint of weak stock or broth, 1 gill of vinegar, salt and pepper to taste, 1 tablespoonful of pounded sugar.

255

Mode. – Cut the cabbage into very thin slices, put it into a stewpan, with the ham cut in dice, the butter, ½ pint of stock, and the vinegar; cover the pan closely, and let it stew for 1 hour. When it is very tender, add the remainder of the stock, a seasoning of salt and pepper, and the pounded sugar; mix all well together, stir over the fire until nearly all the liquor is dried away, and serve. Fried sausages are usually sent to table with this dish: they should be laid round and on the cabbage, as a garnish.

Time. – rather more than 1 hour. Average cost, 4d. each.

Sufficient for 4 persons.

Seasonable from September to January.

STEWED CELERY À LA CRÈME

INGREDIENTS. – 6 heads of celery; to each ½ gallon of water allow 1 heaped tablespoonful of salt, 1 blade of pounded mace, ⅓ pint of cream.

Mode. – Wash the celery thoroughly; trim, and boil it in salt and water until tender. Put the cream and pounded mace into a stewpan; shake it over the fire until the cream thickens, dish the celery, pour over the sauce, and serve.

Time. – Large heads of celery, 25 minutes; small ones, 15 to 20 minutes.

Average cost, 2d. per head.

Sufficient for 5 or 6 persons.

Seasonable from October to April.

FRIED CUCUMBERS

INGREDIENTS. – 2 or 3 cucumbers, pepper and salt to taste, flour, oil or butter.

Mode. – Pare the cucumbers and cut them into slices of an equal thickness, commencing to slice from the thick, and not the stalk end of the cucumber. Wipe the slices dry with a cloth, dredge them with flour, and put them into a pan of boiling oil or butter; keep turning them about until brown; lift them out of the pan, let them drain, and serve, piled lightly in a dish. These will be found a great improvement to rump-steak: they should be place on a dish with the steak on the top.

Time. – 5 minutes. Average cost, when cheapest, 4d. each.

Sufficient for 4 or 5 persons.

Seasonable. – Forced from the beginning of March to the end of June; in full season in July and August.

Beeton has a theory that a cucumber must be cut from the end away from the stalk as it will be better. I've tried cutting from either end and to be honest it doesn't seem to be much different to me.

The potato has clearly now taken hold – Beeton offers them fried, boiled, mashed and baked. ('Do not forget to send to table with them a piece of cold butter' – I nearly fell out with a friend for life after she gave me baked potato with margarine for supper.) They are also now included in salads.

ELIZABETH DAVID

David does include fairly straightforward recipes for carrots and potatoes, but it is for her introduction to rare vegetables that she is more known. Even sweet potatoes would have been unknown to most

English in the fifties – unless they had served in the army in the Middle East and been given them in chip form. David suggests simply baking them and eating them with butter and salt, as a course on their own.

AUBERGINE DOLMAS
(A TURKISH AND MIDDLE EASTERN DISH)

8 small round aubergines (or 4 large ones), a cup of cooked rice, ¼ lb. of minced mutton (either raw or cooked), 2 tomatoes, salt, pepper, onions, lemon juice, herbs, a few pine nuts or walnuts, olive oil.

Mix the cooked rice with the well seasoned meat, a chopped fried onion or two, the chopped tomatoes, and some marjoram, mint, or basil.

Cut about an inch off the thin end of the aubergines, and with a small spoon scoop out most of the flesh. Cut this into dice and mix it with the prepared stuffing. Fill the aubergines with the stuffing (not too full), put the tops in, inverted, so that they fit like corks, lay them in a pan with a little olive oil; let this get hot and then pour hot water over them to come halfway up. Simmer for 30 minutes, add the juice of a lemon, and cook very slowly another 30 minutes. There should be just a very little sauce left by the time they are ready. If there is any stuffing over, use it to fill tomatoes, which can be baked and served with the aubergines.

FENNEL

An absolutely delicious vegetable.

Cut the fennel roots in half and throw them into boiling water. When they are tender arrange them in a buttered fire-proof dish, spread grated Parmesan and breadcrumbs on the top and put them in the oven until the cheese has melted.

In the south of France the very young fennel is cut in half and eaten raw, like celery, with salt and lemon juice.

FASOULIA

The Greek name for haricot beans. People who appreciate the taste of genuine olive oil in their food will like this dish. Soak ½ lb. of beans for 12 hours. Heat half a tumbler of olive oil in a deep pan; put in the strained beans; lower the heat; stir the beans and let them simmer gently for 10 minutes, adding 2 cloves of garlic, a bayleaf, a branch of thyme, and a dessertspoonful of tomato paste. Add boiling water to cover the beans by one inch. Cook them over a moderate fire for 3 hours. The liquid should have reduced sufficiently to form a thickish sauce. Squeeze in the juice of a lemon, add some raw onion cut into rings, some salt and black pepper, and leave them to cool.

SAUCES, FORCEMEATS ETC.

Some of the sauces referred to by the cookery writers I quote are still familiar to us, some occur under other names and others are lost to us. I have included any which are mentioned in other recipes, or which I think we could still use to greedy advantage.

HANNAH WOOLLEY

SEVERAL EXCELLENT SAUCES FOR SEVERAL DISHES, AND FIRST FOR GREEN-GEESE

Take the juice of Sorrel mixed with scalded Gooseberries, beaten Butter and Sugar, then serve it on Sippets. Or fill their bellies with Goosberries, and so roast them, then take them out, and mingle them with Sugar, Butter, Vinegar, Cinamon and served on sippets.

Sorrel and gooseberries are both flavours used a great deal more in old recipes than they are today; the tartness of the gooseberry makes it an ideal and more unusual accompaniment to goose than the more commonly used apples and pears.

A variety of sauces are listed, and are almost more ideas than recipes. I've included a few of the more unusual ones.

For roast Mutton divers sorts of Sawces: Whole Onions stewed in Gravy, White-wine, Pepper, pickled Capers, Mace and three or four slices of Lemon; Salt, Pepper, juice of Oranges and an A[n]chovee.

260

For roast Veal several Sawces. 1. Gravy, Claret, Nutmeg, Vinegar, Butter, Sugar and Oranges. 2. Only Vinegar and Butter. 3. All manner of sweet Herbs chopped small, with the yolks of three or four Eggs, and boil them in Vinegar and Butter, a few bread-crumbs, Currans, beaten Cinamon, Suggar, and a whole Clove or two, put it under the Veal with slices of Orange and Lemon to garnish the Dish.

For Rabbets…1. Beaten Butter, with the Liver, and Parsley cut very small. 2. Sage and Parlsey minced, rowl it in a ball of Butter, and stuff the belly therewith.

For roast Hens…1. Take the yolks of three hard Eggs minced small, salt, grated Bread, Gravy, juice of Oranges, with Lemon-peel shred small. 2. Oyster-liquor, an Anchovee or two, Nutmeg and Gravy, and rub the Dish with a Clove of Garlick.

These sauces show clearly how, contrary to popular misconception, garlic and anchovies have been used in English cooking for centuries.

TO MAKE EXCELLENT SAUCE FOR MUTTON, EITHER CHINES, LEGS, OR NECKS

Take half a dozen Onions shred very small, a little strong Broath, and a glass of White-wine; boyl all these well together: Then take half a pint of Oysters, and mince them, with a little Parsley, and two or three small bunches of Grapes, if in season, with a Nutmeg sliced, and the Yolks of two or three Eggs; put in all these together with the former, and boyl it, and pour it all over your Meat, and then pour some melted butter on the top, and strew on the Yolks of two or three hard Eggs minced small.

We don't eat mutton any more; its strong taste is too much for our refined stomachs, or so the butchers and supermarkets seem to think. I had a romance with a sheep farmer, who used to keep a couple of lambs for a year longer. In these parts we call it 'wether', elsewhere it is known as 'hog'. It is delicious – stronger than lamb, and darker, but not as strong as the mutton of the olden days. You need to cook it differently, more slowly, but it is worth the wait. I wonder how many other sheep farmers still hold to this tradition. If you know one, ask if you can buy a joint next time he slaughters his wether. It will be worth it. Woolley's recipes for sauces to go with mutton would be delicious with wether – the strong taste of the meat can hold up to a good bold sauce.

ANOTHER GOOD SAUCE FOR MUTTON

Take a handful of Pickled Cucumbers, as many Capers, and as much Samphire; put them into a little Verjuice, White-wine and strong Broth, and a Limon cut in small pieces, and a little Nutmeg grated; let them boyl together, and then beat them up thick, with a Ladleful of Butter melted, and a couple of Yolks of Eggs, and a little sugar; Dish your Meat upon Sippets, pour on your sauce, and Garnish it with Samphire, Capers, and Barberries.

TO MAKE A SAUCE FOR TURKIES, OR CAPONS

Take a two-penny white loaf, and lay it a soaking in strong broth, with Onions sliced therein; then boyl it in Gravy, together with a Limon cut in small pieces, a little Nutmeg sliced, and some melted butter, put this under your Turkey, or Capon, and so serve it; you will find it Excellent Sauce.

'In England,' wrote the eighteenth-century diplomat Francesco Caracciolo, 'there are sixty different religions, and only one sauce.' It is thought he was referring either to bread sauce, of which this is a very early version, or melted butter.

HANNAH GLASSE

TO MAKE FORCE-MEAT BALLS

Now you are to observe, that force-meat balls are a great addition to all made dishes; made thus: take half a pound of veal, and half a pound of suet, cut fine, and beat in a marble mortar or wooden bowl; have a few sweet-herbs shred fine, a little mace dried and beat fine, a small nutmeg grated, or half a large one, a little lemon-peel cut very fine, a little pepper and salt, and the yolks of two eggs; mix all these well together, then roll them in little round balls, and some in little long balls; roll them in flour, and fry them brown. If they are for anything of white sauce, put a little water on in a sauce-pan, and when the water boils put them in, and let them boil for a few minutes, but never fry them for white sauce.

Veal being so expensive and not always easy to find, you can substitute pork. Suet is fat found around the kidneys, and of course we can now buy it dried. However I have used the real thing for a suet pudding and it was totally amazing. Incredibly light and utterly delicious. The butcher will usually give it to you free, but the trick is to put it into the fridge and grate it really cold, so it's easier to manipulate. You use it in exactly the same way as you would good old Atora.

TRUFFLES AND MORELS GOOD
IN SAUCES AND SOUPS

Take half an ounce of truffles and morels, simmer them in two or three spoonfuls of water for a few minutes, then put them with the liquor in the sauce. They thicken both sauce and soup, and give it a fine flavour.

TO MAKE A MUSHROOM-SAUCE
FOR WHITE FOWLS OF ALL SORTS

Take a pint of mushrooms, wash and pick them very clean, and put them into a saucepan, with a little salt, some nutmeg, a blade of mace, a pint of cream, and a good piece of butter rolled in flour. Oil these all together, and keep stirring them; then pour your sauce into your dish, and garnish with lemons.

MUSHROOM-SAUCE FOR WHITE FOWLS BOILED

Take half a pint of cream, and a quarter of a pound of butter, stir them together one way till it is thick, then add a spoonful of pickled mushrooms, or fresh if you have them. Garnish only with lemon.

TO MAKE CELERY-SAUCE, EITHER FOR ROASTED OR BOILED FOWLS, CURKIES, PARTRIDGES, OR ANY OTHER GAME

Take a large bunch of celery, wash and pare it very clean, cut it into little thin bits, and boil it softly in a little water till it is tender; then add a little beaten mace, some nutmeg, pepper, and salt, thickened with a good piece of butter rolled in flour, then boil it up, and pour in your dish.

You may make it with cream thus: boil your celery as above, and add some mace, nutmeg, a piece of butter as big as a walnut rolled in flour, and half a pint of cream; boil them all together, and you may add, if you will, a glass of white wine, and a spoonful of catchup.

Celery is delicious with game birds such as pheasant or wild duck. Good luck with finding curkies. Could it be a misprint for turkies?

A PRETTY LITTLE SAUCE

Take the liver of the fowl, bruise it with a little of the liquor, cut a little lemon-peel fine, melt some good butter, and mix the liver by degrees; give it a boil, and pour it into the dish.

TO MAKE LEMON-SAUCE FOR BOILED FOWLS

Take a lemon, pare off the rind, then cut it into slices, and cut it small; take all the kernels out, bruise the liver with two or three spoonfuls of good gravy, then melt some butter, mix it all together, give them a boil, and cut in a little lemon-peel very small.

265

FRENCH BATTER
(FOR FRYING VEGETABLES, AND FOR
APPLE, PEACH, OR ORANGE FRITTERS)

Cut a couple of ounces of good butter into small bits, pour on it less than a quarter of a pint of boiling water, and when it is dissolved add three-quarters of a pint of cold water, so that the whole shall not be quite milk warm; mix it then by degrees and very smoothly with twelve ounces of fine dry flour and a *small* pinch of salt if the batter be for fruit fritters, but with more if for meat or vegetables. Just before it is used, stir into it the whites of two eggs beaten to a solid froth; but previously to this, add a little water should it appear too thick, as some flour requires more liquid than other to bring it to the proper consistence; this is an exceedingly light batter, excellent for the purposes for which it is named.

Butter, 2 oz.; water, from ¾ to nearly 1 pint; little salt; flour, ¾ lb.; white of 2 eggs, beaten to snow.

ELIZA ACTON

It is with her usual sternness that Eliza Acton offers up her 'introductory remarks' on sauces. But she is right – sauces do often make the difference between a good or bad dish. And the answer is not, as many insecure cooks feel, just to throw jugs of cream or bottles of wine into the mix. 'Coarsely or carelessly prepared' sauces 'greatly discredit the cook, and are anything but acceptable to the eaters.' She recommends that the reader 'strictly follows' her instructions, so that at the very least they will be able to prepare 'tolerably palatable sauces'. I am not entirely sure that such a frightening introduction might not put off her audience.

Melted butter was a sauce much used in Acton's day. Indeed she refers to '"the one sauce of England" as it is called by foreigners', and she has no fewer than seven variations on the sauce.

SAUCE TOURNEE, OR PALE THICKENED GRAVY

Sauce tournée is nothing more than rich pale gravy made with veal or poultry and thickened with delicate white *roux*. The French give it a flavouring of mushrooms and green onions, by boiling some of each in it for about half an hour before the sauce is served: it must then be strained, previously to being dished…Blend the flour and butter perfectly with a knife before they are thrown into the stewpan, and keep them stirred without ceasing over a clear and gentle fire until they have simmered for some minutes, then place the stewpan high over the fire, and shake it constantly until the *roux* has lost the raw taste of the flour; next, stir very gradually to it a pint of the gravy, which should be boiling. Set it by the side of the stove for few minutes, skim it thoroughly, and serve it without delay.

Butter, 1 oz.; flour, ¾ oz.; strong pale gravy, seasoned with mushrooms and green onions, 1 pint.

<u>OBS</u>. – With the addition of three or four yolks of very fresh eggs, mixed with a seasoning of mace, cayenne, and lemon-juice, this becomes *German sauce*, now much used for fricassées, and other dishes; and minced parsley (boiled) and chili vinegar, each in sufficient quantity to flavour it agreeably, convert it into a good fish sauce.

GOOSEBERRY SAUCE FOR MACKEREL

Cut the stalks and tops from half to a whole pint of quite young gooseberries, wash them well, just cover them with cold water, and boil them very gently indeed, until they are tender; drain and mix them with a small quantity of melted butter, made with rather less flour than usual. Some eaters prefer the mashed gooseberries without any addition; others like that of a little ginger. The best way of making this sauce is to turn them into a hair-sieve to drain, then to press them through it with a wooden spoon, and to stir them in a clean stewpan or saucepan over the fire with from half to a whole teaspoonful of sugar, just to soften their extreme acidity, and a bit of fresh butter about the size of a walnut. When the fruit is not passed through the sieve it is an improvement to seed it.

Gooseberries remind me intensely of my childhood. There were a few big bushes in the garden and it was of course the children's job to fight our way through the prickles to the fruit. The pain was made worse by not really liking the end product, except possibly in a crumble.

The French only really use gooseberries with mackerel, and not that often. But this is a classic recipe, definitely improved with the hint of ginger.

GENEVESE SAUCE, OR SAUCE GENEVOISSE

Cut into dice three ounces of the lean of a well-flavoured ham, and put them with half a small carrot, four cloves, a blade of mace, two or three very small sprigs of lemon thyme and of parsley, and rather more than an ounce of butter, into a stewpan; just simmer them from three-quarters of an hour to a whole hour, then stir in a teaspoonful of flour; continue the slow stewing for about five minutes, and pour in by degrees a pint of good boiling veal gravy, and let the sauce again simmer softly for nearly an hour. Strain it off, heat it in a clean saucepan, and when it boils, stir in a wineglassful and a half of good sherry or Madeira, two tablespoonsful of lemon-juice, some cayenne, a little salt if needed, and a small tablespoonful of flour very smoothly mixed with two ounces of butter. Give the whole a boil after the thickening is added, pour a portion of the sauce over the fish (it is served principally with salmon and trout), and send the remainder very hot to table in a tureen.

Lean of ham, 3 oz.; ½ small carrot; 4 to 6 cloves; mace, 1 large blade; thyme and parsley, 3 or 4 small sprigs of each; butter, 1 to 1 ½ oz.; 50 to 60 minutes. Veal gravy, 1 pint; ¾ to 1 hour. Sherry or Madeira, 1 ½ glassful; lemon-juice, 2 tablespoonsful; seasoning of cayenne and salt; flour, 1 tablespoonful; butter, 2 oz.: 1 minute.

This is recommended to eat with salmon. The following sauce would also be good with the fish.

COMMON SORREL SAUCE

Strip from the stalks and the large fibres, from one to a couple of quarts of freshly-gathered sorrel; wash it very clean, and put it into a well-tinned stewpan or saucepan (or into an enamelled one, which would be far better), without any water; add to it a small slice of good butter, some pepper and salt, and stew it gently, keeping it well stirred until it is exceedingly tender, that it may not burn; then drain it on a sieve, or press the liquid well from it; chop it as fine as possible, and boil it again for a few minutes with a spoonful or two of gravy, or the same quantity of cream or milk, mixed with a half-teaspoonful of flour, or with only a fresh slice of good butter. The beaten yolk of an egg or two stirred in just as the sorrel is taken from the fire will soften the sauce greatly and a saltspoonful of pounded sugar will also be an improvement.

It's worth growing sorrel if you have any space. It's a delicious and overlooked herb. My cousin had an old handwritten cookbook handed down through the family and the sorrel soup from it was always a triumph.

CAPER SAUCE

Stir into the third of a pint of good melted butter from three to four dessertspoonsful of capers; add a little of the vinegar, and dish the sauce as soon as it boils. Keep it stirred after the berries are added; part of them may be minced and a little chili vinegar substituted for their own. Pickled nasturtiums make a very good sauce, and their flavour is sometimes preferred to that of the capers. For a large joint, increase the quantity of butter to half a pint.

Melted butter, third of pint; capers, 3 to 4 desertspoonsful.

My eldest daughter's passions for capers is such that when asked what food she wanted for her fourth birthday party she said bowls of capers. Acton seems almost as keen; she has three different caper sauces in her book, this one, a brown one (made with thickened gravy and cayenne rather than butter) and another for fish, which includes mushroom catsup.

A COMMON SAUCE OF CUCUMBERS

Cucumbers which have the fewest seeds are best for this sauce. Pare and slice two or three, should they be small, and put them into

270

a saucepan, in which two ounces, or rather more, of butter have been dissolved, and are beginning to boil; place them high over the fire, that they may stew as softly as possible, without taking colour, for three–quarters of an hour, or longer should they require it; add to them a good seasoning of white pepper and some salt, when they are half done; and just before they are served stir to them half a teaspoonful of flour, mixed with a morsel of butter; strew in some minced parsley, give it a boil, and finish with a spoonful of good vinegar.

'Place them high over the fire', rather than 'place them over a high fire'. The word order sums up the difference between a nineteenth century open fire and a twenty-first century hob.

Of course Acton has many other sauces – mushroom, onion, apple – but they are too much in our common way of cooking to need inclusion. Her recipes for tomato sauces are only interesting by virtue of their being there at all, as tomatoes took some time to make the move from ornamental to culinary plant. She spells them 'tomata', which is agreeable. Another sauce which is interesting, given our belief that the English never went near garlic until Elizabeth David told us about it, is the following – totally delicious – garlic sauce. Don't be lazy about changing the water.

MILD RAGOUT OF GARLIC, OR, L'AIL À LA BORDELAISE

Divide some fine cloves of garlic, strip off the skin, and when all are ready throw them into plenty of boiling water slightly salted; in five minutes drain this from them, and pour in as much more, which should also be quite boiling; continue to change it every five or six minutes until the garlic is quite tender: throw in a moderate proportion of salt the last time to give it proper flavour. Drain it thoroughly, and serve it in the dish with roast mutton, or put it into good brown gravy or white sauce for table. By changing very frequently the water in which it is boiled, the root will be deprived of its naturally pungent flavour and smell, and rendered extremely mild: when it is not wished to be quite so much so, change the water every ten minutes only.

Garlic, 1 pint: 15 to 25 minutes, or more. Water to be changed every 5 or 6 minutes; or every 10 minutes when not wished so *very* mild. Gravy, or sauce, 1 pint.

COLD SAUCES

The French still don't understand our passion for mint with lamb.

SUPERIOR MINT-SAUCE (TO SERVE WITH LAMB)

The mint for this sauce should be fresh and young, for when old it is tough and indigestible. Strip the leaves from the stems, wash them with great nicety, and drain them on a sieve, or dry them in a cloth; chop them very fine, put them into a sauce-tureen, and to three heaped tablespoonsful of the mint add two of pounded sugar; let them remain a short time well mixed together, then pour to them gradually six tablespoonsful of good vinegar. The sauce thus made is excellent, and far more wholesome than when a larger proportion of vinegar and a smaller one of sugar is used for it; but, after the first trial, the proportions can easily be adapted to the taste of the eaters.

272

FINE HORSERADISH SAUCE
(TO SERVE WITH COLD, ROAST,
STEWED, OR BOILED BEEF)

The root for this excellent sauce should be young and tender, and grated down on a very fine bright grater, quite to a pulp, after it has been washed, wiped, and scraped free from the outer skin.

Horseradish, 2 heaped tablespoonsful; salt, 1 moderate teaspoonful; rich cream, 4 tablespoonsful; good vinegar, 3 dessertspoonsful (of which one may be chili vinegar when the root is mild).

When the other ingredients are smoothly mingled, the vinegar must be stirred briskly to them in very small portions. A few drops of garlic or shalot vinegar can be added to them when it is liked.

Of course we mostly buy standard sauces like horseradish and mint in a jar, but it is a shame.

ISABELLA BEETON

Many of Beeton's – and the earlier writers' – recipes use a gravy in the cooking, as an ingredient its own right. The earlier writers produce the gravies from quantities which would frankly terrify a modern cook. I have included a basic gravy from Mrs Beeton which you could use for verisimilitude, or use any of your own gravy. But whatever you do, please don't use anything from a cube.

A QUICKLY-MADE GRAVY

INGREDIENTS. – ½ lb. shin of beef, ½ onion, ¼ carrot, 2 or 3 sprigs of parlsely and savoury herbs, a piece of butter about the size of a walnut; cayenne and mace to taste, ¾ pint of water.

Mode. – Cut the meat up into very small pieces, slice the onion and carrot, and put them into a small saucepan with the butter. Keep stirring over a sharp fire until they have taken a little colour, when add the water and the remaining ingredients. Simmer for ½ hour, skim well, strain, and flavour, when it will be ready for use.

Time. – ½ hour. Average cost, for this quantity, 5d.

Forcemeat – stuffing – is also used a great deal in early kitchens. Rissoles, stuffed joints, beef or veal 'collops' rolled and stuffed, all use forcemeat. The recipe below is the one that Mrs Beeton refers back to most often in her meat recipes. For instance this is the version of forcemeat that she suggests for the stuffed shoulder of lamb.

FORCEMEAT FOR VEAL, TURKEYS, FOWLS, HARE &C.

INGREDIENTS. – 2 oz. of ham or lean bacon, ¼ lb. of suet, the rind of half a lemon, 1 teaspoonful of minced parsley, 1 teaspoonful of minced sweet herbs; salt, cayenne, and pounded mace to taste; 6 oz. of bread crumbs, 2 eggs.

Mode. – Shred the ham or bacon, chop the suet, lemon-peel, and herbs, taking particular care that all be very finely minced; add a seasoning to taste, of salt, cayenne, and mace, and blend all thoroughly together with the bread crumbs, before wetting. Now beat and strain the eggs, work these up with the other ingredients, and the forcemeat will be ready for use. When it is made into balls, fry of a nice brown, in boiling lard or put them on a tin and bake for ½ hour in a moderate oven. As we have stated before, no one flavour should predominate greatly, and the forcemeat should be of sufficient body to cut with a knife, and yet not dry and heavy. For very delicate forcemeat, it is advisable to pound the ingredients together before binding with the egg; but for ordinary cooking, mincing very finely answers the purpose.

Average cost, 8d.

Sufficient for a turkey, a moderate-sized fillet of veal, or a hare.

ITALIAN SAUCE (BROWN)

INGREDIENTS. – A few chopped mushrooms and shalots, ½ pint of stock, ½ glass of Madeira, the juice of ½ lemon, ½ teaspoonful of pounded sugar, 1 teaspoonful of chopped parsley.

Mode. – Put the stock into a stewpan with the mushrooms, shalots, and Madeira, and stew gently for ¼ hour, then add the remaining ingredients, and let them just boil. When the sauce is done enough, put it in another stewpan, and warm it in a *bain marie*. The mushrooms should not be chopped long before they are wanted, as they will then become black.

Time. – ¼ hour. *Average cost*, for this quantity, 7d.

Sufficient for a small dish.

Beeton suggests this sauce with her broiled veal cutlets, but I would leave out the sugar.

ELIZABETH DAVID

TURKISH STUFFING FOR A WHOLE ROAST SHEEP

2 cups partly cooked rice, 1 dozen cooked chestnuts, 1 cup currants, 1 cup shelled pistachio nuts, salt, cayenne pepper, 1 teaspoon ground cinnamon, ¼ lb. butter.

Chop the chestnuts and the pistachio nuts finely, mix with the other ingredients. Melt the butter and cook the stuffing in it gently, stirring until all the ingredients are well amalgamated.

This stuffing can also be used for chicken and turkey.

This was the recipe which convinced John Lehmann that the untidy manuscript with which he had been presented was indeed something out of the ordinary. The meat ration was a few ounces a week, and here was a writer telling the world how to stuff a whole sheep.

SAUCE ESPAGNOLE

Sauce Espagnole being the basic brown sauce from which many others derive, for it was usually made in considerable quantity, and kept for several days. This being no longer possible, I give the quantities for making about 1 pint.

2 oz. bacon or ham, 1 ½ oz. butter, 1 oz. carrots, ½ gill white wine, ½ oz. onion, 1 ¼ pints good brown stock, thyme, bay leaf, salt and pepper, ½ lb. tomatoes.

Melt the bacon or ham cut in dice in a little of the butter; add the carrots, also cut in dice, the onions and the herbs and seasonings; when they turn golden add the white wine and reduce.

In another pan put the rest of the butter and when it is melted

276

put in the flour; let it brown very gently, stirring to prevent burning. When it is smooth and brown add half the brown stock, bring to the boil, transfer the mixture from the other pan, and let the whole cook very slowly for 1 ½ hours. Put the sauce through a fine sieve; return to the saucepan and add the chopped tomatoes and the rest of the stock; let it cook slowly another 30 minutes and strain it again; the sauce should now be of the right consistency, but if it is too thin cook it again until it is sufficiently reduced.

MOHAMMED'S SAUCE FOR FISH

Mayonnaise, 2 hard-boiled eggs, 3 anchovies (boned and chopped), juice of onions, capers, celery, fresh cucumber.

Chop all the ingredients finely and stir into the mayonnaise.

PUDDINGS

'BLESSED BE HE THAT INVENTED PUDDING for it is a manna that hits the palates of all sorts of people...Ah what an excellent thing is an English pudding!' wrote Henri Misson, a French traveller to England in Tudor times. He is right, of course. The pudding is a gloriously English invention – but by 'Pudding' Misson, and people for generations, meant the boiled pudding as in a suet pudding, either sweet or savoury. You don't see them much anymore, which is a great sadness. Anyone who spends an English winter without a proper steak and kidney pudding has not yet lived. Even more delicious to my not usually sweet tooth is Apple Hat, where the suet is filled with cox apples and golden syrup. We used to have it when we went to stay with my grandmother in Somerset, and my mother later took up the flag. My younger brother, who lives in France, almost cried with greed and nostalgic happiness when I made him one on a visit home.

This chapter, though, is taking puddings in its more general, English sense. This is a book dedicated to the great cookery writers of England, so I will not ignore the ghosts of Woolley, Acton et al by using a French word – desserts – where an English one will do.

The English are still one of the great countries for a pudding. The French may beat us at patisserie, and the Italians and Germans may be proud of various dry cakey biscuit confections, but for my money we still make the best puddings. Their very names remind us of a different time – Queen of Puddings, Eve's Pudding, Royal Curd Tart, Treacle Tart (the French don't even know what treacle is, but my how they lap it up once introduced), mincemeats, crumble, syllabubs, possets. It is perhaps in these old favourites that we can most recognise the kitchens of centuries ago. Some people still make junket, including the mother of an old flame.

His was an old-fashioned Exmoor farmhouse, where after hunting everyone gathered for huge teas and whisky, leading more or less smoothly on into dinner. The larder was a beautiful, huge, flagstoned, slate-shelved room where occasionally one found slightly worrying offcuts or bowls of mysterious leftovers. And junket. Junket is a pudding, particular to the West Country, made of heated milk (preferably, according to Hannah Woolley, ewes' or goats' milk) and rennet (the digestive juices from a calf's stomach), put into individual moulds and set, sometimes with nutmeg or cinnamon dusted on to it. Served with stewed fruit and/or clotted cream, it should be delicious. But to me, I just can't get beyond the hot milk and digestive enzymes. Sorry. We're all allowed to be fussy about something.

HANNAH WOOLLEY

AN ALMOND-TART

Strain beaten Almonds with Cream, yolks of Eggs, Sugar, Cinnamon and Ginger, boil it thick, and fill your Tart therewith.

Very simple instructions, with not a lot by way of detail. It doesn't even mention cooking the tart, which ideally should be blind-baked and then baked again until the custard sets. But the ingredients – ground almonds, cinnamon, ginger – are all ingredients we would still find in many a pudding today. Delicious.

APPLE-CREAM

Take a dozen Pippins, or more, pare, slice, or quarter them, put them into a Skillet, with some Claret-wine, and a trace of Ginger sliced thin, a little Lemmon-peel cut small, and some Sugar; let all these stew together till they be soft, then take them off the fire, and put them into a Dish, and when they be cold, take a quart of boil'd cream, with a little Nutmeg, and put in of the Apple as much as will thicken it; and so serve it up.

The French call it apple compote, but whichever you way you name it stewed apple is one of the simplest and most delicious of puddings. We used to have it with whipped egg whites so that it was all fluffy and became Apple Snow.

A NORFOLK-FOOL

Take a quart of thick sweet Cream, and set it a-boiling in a clear scoured Skillet, with some large Mace and whole Cinamon; having boiled a little while, take the yolks of five or six Eggs beaten well and put to it; being off the fire, take out the Cinamon and Mace; the Cream being pretty thick, slice a fine Manchet into thin slices as many as will cover the bottom of the Dish, and then pour on the Cream; trim the Dish with carved sippets: and stick it with sliced Dates and scrape Sugar all over it.

Bread and butter pudding, as I live and breathe.

POMPION-PYE

Take a pound of Pompion [pumpkin], and slice it; an handful of Time, a little Rosemary, sweet Marjoram stripped off the stalks, cut them small; then take Cinamon, Nutmeg, Pepper, and a few

280

Cloves, all beaten; also ten Eggs, and beat them all together, with as much Sugar as you shall think sufficient; then fry them like a Froise [*type of pancake or omelette*]; and being fried, let them stand till they are cold; Then fill your Pye after this manner; Take Apples sliced thin round-wise, and lay a layer of the Froise, and another of the Apples, with Currans betwixt the layers; be sure you put in good store of sweet [*unsalted*] Butter before you close it. When the Pye is baked, take six yolks of Eggs, some White-wine of Verjuice, and make a Caudle thereof, but not too thick; cut up the lid and put it in, and stir them well together whilst the eggs and Pompions are not perceived, and so serve it up.

QUAKING PUDDING

Slice the Crum of a Peny-manchet, and infuse it three or four hours in a pint of scalding hot Cream, covering it close, then break the bread with a spoon very small, and put to it eight Eggs (but four whites) and beat them together very well, then season it with Sugar, Rosewater and grated Nutmeg; if you think it too stiff, qualifie that fault with cold Cream, and beat them well together, then wet the bag or napkin, and flower it, put in the Pudding, and tye it hard, boil it half an hour, then dish it and put Butter to it, Rosewater and Sugar, and so serve it to the Table.

This is a proper boiled pudding, of the type the English were famed for across Europe. I'd leave out the Rosewater, but that's a personal hatred. Here's another traditional boiled pudding, as close to spotted dick as be-damned. I think that for our tastes it is better boiled or steamed in water than beef broth.

TO MAKE A HEDGE-HOG PUDDING

Put some Raisins of the Sun into a deep wooden Dish, and then take some grated Bread, and one pint of sweet Cream, three Yolks of Eggs, with two of the whites, and some Beef-suet, grated Nutmeg, and Salt; then sweeten it with Sugar, and temper all well together, and so lay it into the Dish upon the Raisins, then tye a Cloath about the Dish, and boyl it in Beef-broth, and when you take it up lay it in a pewter Dish, with the Raisins uppermost, and then stick blanched Almonds very thick into the Pudding, then melt some butter, and pour it upon the Pudding, then strew some Sugar about the Dish, and Serve it.

And if that was a spotted dick by another name, here's another bread and butter pudding:

TO MAKE A FINE PUDDING IN A DISH

Take a penny white loaf, and pare off all the Crust, and slice it thin into a Dish, over a Chafing-Dish of Coals, till the bread be almost dry; then put in a piece of sweet butter, and take it off, and let it stand in the Dish till it be cold, then take the yolks of three Eggs, and the quantity of one with some Rose-water, and Sugar, and stirring them all together, put it into another Dish well butter'd, and bake it.

TO MAKE A DAMSON-TART

Take Damsons, and seeth them in Wine, and strain them with a little Cream, then boyl your stuff over the fire, till it be thick, and put thereto Sugar, Cinamon, and Ginger, but set it not in the Oven after, but let your Paste be baked before.

TO MAKE A RARE CITRON-PUDDING

Take a penny-loaf, and grate it, a pint and half of Cream, half a dozen of Eggs, one Nutmeg sliced, a little salt, an Ounce of Candyed Citron sliced small, a little Candyed Orange-peel sliced, three Ounces of Sugar; put these into a wooden dish well Flowered, and covered with a Cloath, and when the water boyleth put it in, boyl it well, and serve it up with Rose-Water and Sugar, and stick it with Wafers, or blanched Almonds.

TO MAKE A VERY FINE CUSTARD

Take a quart of Cream, and boyl it with whole Spice; then beat the Yolks of ten Eggs, and five whites, mingle them with a little Cream, and when your Cream is almost cold, put your Eggs into it, and stir them very well, then sweeten it, and put out your Custard into a deep Dish, and bake it; then serve it in with *French* Comfits strewed on it.

TO MAKE APPLE-PYES, TO FRY

Take about twelve Pippins, pare them, cut them, and almost cover them with water, and almost a pound of Sugar, let them boyl on a gentle Fire close covered, with a stick of Cinamon, minced Orange-peel, a little Dill seed beaten, and Rose-water, when this is cold and stiff, make them into little Pasties, with rich Paste, and so fry them.

283

HANNAH GLASSE

Glasse has a lovely line in puddings: cheesecakes, syllabubs, custards and creams. She uses almonds and lemons and cinnamon; more esoterically she also uses powdered ivory, amber and hartshorn, ingredients with which we are less familiar. There is something both ladylike and comforting about these puddings.

TO MAKE LEMON CHEESECAKES

Take the peel of two large lemons, boil it very tender, then pound it well in a mortar, with a quarter of a pound or more of loaf sugar, the yolks of six eggs, and half a pound of fresh butter; pound and mix all well together, lay a puff-paste in your patty-pans, fill them half full, and bake them. Orange cheesecakes are done the same way, only you boil the peel in two or three waters, to take out the bitterness.

TO MAKE ALMOND CHEESECAKES

Take half a pound of Jordan almonds, and lay them in cold water all night, the next morning blanch them into cold water, then take them out, and dry them in a clean cloth, beat them very fine in a little orange-flower water, then take six eggs, leave out four whites, beat them and strain them, then half a pound of white sugar, with a little beaten mace; beat them well together in a marble mortar, take ten ounces of good fresh butter, melt it, a little grated lemon-peel, and put them in the mortar with the other ingredients; mix all well together, and fill your patty-pans.

TO MAKE ALMOND CUSTARDS

Take a pint of cream, blanch and beat a quarter of a pound of almonds fine, with two spoonfuls of rose-water. Sweeten it to your palate; beat up the yolks of four eggs, stir all together one way over the fire till it is thick, then pour it out into cups. Or you may bake it in little china cups.

TO MAKE BAKED CUSTARDS

One pint of cream boiled with mace and cinnamon; when cold take four eggs, two whites left out, a little rose and orange-flower water and sack, nutmeg and sugar to your palate; mix them well together, and bake them in china cups.

The 'cream' dishes, of which Glasse includes quite a few, are an English version of the Italian 'panna cotta', which translates literally as 'cooked cream'. An advantage of the Glasse versions are that they do not contain gelatine, which makes them suitable for aggressive vegetarians. Early Italian versions don't include gelatine either, but involve a preparation of boiled fish bones which would have had the same jellifying effect.

A LEMON-CREAM

Take the juice of four large lemons, half a pint of water, a pound of double-refined sugar beaten fine, the whites of seven eggs, and the yolk of one beaten very well, mix all together, strain it, and set it on a gentle fire, stirring it all the while, and scum it clean, put into it the peel of one lemon, when it is very hot, but don't boil, take out the lemon-peel, and pour it into china dishes. You must observe to keep it stirring one way all the time it is over the fire.

TO MAKE ALMOND CREAM

Take a quart of cream, boil it with a nutmeg grated, a blade or two of mace, a bit of lemon-peel, and sweeten to your taste: then blanch a quarter of a pound of almonds, beat them very fine, with a spoonful of rose or orange-flower water, take the whites of nine eggs well beat, and strain them to your almonds, beat them together, rub very well through a coarse hair-sieve; mix all together with your cream, set it on the fire, stir it all one way all the time till it boils, pour it into your cups or dishes, and when it is cold serve it up.

TO MAKE WHIPT SYLLABUBS

Take a quart of thick cream, and half a pint of sack, the juice of two Seville oranges or lemons, grate in the peel of two lemons, half a pound of double refined sugar, pour it into a broad earthen pan, and whisk it well; but first sweeten some red wine or sack, and fill your glasses as full as you chuse, then as the froth rises take it off with a spoon, and lay it carefully into your glasses till they are as full as they will hold. Don't make these long before you use them. Many use cyder sweetened, or any wine you please, or lemon, or orange whey made thus: squeeze the juice of a lemon or orange into a quarter of a pint of milk, when the curd is hard, pour the whey clear off, and sweeten it to your palate. You may colour some with the juice of spinach, some with saffron, and some with cochineal, just as you fancy.

Syllabubs were popular from the sixteenth century onwards. As Glasse says, various different wines or ciders could be used; now we are likely to use sherry or sweet vermouth. 'Sack' (or 'canary', which is sack from the Canary Islands) most closely resembles today's sweet sherry. Serving them in various different colours sounds more eighteenth century than anything we would want now – although maybe a rainbow of syllabubs would be amusing.

Our sixth form English teacher used to give supper parties for her girls. The menu was always the same – not very good boeuf bourguigon followed by delicious syllabub. We sat around her little sitting room, eating off our knees and making awkward conversation. We were fond of her but foul about her, laughing behind her back at her spinsterhood and her supper parties, assuming that she asked us because she had no friends. I feel guilty every time I think of syllabub.

I doubt she used the recipe, very popular in early cooking, which involved milking the cow directly into the dish of sack and cream.

Another English favourite is the trifle. For years, brought up on school trifles and a Francophile mother who thought trifles were something faintly disgusting and English, I did not see the point of them. My mother-in-law, however, queen of English cooking, taught me differently. A good trifle is an excellent pudding indeed.

Originally a trifle was just another name for a thickened and flavoured cream. By the time Glasse was writing, though, eggs were added to make a custard and poured over alcohol-soaked bread. As the jelly remains my least favourite part of a modern trifle, this recipe suits me very well.

TO MAKE A TRIFLE

Cover the bottom of your dish or bowl with Naples biscuits broke in pieces, mackeroons broke in halves, and ratafia cakes. Just wet them all through with sack, then make a good boiled custard not too thick, and when cold pour it over it, then put a syllabub over that. You may garnish it with ratafia cakes, currant jelly, and flowers.

ELIZA ACTON

Taken all in all, Acton's puddings take up almost a quarter of her book. She has sections on pastries, soufflés, boiled puddings, baked puddings, and 'sweet dishes, or entremets'. She is particularly fond of pies, both meat and fruit, although she apologises for not including more: 'we have rejected those which may be found in almost every English cookery book'. I've taken a leaf from her book and not put in many either, as we do all know what an apple pie is and her instructions are not that dissimilar from what we make now. I'm always a bit cross at the phrase 'as American as apple pie', as in fact the apple pie is ours entirely. The settlers had to wait for apple trees to be sent over and bear fruit before they could recreate their favourite pie from home. I'll give them the pumpkin pie for sure, but the apple? Hands off.

PUDDING-PIES

This form of pastry (or its name at least) is, we believe, peculiar to the county of Kent, where it is made in abundance, and eaten by all classes of people during Lent. Boil for fifteen minutes three ounces of ground rice (or rice flour) in a pint and a half of new milk and when taken from the fire stir into it three ounces of butter and four of sugar; add to these six well-beaten eggs, a grain or two of salt, and a flavouring of nutmeg or lemon-rind at pleasure. When the mixture is nearly cold, line some large patty-pans or some saucers with thin puff-paste, fill them with it three parts full, strew the tops thickly with currants which have been cleaned and dried, and bake the pudding-pies from fifteen to twenty minutes in a gentle oven.

Milk, 1 ½ pint; ground rice, 3 oz.: 15 minutes. Butter, 3 oz.; sugar ¼ lb. nutmeg or lemon-rind; eggs, 6; currants, 4 to 6 oz.: 15 to 20 minutes.

COCOA-NUT CHEESE-CAKES (JAMAICA RECEIPT)

Break carefully the shell of the nut, that the liquid it contains may not escape. (This, as we have elsewhere stated, is best secured by boring the shell before it is broken. The milk of the nut should never be used unless it be very fresh.) Take out the kernel, pare thickly off the dark skin, and grate the nut on a delicately clean grater; put it, with its weight of pounded sugar, and its own milk, or a couple of spoonsful or rather more of water, into a silver or block-tin saucepan, or a very small copper stewpan perfectly tinned, and keep it gently stirred over a quite clear fire until it is tender: it will sometimes require an hour's stewing to make it so. When a little cooled, add to the nut, and beat well with it, some eggs properly whisked and strained, and the grated rind of half a lemon. Line some patty-pans with fine paste, put in the mixture, and bake the cheese-cakes from thirteen to fifteen minutes.

Grated cocoa-nut, 6 oz.; sugar, 6 oz.; the milk of the nut, or of water, 2 large tablespoonsful: ½ to 1 hour. Eggs, 5; lemon-rind, ½ of 1: 13 to 15 minutes.

As a child, I once gave my brother a coconut for Christmas. I can't think why. And then, running up the stairs to hide it from him, I slipped and knocked myself out on it and had to explain the monstrous bruise on my head away. I wish we had instead made this cheesecake with it.

Acton is absolutely right about the freshness of coconut milk. It is the most extraordinary drink. Fresh from the nut, it is incredibly thirst-quenching and peculiarly delicious. We drank it in Ghana where it took the edge off the very humid heat. We were then given milk that had been fermenting for one day, then two, then three. By the third day it is the most terrifying alcoholic drink I've ever encountered, driving grown men to madness (albeit a temporary one).

MADAME WERNER'S ROSENVIK CHEESE-CAKES

Blanch and pound to the finest possible paste, four ounces of fine fresh Jordan almonds, with a few drops of lemon-juice or water, then mix with them, very gradually indeed, six fresh, and thoroughly well-whisked eggs; throw in by degrees twelve ounces of pounded sugar, and beat the mixture without intermission all the time; add then the finely grated rinds of four small, or of three large lemons, and afterwards, by very slow degrees, the strained juice of all. When these ingredients are perfectly blended, pour to them in small portions, four ounces of just liquefied butter (six of clarified if exceedingly rich cheese-cakes are wished for), and again whisk the mixture lightly for several minutes; thicken it over the fire like boiled custard, and either put into small pans or jars for storing, or fill with it, one-third full, some patty-pans lined with the finest paste; place lightly on it a layer of apricot, orange, or lemon-marmalade, and on this pour as much more of the mixture. Bake the cheese-cakes from fifteen to twenty minutes in a a moderate oven. They are very good *without* the layer of preserve.

Jordan almonds, 4 oz.; eggs, 6; sugar, 12 oz.; rinds and strained juice of 4 small, or of 3 quite large lemons; butter, 4 oz. (6 for

290

rich cheese-cakes); layers of preserve. Baked 15 to 20 minutes, moderate oven.

APPEL KRAPFEN (GERMAN RECEIPT)

Boil down three-quarters of a pound of good apples with four ounces of pounded sugar, and a small glass of white wine, or the strained juice of a lemon; when they are stewed quite to a pulp, keep them stirred until they are thick and dry; then mix them gradually with four ounces of almonds, beaten to a paste, or very finely chopped, two ounces of candied orange or lemon-rind shred extremely small, and six ounces of jar raisins stoned and quartered: to these the Germans add a rather high flavouring of cinnamon, which is a very favourite spice with them, but a grating of nutmeg, and some fresh lemon-peel, are, we think, preferable for this composition. Mix all the ingredients well together; roll out some butter-crust a full back-of-knife thickness, cut it into four-inch squares, brush the edges to the depth of an inch round with beaten egg, fill them with the mixture, lay another square of paste on each, press them very securely together, make, with the point of a knife, a small incision in the top of each, glaze them or not at pleasure, and bake them rather slowly, that the raisins may have time to become tender. They are very good. The proportion of sugar must be regulated by the nature of the fruit; and that of the almonds can be diminished when it is thought too much. A delicious tart of the kind is made by substituting for the raisins and candied orange-rind, two heaped tablespoonsful of very fine apricot jam.

VENETIAN FRITTERS (VERY GOOD)

Wash and drain three ounces of whole rice, put it into a full pint of cold milk, and bring it very slowly to boil; stir it often, and let it simmer gently until it is quite thick and dry. When about three parts done, add to it two ounces of pounded sugar, and one of fresh butter, a grain of salt, and the grated rind of half a small lemon. Let it cool in the saucepan, and when only just warm, mix with it thoroughly three ounces of currants, four of apples chopped fine, a teaspoonful of flour, and three large or four small well-beaten eggs. Drop the mixture in small fritters, fry them in butter from five to seven minutes, and let them become quite firm on one side before they are turned: do this with a slice. Drain them as they are taken up, and sift white sugar over them after they are dished.

Whole rice, 3 oz.; milk, 1 pint; sugar, 2 oz.; butter, 1 oz.; grated rind of ½ lemon; currants, 3 oz.; minced apples, 4 oz.; flour, 1 teaspoonful; a little salt; eggs, 3 large, or 4 small: 5 to 7 minutes.

RHUBARB FRITTERS

The rhubarb for these should be of a good sort, quickly grown, and tender. Pare, cut it into equal lengths, and throw it into French batter [see 'Sauces']; with a fork lift the stalks separately, and put them into a pan of boiling lard or butter: in from five to six minutes they will be done. Drain them well and dish them on a napkin, or pile them high without one, and strew sifted sugar plentifully over them: they should be of a very light brown, and quite dry and crisp. The young stalks look well when left the length of the dish in which they are served and only slightly encrusted with the batter, through which they should be merely drawn.

My Australian friend, visiting me in the south of France, wrinkled her nose after three days and asked, 'It's all very well, but where do they get their roughage?' Going through these early cookery books I have sometimes wondered the same thing. With over-cooked (by our standards) vegetables, sugar strewn willy-nilly over almost everything, boiled puddings, pastries, and huge hunks of meat, where did these people get their vitamins? They must have longed for the acidity of rhubarb or gooseberries (which also feature fairly regularly). Rhubarb is often sadly overlooked. Maybe it's something to do with the way it lurks under those clay cloches; there's something sinister about growing above ground, but insisting on the dark. Good rhubarb is, however, heavenly.

Acton also suggests using other fruit with the batter: apples peeled and cored whole and cut in thick slices, oranges peeled, de-pithed and pipped and likewise cut into slices, peaches and apricots skinned, halved and stoned.

BATTER FRUIT PUDDING

Butter thickly a basin which holds a pint and a half, and fill it nearly to the brim with *good* boiling apples pared, cored, and quartered; pour over them a batter made with four tablespoonsful of flour, two large or three small eggs, and half a pint of milk. Tie a buttered and floured cloth over the basin, which ought to be quite full, and boil the pudding for an hour and a quarter. Turn it into a hot dish when done, and strew sugar thickly over it; this, if added to the batter at first, renders it heavy. Morella cherries make a very superior pudding of this kind; and green gooseberries, damsons, and various other fruits, answer for it extremely well: the time of boiling must be varied according to their quality and its size.

293

For a pint and half mould or basin filled to the brim with apples or other fruit; flour, 4 tablespoonful; eggs, 2 large or 3 small; milk, ½ pint: 1 ¼ hour.

OBS. – Apples cored, halved, and mixed with a good batter, make an excellent baked pudding, as do red currants, cherries, and plums of different sorts likewise.

This is an English version of a clafoutis – apples rather than black cherries and boiling rather than baking.

The names of some of Acton's boiled puddings are wonderful and give some idea as to the preoccupations and aspirations of her readership: The Publisher's Pudding, Her Majesty's Pudding, Prince Albert's Pudding, the Elegant Economist's Pudding and The Welcome Guest's Own Pudding (which, with a small addition, can be turned into Sir Edwin Landseer's Pudding). They are all variations on a theme: suet, breadcrumbs, candied peel, macaroons, sultanas, fortified wines and milk all feature heavily. One pudding (German) mixes suet and rice, which is really too much of a good thing, and another 'Vegetable Plum Pudding (Cheap and good)' uses mashed potato, mashed carrots, flour, currants, and suet. I couldn't bring myself to cook that one. Often the puddings are served with a fruit syrup – a forerunner of the more healthy and fruit-heavy coulis that are so merrily drizzled around puddings nowadays.

I will give you one of the many boiled puddings (you can steam them) for a flavour of the Victorian era one winter's Sunday lunch.

SNOWDON PUDDING (GENUINE RECEIPT)

Ornament a well buttered mould or basin with some fine raisins split open and stoned, but not divided, pressing the cut side on the butter to make them adhere; next, mix half a pound of *very* finely minced beef kidney suet, with half a pound of bread-crumbs, and an ounce and a half of rice-flour, a pinch of salt, and six ounces of lemon marmalade, or of orange when the lemon cannot be procured; add six ounces of pale brown sugar, six thoroughly whisked eggs, and the grated rinds of two lemons. Beat the whole until all the ingredients are perfectly mixed, pour it gently into the mould, cover it with a buttered paper and floured cloth, and boil it for one hour and a half. It will turn out remarkably well if carefully prepared. Half the quantity given above will fill a mould or basin which will contain rather more than a pint, and will be sufficiently boiled in ten minutes less than an hour. To many tastes a slight diminution in the proportion of suet would be an improvement to the pudding; and the substitution of pounded sugar for the brown, might likewise be considered so. Both the suet and the eggs used for it, should be as fresh as possible.

This pudding is constantly served to travellers at the foot of the mountain from which it derives its name. It is probably well known to many of our readers in consequence. Wine sauce... or any other... sweet pudding sauce...may be poured over, or sent to table with it.

WINE SAUCE FOR SWEET PUDDINGS

Boil gently together for ten or fifteen minutes the very thin rind of a small lemon, about an ounce and a half of sugar, and a wineglassful of water. Take out the lemon-peel and stir into the sauce until it has boiled for one minute, an ounce of butter smoothly mixed with a large half-teaspoonful of flour; add a wineglassful and half of sherry or Madeira, or other good white wine, and when quite hot serve the sauce without delay. Port wine sauce is made in the same way with the addition of a dessertspoonful of lemon-juice, some grated nutmeg and a little more sugar. Orange-rind and juice may be used for it instead of lemon.

If we're looking at suet – and if we're looking at nineteenth-century puddings, we definitely are looking at suet – then we cannot forget the dumpling. I pray the dumpling never entirely disappears from English cooking. We very occasionally still see them in a beef stew, but let's not overlook the sweet version.

LEMON DUMPLINGS (LIGHT AND GOOD)

Mix, with ten ounces of fine bread-crumbs, half a pound of beef-suet, chopped extremely small, one large tablespoonful of flour, the grated rinds of two small lemons, or a a very large one, four ounces of pounded sugar, three large or four small eggs beaten and strained. Divide these into four equal portions, tie them in well-floured cloths, and boil them an hour. The dumplings will be extremely light and delicate: if wished very sweet, more sugar must be added to them. The syrup of preserved ginger would be both a wholesome and appropriate sauce for them.

Acton's baked puddings have names as wonderful as her boiled ones: The Printer's Pudding, the Young Wife's Pudding (Author's receipt), The Poor Author's Pudding, The Curate's Pudding, The Good Daughter's Mincemeat Pudding and another Elegant Economist's Pudding ('We have already given a recipe for an exceedingly good boiled pudding bearing this title, but we think the baked one answers even better, and it is made with rather more facility'). It is in the section on baked puddings that we really see the puddings which have survived in pretty much the same form to the present day: bread and butter puddings, castle puddings and Bakewell pudding, which she dismisses as 'a rich and expensive, but not very refined pudding.' Above all there is of course the pudding which started me on this trek into the past … the best rice pudding you will ever eat.

RICH RICE PUDDING

Wash very clean four ounces of whole rice, pour on it a pint and a half of new milk, and stew it slowly till quite tender; before it is taken from the fire, stir in two ounces of good butter, and three of sugar; and when it has cooled a little, add four well-whisked eggs, and the grated rind of half a lemon. Bake the pudding in a gentle oven from thirty to forty minutes. As rice requires long boiling to render it soft in milk it may be partially stewed in water, the quantity of milk diminished to a pint, and a little thick sweet cream mixed with it, before the other ingredients are added.

Rice, 4 oz.; new milk, 1 ½ pint; butter, 2 oz.; sugar, 3 oz.; eggs, 4; rind of ½ lemon: 30 to 40 minutes, slow oven.

THE GOOD DAUGHTER'S MINCEMEAT PUDDING (AUTHOR'S RECEIPT)

Lay into a rather deep tart-dish some thick slices of French roll very slightly spread with butter and covered with a thick layer of mincemeat, place a second tier lightly on these, covered in the same way with the mincemeat; then pour gently in a custard made with three well-whisked eggs, three-quarters of a pint of new milk or thin cream, the slightest pinch of salt, and two ounces of sugar. Let the pudding stand to soak for an hour, then bake it gently until it is quite firm in the centre: this will be in from three-quarters of an hour to a full hour.

THE AUTHOR'S CHRISTMAS PUDDING

To three ounces of flour, and the same weight of fine, lightly-grated bread-crumbs, add six of beef kidney-suet, chopped small, six of raisins weighed after they are stoned, six of well-cleaned currants, four ounces of minced apples, five of sugar, two of candied orange-rind, half a teaspoonful of nutmeg mixed with pounded mace, a very little salt, a small glass of brandy, and three whole eggs. Mix and beat these ingredients well together, tie them tightly in a thickly-floured cloth, and boil them for three hours and a half. We can recommend this as a remarkably light small rich pudding: it may be served with German, wine, or punch sauce.

Flour, 3 oz.; bread-crumbs, 3 oz.; suet, stoned raisins, and currants, each, 6 oz.; minced apples, 4 oz.; sugar, 5 oz.; candied peel, 2 oz.; spice, ½ teaspoonful; salt, few grains; brandy, small wineglassful; eggs, 3: 3 ½ hours

GREEN GOOSEBERRY PUDDING

Boil together, from ten to twelve minutes, a pound of green gooseberries, five ounces of sugar, and rather more than a quarter of a pint of water: then beat the fruit to a mash, and stir to it an ounce and a half of fresh butter; when nearly, or quite, cold, add two ounces and a half of very fine bread-crumbs, and four well whisked eggs. Bake the pudding gently from half to three-quarters of an hour. To make a finer one of the kind, work the fruit through a sieve, mix it with four or five crushed Naples biscuits, and use double the quantity of butter.

Green gooseberries, 1 lb.; sugar, 5 oz.; water, full ¼ pint: 10 to 12 minutes. Bread-crumbs, 2 ½ oz.; eggs, 4: ½ to ¾ hour.

ISABELLA BEETON

RICH BAKED APPLE PUDDING

INGREDIENTS. – ½ lb. of the pulp of apples, ½ lb. of loaf sugar, 6 oz. of butter, the rind of 1 lemon, 6 eggs, puff-paste.

Mode. – Peel, core, and cut the apples, as for sauce; put them into a stewpan, with only just sufficient water to prevent them from burning, and let them stew until reduced to a pulp. Weigh the pulp, and to every ½ lb. add sifted sugar, grated lemon-rind, and 6 well-beaten eggs. Beat these ingredients well together; then melt the butter, stir it to the other things, put a border of puff-paste round the dish, and bake for rather more than ½ hour. The butter should not be added until the pudding is ready for the oven.

Time. – ½ to ¾ hour. Average cost, 1s. 10d.

Sufficient for 5 or 6 persons.

Seasonable from August to March.

APPLE TOURTE OR CAKE (GERMAN RECIPE)

INGREDIENTS. – 10 or 12 apples, sugar to taste, the rind of 1 small lemon, 3 eggs, ¼ pint of cream or milk, ¼ lb. of butter, ¾ lb. of good short crust, 3 oz. of sweet almonds.

Mode. – Pare, core and cut the apples into small pieces; put sufficient moist sugar to sweeten them into a basin; add the lemon-peel, which should be finely minced, and the cream; stir these ingredients well, whisk the eggs, and melt the butter; mix altogether, add the sliced apple, and let these be well stirred into the mixture. Line a large round plate with the paste, place a narrow rim of the same round the outer edge, and lay the apples thickly in the middle. Blanch the almonds, cut them into long shreds, and strew over the top of the apples, and bake from ½ to ¾ hour, taking care that the almonds do not get burnt: when done, strew some sifted sugar over the top, and serve. This tourte may be eaten either hot or cold, and is sufficient to fill 2 large-sized plates.

Time. – ½ to ¾ hour. Average cost, 2s. 2d.

Sufficient for 2 large-sized tourtes.

Seasonable from August to March.

Remember the pastry-cook in Germany, and you will see where this recipe came from. Not Eliza Acton, on this occasion.

Like Acton, Beeton has puddings with interesting names – A Bachelor's Pudding or Chancellor's Pudding, for instance, which are boiled puddings, and 'Baroness Pudding', which is billed as 'Author's Recipe', although the explanatory note says that it 'was kindly given to [the editress's] family by a lady who bore the title here prefixed to it'. Snobbish and unnecessary, maybe, but probably just the thing that would cheer up an upwardly-mobile middle-class lady of the house.

MARMALADE AND VERMICELLI PUDDING

INGREDIENTS – 1 breakfastcupful of vermicelli, 2 tablespoonfuls of marmalade, ¼ lb. of raisins, sugar to taste, 3 eggs, milk.

Mode. – Pour some boiling milk on the vermicelli, and let it remain covered for 10 minutes; then mix it with the marmalade, stoned raisins, sugar, and beaten eggs. Stir all well together, put the mixture into a buttered mould, boil for 1 ½ hour, and serve with custard sauce.

Time. – 1 ½ hour. Average cost, 1s.

Sufficient for 5 or 6 persons. *Seasonable* at any time.

Iced puddings had begun to come into fashion, but they were fancy as anything, took days to prepare and involved a plethora of moulds, pounded ice and saltpetre. It must have been very hard to keep up with that fashion, and I wonder how many of Mrs Beeton's young bride readers dared try. Apart from the standard boiled puddings which were still so central to the sweet course, many of the puddings (or desserts, to make the distinction) were indeed incredibly fiddly and seem as much for show as for taste, which is why I have not included many of them. Fritters and jellies are also popular, but most puddings seem to involve at the very least a mould.

The following is an old favourite that you don't see much any longer, and relies again on the glories of the English apple.

CHARLOTTE-AUX-POMMES

INGREDIENTS. – A few slices of rather stale bread ½ inch thick, clarified butter, apple marmalade made with about 2 dozen apples, ½ glass of sherry.

Mode. – Cut a slice of bread the same shape as the bottom of a plain round mould, which has been well buttered, and a few strips the height of the mould, and about 1 ½ inch wide; dip the bread in clarified butter (or spread it with cold butter, if not wanted so rich); place the round piece at the bottom of the mould, and set the narrow strips up the sides of it, overlapping each other a little, that no juice from the apples may

301

escape, and that they may hold firmly to the mould. Brush the *interior* over with white of egg (this will assist to make the case firmer); fill it with apple marmalade, with the addition of a little sherry, and cover them with a round piece of bread, also brushed over with egg, the same as the bottom; slightly press the bread down, to make it adhere to the other pieces; put a plate on the top, and bake the *charlotte* in a brisk oven, of a light colour. Turn it out on the dish, strew sifted sugar over the top, and pour round it a little melted apricot jam.

Time. – 40 to 50 minutes. Average cost, 1s. 9d.

Sufficient for 5 or 6 persons. *Seasonable* from July to March.

ELIZABETH DAVID

David includes very few puddings in Mediterranean Food. *This is because many of the traditional puddings of that region are tiny sticky pastries, candied or fresh fruit. As she says, these dishes are to be made by a pâttisière or a confectioner, not an amateur cook. Most of the few recipes she does suggest involve fruit – watermelon stuffed with blackberries, for instance, baked bananas or fruit salad. My own personal leanings take me towards the French type of pudding (or 'sweet' as David will have it), but even without that favouritism some of the ingredients of her Greek style puddings are even now hard to find – unsalted myzithra, for example, which is a fresh sheeps' cheese definitely unavailable in the wilds of Somerset.*

CRÈME AU CAFÉ

Make some very strong coffee with 2 oz. coffee. Strain it into 1 pint of milk, add 4 oz. powdered sugar, 6 yolks of eggs and 3 whites beaten stiffly with a few spoons of cream. Pour this cream into the serving dish, cover it and place on top of a saucepan of boiling water, stirring until it thickens. When cold pour caramelised sugar over the top.

ESH ES SERAYA, OR PALACE BREAD (AN EGYPTIAN SWEET)

Heat ½ lb. of honey with ¼ lb. of sugar and ¼ lb. of butter until the mixture thickens. Add 4 oz. white breadcrumbs. Cook all together in a saucepan, stirring until it has become a homogeneous mass. Turn out on to a plate and when cold it will be like a soft cake, and can be cut into triangular portions. This sweet is always served with a cream which is skimmed off the top of quantities of milk cooked very slowly until a thick skin forms on the top, so stiff that when separated from the milk it can be rolled up. A little roll of this cream is placed on top of each portion of Palace Bread.

BEIGNETS DE PRUNEAUX

Soak prunes in weak tea for 2 hours and then in rum. Make a frying batter with the addition of a tablespoon of rum and fry the prunes. When golden, roll them in powdered chocolate mixed with vanilla sugar.

Her batter is made with 4 ounces of flour, 3 tablespoons of oil or melted butter, three-quarters of a tumbler of lukewarm water and the beaten white of an egg (and of course, in this instance, the rum). The trick is to beat it smoothly and at the last minute before using.

Here we have an upmarket rice pudding, mixed with dried figs.

GATEAU DE FIGUES SECHES

1 lb. figs, 1 ½ pints milk, 4 tablespoons rice, 3 eggs, 2 oz. butter.

Let the rice soften in the milk. When it is well soaked turn into a basin in the bottom of which are the figs cut up. Leave to cool. Add the eggs one by one, then the butter, mix well. Pour into a buttered mould and cook slowly for 2 hours.

AFTERWORD

The story of English cooking continues, of course. But now the message is disseminated in so many different ways. Boulestin, the dapper Frenchman who, between 1937 and 1939, was the first TV chef, would be astounded at the enormous variety of cooking programmes on television. There are travel/food programmes, food competitions, recreations of historic feasts. Ours is a world which is increasingly obsessed with food, but also alas a world in which so many have forgotten how to cook.

There have been highs and lows in the world of television cookery. The discovery of Jamie Oliver, at that time just a boy in the background of someone else's programme, must be counted a high. Delia began to give the English a new confidence in cooking, but Jamie bought with him a flair, and a social conscience, that means I am sure that his work will survive. For him the books and the television cooking were not enough; with missionary zeal he went out into the school kitchens and houses of the poorer and determinedly took his message of good eating to the masses. His latest book, *Save with Jamie* (2013), takes us right back to Beeton's basics with its emphasis on 'Shop Smart, Cook Clean, Waste Less'. He urges readers to use up leftovers, and shows them how. As Acton wrote so long ago, 'the daily waste of excellent provisions almost exceeds belief', and Jamie carries her torch still.

Many families barely eat together, and when they do it is something they pop into a microwave. We are so impatient that we can hardly wait for that magic ping. An Exmoor GP told me that he hardly ever sees a kitchen table on his house visits any more, that even in rural England the idea of a family eating together is vanishing. I often ask the children I teach about their eating habits; many of them now have fridges and microwaves in their bedrooms, along with their computers and Xboxes and sound systems. Their mothers keep the fridges stocked with ready meals and snacks and sometimes they have 'a roast' together on Sundays. No wonder that so many people will not try anything new, that our nation is getting fatter and fatter. The English are not very brave about civil disobedience, and yet so strongly did one group of mothers feel about their children's school stopping serving chips that they were to be seen pushing packages of fish and chips through the wire fences of the school to their not-so-little darlings. It is our right to fatten our children, they seemed to proclaim, along with the witch in Hansel and Gretel.

We must not be afraid of the less healthy. It is processed foods that are more to blame for our obesity than the butter and cream, red meat and red wine of real cooking. 'Healthy' food is so often bland and tasteless. All the cooks in this book use spices and herbs, anchovies or capers, enriching mushroom sauces or the bones and fat of meat to give a depth of taste.

But nor must we be nervous of the simple. Freshness, good ingredients used in season, clean tastes quickly mingled or stewed together long and slow. Cooking need not be complicated to be delicious.

When my children were small a friend called me a 'food fascist' because I always cooked for my children rather than buying prepared food. (Better than to be called a food pornographer I suppose.) I was not, and this is my final message, one handed down from all the good cookery writers, and all matriarchal lines of domestic advice in history: it does not cost more to cook from scratch. The more people you cook for, the cheaper it is to cook real food. I was poor in those days, and she was not, but I fed my children well.

These cooks – all women, and all English – reassure us now as they did their audiences when they wrote. And there is no reason why we should not put our aprons on, throw our microwaves away and return to daily shopping and daily cooking. We'd all be happier.

GLOSSARY

Béchamel	A béchamel is a white sauce, made from a roux with infused milk added. However in the past a béchamel was made with a mixture of stock and cream. So you will find Eliza Acton, for example, saying you can use one or the other
Broil	To cook by direct heat – either under a grill or on a gridiron
Canary	See 'sack'
Carbonado	Meat or fowl, cut across the grain, seasoned and fried
Catsup	Ketchup. Originally from China, and made of pickled fish and spices, it came to England via Malaya in the eighteenth century. Early recipes were made from mushrooms, walnuts etc. with tomato ketchup arriving in the early nineteenth century
Caudle	A drink, usually made from ale, but could be made from wine, water or milk. It was thickened with egg yolk (sometimes with other ingredients such as breadcrumbs or porridge oats) and was then sweetened and spiced. Mrs Woolley adds a caudle to a pie (see Pompion Pye)
Coffin	A pastry case for a pie
Consommé	A clear soup made of beef and vegetables, which forms the basis of many sauces. You can cheat and buy it in tins

Dutch Oven	A heavy, lidded, cast iron pot
Flea	To flay or strip (skin etc.)
Larding	Using a special needle, strips of firm, fat bacon are sewn through a joint of meat. Needles are easily available from kitchen shops
Lere	A binding (from the French *lier* to thicken)
Manchet	White bread
Marmite	A large metal or earthenware cooking pot with a cover
Patty-pan	A small pan for baking – such as a jam tart pan
Pipkin	A round earthenware pot
Pippins	Apples
Sack	A sweet fortified wine used in puddings (such as trifle). Sweet sherry or sweet vermouth could be used in its stead
Salsify	A root vegetable which looks like a thin parsnip and has a faint oyster-like taste
Sippets	Rounds of toasted or fried bread
Skillet	Now used to mean a frying pan. Originally it meant a lidded serving pan, or a long-handled saucepan
Sweet butter	Unsalted butter
Sweet herbs	Many recipes call for a bundle of 'sweet herbs'. These would be a mixture of thyme, sage, mint, marjoram, savoury and basil
Tammy	A rough textured cloth through which sauces and soups were strained
Verjuice	A sour juice made from crab apples or unripe grapes. Used extensively in the Middle Ages and for some time after. It is making a bit of a comeback and can be bought online and in grand food shops – otherwise use vinegar